D1374632

This book (autographed by the Author) and a thumb-stick, are presented to my loyal friend and helper – Asst. Scoutmaster Henry M. Sherriff – as small tokens of my appreciation of his faithful services to our Troop. And I wish him many happy returns of this day – 11th January 1951.

F.R. Lucas. Group Scoutmaster
10th Chelsea (St. Columba's – Church of Scotland) Troop.

THE

SCOUT MOVEMENT

To Henry Sherriff

With the Author's best wishes

& in recollection of happy days

spent at "Dunedin".

W Reynolds

11. Jan 1951

THE SCOUT MOVEMENT

by

E. E. REYNOLDS
Author of BADEN-POWELL, *&c.*

'Scouting is a Movement, not an Organization'
B.-P.

Geoffrey Cumberlege
OXFORD UNIVERSITY PRESS
London New York Toronto
1950

Oxford University Press, Amen House, London E.C.4
GLASGOW NEW YORK TORONTO MELBOURNE WELLINGTON
BOMBAY CALCUTTA MADRAS CAPE TOWN
Geoffrey Cumberlege, Publisher to the University

PRINTED IN GREAT BRITAIN

PREFACE

THIS BOOK HAS TWO PURPOSES: FIRST TO PROVIDE PRESENT AND future members of the Scout Movement with an account of its development during its first forty years; secondly to explain to all interested in the education and training of boys the principles and methods on which Baden-Powell based his work.

The sources are as follows:

1. The World Chief Guide, Lady Baden-Powell, has kindly allowed me to read the diaries and other private papers of B.-P. that were not accessible when, during the war, I wrote his biography.
2. The Committee of the Council of the Boy Scouts Association has put at my disposal all documents and other material that might be of use. I have been given complete freedom in selecting and using this material.
3. Many of the leaders of the Movement, such as Sir Percy Everett, and Scouters of all ranks, have been good enough to answer my questions and to suggest points that might have eluded me.
4. I have drawn upon my own experience of more than thirty years back to the day when I became a Scoutmaster.

Although the book has been written with the encouragement of the Committee of the Council, I am alone responsible for the treatment of the material and for such comments as seemed to me desirable.

It has not been possible to keep throughout a strictly chronological order; the story is woven backwards and forwards to bring out more clearly the pattern of the development.

Some repetition of material already used in the biography

Baden-Powell is inevitable; that book and this one are complementary to each other.

I am conscious of the omission of the names of many leaders who have helped to build and maintain the Movement, but in the space of one volume it has not proved possible to refer in satisfactory detail to the contributions made even by those whose names are here recorded. I am sure, however, that none will complain of these shortcomings, for we all know that the real achievements of Scouting are not the work of any group of prominent persons, but are the outcome of the devoted and undemonstrative efforts of the many thousands of men and women who followed B.-P. They are content to serve their generation without publicity or award.

E. E. R.

1 November 1949

CONTENTS

LIST OF ILLUSTRATIONS

CHAPTER ONE

THE PRELUDE

THE FIRST ANNUAL REPORT (1910) OF THE BOY SCOUTS ASSOCIATION of the United Kingdom opens with the following statement:

Our aim is to inculcate good citizenship in the future men of the nation by means which will readily appeal to them, viz., 'Scoutcraft'. Scoutcraft includes the qualities of our frontier colonists, such as resourcefulness, endurance, pluck, trustworthiness, etc., plus the chivalry of the Knights; these attributes, both moral and physical, are held up to the boys for imitation and daily practice. In this we supply a *character education* which does not come within the scope of the present book-instruction of the schools. The romance of Scouting appeals to every class, from hooligan to high-born.

This system was originally found valuable when training young soldiers in campaign work, observation, and war-scouting, etc. The small handbook which was only intended for regimental instruction came to be largely adopted by schools, boys' clubs, etc. It seemed more than possible that a training designed on similar lines, but with the military element eliminated, might be of value for education purposes.

The handbook *Scouting for Boys* (1908) was therefore written. It was primarily intended for the Boys' Brigade, Y.M.C.A. Boys, Church Lads' Brigade, and others, and was adopted by them; but the attraction of Scouting also took hold of other boys in large numbers outside these associations, and so a new and independent body started itself, viz., 'The Boy Scouts'. The rapid rise of this corps, and its extension not only through Great Britain, but also in all our chief Overseas Dominions has much exceeded our expectation.

A later passage in the same Report recorded that Scouting had been adopted in the Argentine, Chile, France, Germany, Russia, and Sweden. The second Annual Report (1911) gave the total membership in the United Kingdom as 107,986. All this had come about within three years. Forty years after the publication of *Scouting for Boys* there were four and a half million members of the Movement to be found throughout the British Commonwealth and Empire and in some forty other countries.

The quotation with which this chapter opens was from the pen of Baden-Powell, the Founder of Scouting, and it gives a useful summary of the purposes he had in mind in planning the scheme of training. The last paragraph calls for considerable expansion if we are to understand how this new Movement so quickly became popular with boys.

A number of claimants to be originators of the scheme have come forward from time to time; each could probably maintain that he had thought of one or other of the elements to be found in the training, but the unique appeal of Scouting lies in its fusion of many elements with an unusual method of application. For this successful combination B.-P.'s genius is the only explanation. He found it necessary to set down the facts in a statement endorsed, 'Note for office to keep in case of revival of arguments later when I am dead. R. B.-P. 17.12.13'. It reads:

This man is the 4th to claim that he invented Boy Scouts. I have no recollection of his scheme for training boys which he says he sent me in 1905—but he may have sent it and I may have written to express interest in it: it did not in any case make a great impression on me. My idea of training boys in scouting dates back from 1897 when I applied it to young soldiers in the 5th Dragoon Guards, having for years previously found the good of developing the man's character before putting upon him the dull routine training then considered necessary for a soldier.

The possibility of putting responsibility on to boys and treating them seriously was brought to the proof in Mafeking with the corps of boys raised by Lord Edward Cecil there in 1899 and led me to go into it further.

When I came home from the War in 1902 I found my book *Aids to Scouting* being used in schools and by Boys' Brigade Officers, etc., for teaching boys. As this had been written for soldiers I re-wrote it for boys (after having an experimental camp in 1907). I did not then intend to have a separate organization of Boy Scouts, but hoped that the B.B. and Y.M.C.A. would utilize the idea. However, such a large number of men and boys outside these organizations took it up, that we were obliged to form a directorate to control it.

The movement grew up of itself. In 1910 I had to give up the Army to take charge of it.

The idea of the dress of the Scouts was taken from a sketch of my own dress in Kashmir 1897, in every detail, including hat, staff, shirt, shorts, neckerchief, belt, knife, rolled coat, etc.

The badge was that which I used for Scouts in the 5th Dragoon Guards (since adopted throughout the Army). It was taken from the sign of the North Point of the compass as shown on maps as guide to their orientation.

These two quotations establish the main facts, but they by no means tell the whole story, and if we are to understand the growth of Scouting, it is necessary to know more of the circumstances that provided the soil in which the seeds could germinate. Or, to express the idea in another form, we must trace a number of streams that had to flow into one channel to form the river.

It is important to remember that B.-P. was fifty years old in 1907 when he framed his Boy Scout scheme. He was able to draw upon a rich experience of life in several countries; he had held positions of great responsibility and had been in situations where the course of events largely depended on his own judgement. It was not therefore as a young and enthusiastic philanthropist that he faced the problem of boy training; he was a man of matured mind, accustomed to making accurate observations of facts, and to drawing deductions from them that had to stand the test of practical application. To these powers was added that dramatic sense that can imagine how others, especially boys, look at suggestions put forward for their consideration.

Mention must be made, however briefly, of the tributary streams of influence in B.-P.'s first fifty years.

First must be noted a happy home life. He grew up with the companionship of four brothers, three older than himself. They were allowed to spend holidays camping or canoeing or sailing by themselves under the leadership of the eldest. A love and knowledge of natural history was part of the family life.

Next came Charterhouse and the powerful influence of the headmaster, Haig-Brown, who was 'no theorist about education, no lover of exact rules, and rather one who allowed both boys and masters the largest measure of independence' (*D.N.B.*).

When the school moved to Godalming B.-P. spent many a free afternoon by himself in the surrounding woods (out of bounds) adding to his knowledge of wild life and playing the backwoodsman.

When he went to India as a subaltern in 1876 he was fortunate in having as his Commanding Officer Baker Russell, who encouraged initiative and, like Haig-Brown, was 'no lover of exact rules'. B.-P. specialized in surveying, reconnaissance work, and scouting (a neglected branch of army training), and after trying out various methods of training for young soldiers, he devised a scheme that he published in *Reconnaissance and Scouting* in 1884; in this small book will be found many of the ideas that were to be developed later.

Active service in Ashanti (1895) gave him intensive experience of pioneering; his work as an army scout in the Matabele Campaign of 1896 called out all his powers of observation and deduction with brilliant results.

On his return to India in 1897 in command of the 5th Dragoon Guards, he introduced a scheme of scout training designed to develop in his men their powers of observation, and to encourage initiative and self-reliance. He summarized his scheme and explained his methods in a handbook *Aids to Scouting*; the final proofs of this were sent out of Mafeking just before it was invested by the Boers in 1899. This book should be studied by anyone who wishes to understand the origins of the Scout Movement.

In his note, B.-P. referred to the next important influence in the growth of his ideas—the success of the boy cadets in the siege of Mafeking; he found that they, too, responded, as his young soldiers had done, when trusted and given responsibility.

So all these streams were gradually flowing towards one another; they might not have reached a common channel but for three factors—without these B.-P. might have realized his dream of spending his retirement on a farm in Wales.

The first factor was correspondence with boy admirers who wrote to him after Mafeking; the second was the use made of *Aids to Scouting* by teachers and others; the third was the Boys' Brigade.

It was natural that many boys wrote to the hero of Mafeking to express their admiration or to seek his advice. B.-P. gave thoughtful care to such correspondence, for he always took boys seriously—by that is not meant with a ponderous gravity, for his sense of fun was seldom far below the surface, but he knew that what may be brushed aside by an adult as a trifle may be a matter of urgent importance to a boy. In his replies he was already suggesting principles of conduct that were later to be woven into the Scout scheme, such as Duty to God, and the daily Good Turn.

Some far-seeing teachers had found in *Aids to Scouting* useful hints for attractive activities for boys. The games and practices suggested made a great appeal, though doubtless part of this may be explained by the glamour of the author's name. In November 1900 the editor of *Boys of the Empire* published the first instalment of this book as a serial under the title 'The Boy Scout'.

It was, however, through the Boys' Brigade that B.-P. was, so to speak, brought to bay. Writing in 1914 on the death of Sir William Smith, the Founder of the Boys' Brigade, he recalled a decisive occasion.

> It is already ten years ago since I accepted his invitation to come and review the B.B. at Glasgow on the twentieth anniversary of their existence. They were then 54,000 strong throughout Great Britain. There were between 7,000 and 8,000 boys on parade. It was the finest muster of boys that I had ever seen—all of them keen, alert, clean, and well set-up. I told Sir William that I would willingly change places to be in his shoes and to look upon those splendid lads as my own. Then, in a chaffing way, I said he ought to have ten times that number, and would get them if he only gave more variety and attraction to the training.

Sir William's answer was to propose that B.-P. should put down some suggestions for attractive activities, and rewrite *Aids to Scouting* as a handbook for the training of boys.

That parade of the Boys' Brigade was held in 1903, but some years were to elapse before Sir William's challenge could be taken up.

The basis of the Boys' Brigade was Church membership, and the Bible class was a primary part of its work; drill and physical training were the leading activities and the band was a means of attracting boys as well as of providing a musical training. Since those early days the scheme has broadened without sacrificing any of the original elements; this broadening was, in part, the result of B.-P.'s first suggestions, but his complete scheme was not adopted as a whole. He did not himself recognize for some time that his practical ideas, and particularly his special method, could not be tacked on to any existing organization as he at first intended; what he ultimately did as a result of his thorough investigation of the problem of training boys was to produce a scheme that could only be fully effective when applied in its entirety as a unit.

B.-P.'s relations with the Boys' Brigade were always of the friendliest character and he was a Vice-President up to his death. The Boy Scouts may, in a sense, be regarded as a collateral of the Boys' Brigade, and the two organizations have always worked in complete harmony.

CHAPTER TWO

FIRST PLANS

B.-P.'S APPOINTMENT AS INSPECTOR-GENERAL OF CAVALRY IN 1903 left him little time for other interests. He visited Germany, France, and the United States to study methods of cavalry training before founding the British Cavalry School at Netheravon in 1904. In 1906 he was in South Africa with the Duke of Connaught. He had not, however, forgotten his promise to Sir William Smith, and he drew up a preliminary scheme of activities that seemed to him more attractive to boys than existing organizations provided. This was published in *The Boys' Brigade Gazette* in June 1906.[1] In this he was chiefly concerned with practices to develop the powers of observation and deduction; he mentioned a number of other possible activities such as fire-lighting, cooking out of doors, first aid, and compass work, but he gave no indications of how these were to be taught. A series of tests further emphasized training in observation. In this list of practices—for it was little more—he hoped that the men training boys would find new ways of attracting recruits.

Meanwhile he was studying various schemes of training already in use, such as Jahn's work in Germany and some American boys' organizations, but these brought very little grist to the mill. He circulated copies of his scheme to friends for their comments, and discussed the subject with anyone who would listen to him. One lady, for instance, recorded that he was so full of the subject that he talked to her about it for a long time at a garden-party and then offered to give her a practical lesson in tracking in the neighbouring woods.

In October 1906 he met Ernest Thompson Seton, the founder of the Woodcraft Indians in the United States. Here was a scheme that came nearer in conception to his own ideas

[1] This document is printed in full in my *Baden-Powell* (Oxford, 1942), pp. 140–2.

than anything so far studied. A note in B.-P.'s diary reads:

> Oct 30. Lunched with Thompson Seton who told me all about his Red Indian Boys scheme. Each 'camp' ruled by its own Council. Each boy begins with a scalp which he loses if he fails to do a thing, and can only redeem by payment. He gains feathers and badges by qualifying in various subjects (all outdoor) and no competition only qualifying. Scouting practising very good.

Seton's scheme was based entirely on the practices of the North American Indians, or, it would be more true to say, on a romantic notion of their manners and customs. Catlin's *North American Indians* had been one of B.-P.'s favourite books as a boy and he had a more correct idea of the Red Indian than the idealized figure of Seton's imagination. Moreover B.-P. had a wide first-hand knowledge of primitive races especially of those in west and south Africa, and while he recognized their admirable qualities, he did not blind himself to their limitations; he certainly did not regard them as models to hold up to boys. There was, he saw, an even greater objection to basing a scheme on one race whether Red Indians or Zulus. As he wrote in later years of the Red Indian cult, 'its appeal must not always be relied on to be a lasting one, and boys are apt to tire of it, and to be ridiculed out of it'. So he looked for a more enduring and universal type that could satisfy a boy's romantic longings, and he found it in 'the work and attributes of backwoodsmen, explorers, and frontiersmen'. Had he followed or even adapted Seton's Red Indian scheme, Scouting would have had a restricted appeal, and would certainly not have become a world-wide Movement. He took every opportunity he could to explain his ideas. In November 1906, for instance, he reluctantly declined an invitation to meet the Guild of Undergraduates of Liverpool University. He wrote,

> I have designs on the Universities with a view to enlisting their help in a scheme which I want to put forward regarding the training of all boys to be Scouts. I believe that if I could get a chance some day of explaining it to undergraduates they would see in it an interesting occupation for themselves and one in which they could be doing work of national importance in training 'patrols' of half-a-dozen lads to be really useful men, by teaching them observation, tracking, alertness, discipline, self-reliance, self-sacri-

fice, and patriotism, etc., by means of the fascinating sport of Scouting.

By the beginning of 1907 he had at last got his scheme in outline. A draft was sent in February to a few friends; it was headed 'Boy Patrols'—a clear indication of the lines of his thinking. In May a slightly revised form of this was published with a leaflet of explanation. These two documents are so important that they must be reproduced in full.

I. BOY SCOUTS

A SUGGESTION

'The same causes which brought about the downfall of the great Roman Empire are working to day in Great Britain.'

These words were spoken the other day by one of our best-known democratic politicians, and their truth is practically admitted by those who have studied and compared the general conditions of both countries.

The main cause of the downfall of Rome was the decline of good citizenship among its subjects, due to want of energetic patriotism, to the growth of luxury and idleness, and to the exaggerated importance of local party politics, etc.

Personally I am not pessimistic enough to think with some people that we are already so far on the downward grade as to be hopeless; on the contrary, I think that we are only near to the parting of the ways where it becomes incumbent upon every one of us who has the slightest patriotism in him to earnestly help, in however small a way, to turn the rising generation on to the right road for good citizenship.

To this end the following scheme is offered as a possible aid towards putting on a positive footing the development, moral and physical, of boys of all creeds and classes, by a means which should appeal to them while offending as little as possible the susceptibilities of their elders.

It is intended to be applicable—and not in opposition—to any *existing* organisation for boys such as Schools, Boys' Brigades, Messengers, Cricket Clubs, Cadet Corps, etc., or it can supply an organisation of its own where these do not exist.

Many officers of such organisations have asked me for suggestions for developing and keeping up the interest of their boys in their training, and a small handbook, which I published for teaching Scouting in the Cavalry has, I find, been used to a very considerable extent in teaching children in England. For these reasons it occurred to me to frame a scheme of scouting, such as this, specially adapted for boys.

Under the term 'Scouting', with its attributes of romance and adventure, I suggest instruction in the many invaluable qualities which go to make a good citizen equally with a good scout. These include observation and deduction, chivalry, patriotism, self-sacrifice, personal hygiene, saving life, self-reliance, etc., etc.

A somewhat similar idea was started in America a short time back by Mr. Ernest Thompson Seton, and has already attained phenomenal success.

I append herewith for consideration a short summary of my scheme.

I propose to give the full details in a small handbook which is intended to serve either as a text-book for instructors or as a self-educator for individual boys.

In the meantime I should be very grateful for any suggestions or criticisms.

R. S. S. Baden-Powell,
Major-General.

32 Prince's Gate,
London, S.W.
May, 1907.

II. BOY SCOUTS

SUMMARY OF SCHEME

For Schoolmasters, Clergymen, Country Squires, Officers of Boys' Organisations, Cadet Corps, Y.M.C.A., Cricket and Football Clubs, Boy Messengers, etc.

Scouts.—Men Scouts are of two kinds: War Scouts and Peace Scouts.

A War Scout is a man selected for his reliability, courage, and intelligence to go ahead of a force to find out all about the enemy and the country. On his good work and sense of duty depends very largely the success or failure of the expedition.

A Peace Scout is the kind of man we find among the Pioneers and Trappers of North-West Canada, Explorers and Hunters of Africa, Prospectors, Drovers, and Bushmen of Australia, and above all in the Canadian North-West Mounted Police, the South African Constabulary, Royal Irish Constabulary, British South African and numerous other Police Forces.

For all, whether War or Peace scouts, the following qualities are essential:

Woodcraft.—That is, ability to live in the open, to kill and cook for themselves, to find their way in unknown countries, to look after their health, and to understand the ways of animals, and to have general resourcefulness and self-reliance.

The Power of Observation must be well developed so that nothing escapes their attention. They must be able to track and to read meaning, from footprints and other slightest signs.

Loyalty to their Duty must guide their actions when away from the immediate direction of their officers or employers.

Chivalry must rule their dealings with other people; that is a kindly comradeship for all others of their kind, and a respect and helpfulness to all women, children, and helpless people.

Courage and Endurance are essential; and the men must at all times be prepared to take their lives in their hands and to fling them away without thinking it too great a sacrifice if duty or circumstances demand it.

These are the qualities which a Scout must possess, whether it be for Peace or for War. But they are also the qualities which make the best citizens in a peaceful community. They can all be acquired under instruction; and they cannot be learned too early in life.

At present there is only too little instruction in these among boys, especially town-bred boys, and this scheme is offered as a small step towards supplying the want.

Object of Scheme. To help in making the rising generation, of whatever class or creed, into good citizens at home or for the Colonies.

Reasons. Designed to fill the following wants:

1. The existing want of instruction among our boys in manly qualities tending to good citizenship.
2. The want of attractiveness in some of the existing organisations for boys.
3. The want of novelty in all for permanently keeping up the boys' interest.

Method. Under the attractive name of 'Scouting' a novel form of instruction is given in citizenship, *applicable to any existing organisation.*

Or where such organisation does not exist a special one can easily be formed.

It is applicable to town or country, Great Britain or a Colony.

It includes games and competitions for the maintenance of continued interest.

Instruction. Partly indoor, mostly outdoor; adapted to town as well as to country; easy, inexpensive, and useful; developing character and health, not only in the boys but in the Instructor as well by instruction in 'Scoutcraft'.

Scoutcraft includes the following subjects and their respective details which are taught theoretically, and also practically by certain tests and games;

1. *Discipline.*—Self-discipline; Obedience to Scout Law; Self-sacrifice and Sense of Duty, etc.
2. *Observation.*—Noticing details; Tracking; Quick sight; Deducing meaning from small signs; Judging distances; heights, and numbers.
3. *Woodcraft.*—Camping; Cooking; Natural History; Resourcefulness; Map-reading; Finding the way; Boating; Swimming; Carpentering; Cycling; Marksmanship; Astronomy, etc.
4. *Health and Endurance.*—Physical development; Exercises and Games; Cleanliness; Non-smoking; Continence; Sobriety; Food; Sanitation, etc.
5. *Chivalry.*—Courtesy and helpfulness to women and children; The Knights and their Code; Charity; Thrift; Honour; Courage; Cheerfulness.
6. *Patriotism.*—History and Geography of Britain and her Colonies; The Flag; H.M. Services; Deeds that won the Empire; Nature of government, etc.
7. *Saving Life.*—Ambulance work; Saving Life in cases of fire, gas-fumes, drowning, street accidents, panics, etc. The Albert Medal.

Games. After first instruction in the above details, interest is maintained by games and competitions in Scoutcraft.

Handbook. An inexpensive handbook called *Scouting for Boys* is being prepared. It contains a progressive course of lessons and practices in each of the above subjects, such as will enable an Instructor, though untrained himself, to teach his boys; or it can be used as a self-instructor by an individual boy wishing to teach himself.

Expense. Expense should be very small. No apparatus or uniform is absolutely necessary beyond badges.

Chief items of expense where a boys' organisation does not exist already would be hire and lighting of room, stationery, a few books, badges, etc., which could be met by a small subscription from members.

ORGANISATION. 'Patrols' of six Scouts are formed under a senior boy as 'Patrol Leader'.

Four or more Patrols, up to ten, form a 'Troop' under an officer called a 'Scout Master'.

HOW TO START. The Scout Master would select six or eight special boys to act as Patrol Leaders of his Troop. These he would put through a course of instruction of about three weeks or a month, with the help of the Handbook. If Saturdays and Sundays only are available it will take a little longer.

After this each Patrol Leader would form and instruct his Patrol of six scouts on the same lines, under the supervision of the Scout Master, to pass a standard test for the privilege of wearing the badge of a Scout.

Similarly where there are not enough boys to form a troop, a man or boy can form a patrol of six and instruct them.

After which further development could be carried out by games and competitions.

UNDERSTUDY. Each Scout Master should have an 'Adjutant'—i.e. an officer under him as second in command and general assistant, ready to take his place at any time.

Similarly in each Patrol there should be a 'Corporal' trained to help the Patrol Leader and to act for him when necessary.

Responsibility is thus given to a number of boys.

DISCIPLINE. The principle is that each scout is put *on his honour* to carry out orders whether his officer is present or not.

There is one important difference between this second leaflet and the draft of four months earlier. The draft ends with the following paragraph:

A Court of Honour is formed in each troop of the officers and two Patrol Leaders for awarding praise or blame, conducting tests and competitions, maintaining Scout Law, and carrying on general business of the Troop.

There is no indication of why this was omitted in the published leaflet; its ideas were restored in the final scheme.

⚜ ⚜ ⚜ ⚜ ⚜ ⚜ ⚜ ⚜ ⚜ ⚜ ⚜ ⚜ ⚜ ⚜ ⚜ ⚜ ⚜

CHAPTER THREE

BROWNSEA ISLAND

IT HAS BEEN NOTED THAT THE NAME 'BOY SCOUT' HAD BEEN USED as early as 1900 as the title under which *Aids to Scouting* was serialized in a boys' magazine. Probably the first use of the name was in February of that year for a series of boys' yarns, or Penny Dreadfuls, the opening number being entitled 'The Boy Scout of Scarlett's'. Other Boy Scout adventures appeared in the New Buffalo Bill Library and in Tip Top Tales. During the Boer War boys dramatized themselves as Boy Scouts just as they played at the Siege of Mafeking, or wore B.-P. button-hole badges. We have seen that the second of the two leaflets printed in the last chapter originally bore the heading 'Boy Patrols', and when it seemed likely that the Movement would develop as a separate entity, B.-P. thought of using the name 'Imperial Scouts'; fortunately he was persuaded not to adopt this restrictive term, and 'Boy Scouts' won the day.

The second leaflet stated that 'an inexpensive handbook called *Scouting for Boys* is being prepared'. B.-P.'s term of office as Inspector-General of Cavalry ended with a tour in Egypt and the Sudan at the beginning of 1907; he was then free from military duties to devote himself to the writing of the handbook.

Part of his manuscript has survived, and from this, and from entries in his diary, it is possible to follow the course of composition. The first date that can be given is 18 June 1907 when he sent to the typist the manuscript of part of the chapter on 'Tracking'. At that date he was staying at the Izaak Walton Hotel, Dovedale. His diary of 19 June records: 'Wrote *Scouting for Boys* most of the day—writing 9 hours.'

It was about this time that he met Arthur Pearson (later Sir Arthur) and discussed with him the best means of bringing the Boy Scout scheme to the attention of those interested in the training of boys. Pearson was at once interested and they worked out a programme for the next twelve months. They decided that a trial camp should be run by B.-P. in the summer of 1907; if that should prove a success, then he should tour the country during the winter of 1907–8 and expound the scheme; meanwhile *Scouting for Boys* should be finished and Pearson would arrange for publication as cheaply as possible. He further gave £1,000 to cover initial expenses, and provided an office in Henrietta Street. They also made plans for launching in 1908 a new boys' paper to be called 'The Scout'. It seems that Pearson probably realized that B.-P.'s original idea of providing additional activities for existing organizations would not meet the needs of boys. This idea, however, was not abandoned until events proved that boys insisted on being Boy Scouts and not Something-else-plus-Scouting.

In the middle of July 1907, B.-P. went to stay at Mill House, Wimbledon Common, in order to concentrate on his book. From there he wrote to his mother:

> It is perfectly delightful here and I am getting on with my writing very well—being entirely my own master—and very quiet sitting out in the garden all day.

His preparations for the proposed camp were now made. A site had been secured at the south-west corner of Brownsea Island in Poole Harbour.

B.-P. decided that he wanted a mixed company of boys to see how they would get on together; so he formed his party out of sons of his own friends and some boys selected by the Boys' Brigade officers of Poole and Bournemouth; in this, and in helping to organize the camp, he received great assistance from Mr. (later Alderman) H. Robson and from Mr. G. W. Green, both of the B.B.; the latter was mainly responsible for collecting stores and gear. They were a bit surprised at some of B.-P.'s requirements, for this was not a camp along normal lines to which they had been accustomed.

In a long letter to the parents of the boys he invited, B.-P. described the scheme of training he proposed to follow at the camp—this was under the headings of woodcraft, observation, discipline, health and endurance, chivalry, saving life, and patriotism. He gave the daily time-table with lists of the personal equipment each boy would need. Details were also given of the site and of the means of transport. He asked that each boy before coming should learn how to tie a reef knot, a sheet bend, and a clovehitch, of which he gave sketches. It is indeed a model letter for a Scoutmaster to send to parents before camp.

Major Kenneth Maclaren, an old Army friend, was there to help, and P. W. Everett (now Sir Percy Everett, Deputy Chief Scout for Great Britain) assisted in running the camp. Donald Baden-Powell, B.-P.'s very young nephew, was also there.

The following is the list of the boys in their four Patrols; the first name of each five is that of the Patrol Leader.

WOLVES (Blue)	CURLEWS (Yellow)
H. Wroughton	G. Rodney
C. I. Curteis	H. H. Watts
J. M. Evans-Lombe	A. Vivian
P. Medway	T. Bonfield
R. Giles	R. Grant

BULLS (Green)	RAVENS (Red)
T. B. A. Evans-Lombe	H. B. Emley
A. Primmer	B. Tarrant
B. Blandford	S. Rodney
J. Rodney	B. Collingbourne
M. Noble	H. Noble

These fortunate boys did not, of course, realize what the camp was all about; to them it was just a good holiday with the added thrill of having the hero of Mafeking to themselves for a week, for that was to have been the length of the camp, but everyone enjoyed it so much that the time was extended; the dates were 29 July to 9 August.

News of the camp had got about, and the newspapers were soon looking for copy, but B.-P. put them off. To one editor he wrote:

> I write to say that the camp is quite a small experimental one, and in no way worth public attention as far as it goes. I certainly hope to evolve a big scheme eventually, but this is a very partial experiment, and undue advertisement of it can only do harm to the whole. I hope, therefore, that you will help me by not giving it any more publicity.

LORD BADEN-POWELL OF GILWELL, O.M.
A photograph taken in Copenhagen, 1924

18

One great point about them was that every day they had to do a good turn to somebody, and that is one of our rules.

When you get up in the morning remember that you have got to do a good turn to someone during the day; tie a knot in your handkerchief to remind yourself of it; and when you go to bed at night think who you did the good turn to.

If you should ever find that you had forgotten to do it, you must do two good turns the next day instead. Remember that by your Scout's Oath you are on your Honour to do it.

or leave the tail of your necktie outside your waistcoat

A good turn need only be a very small one; if it is only to put half a penny in a poor box, or to help an old woman to cross the street, or to give water to a thirsty horse it is a good turn. But one must be done every day; and it only counts as a good turn when you do not accept any reward in return.

[Make each scout tie knot in handkerchief or to remind him to do good turn next day]

A PAGE OF THE ORIGINAL MANUSCRIPT OF *SCOUTING FOR BOYS*

See pages 36–7 of 40th Anniversary Edition

We may regret that only a few photographs were taken, and surviving copies of some are so faded as to make reproduction difficult, but on the other hand the boys were not distracted by the attentions of the press.

One newspaper did publish a description of the camp site, but the facts for this were gathered before the camp had really opened. A few of the boys had arrived, and with B.-P. and Major Maclaren were helping to pitch the tents. These were bell tents; this was almost the only type available at that time, and indeed for some years to come. Scouting and the rising interest in camping helped to make the ridge tent known, until it ousted the Army tent. Straw palliasses were used for beds, but the boys also made mattresses on looms as described in *Scouting for Boys*. These were used when on night picket. A marquee provided the dining-quarters. Cooking, with an exception to be noted later, was done centrally by an Army cook. The organization in these respects was on the usual plan of a Boys' Brigade camp. Each Patrol had its own tent.

The boys did not wear uniform; they were asked, however, to bring flannel 'shorts'; the fact that this word was put in quotation marks indicates that it was an unusual request in 1907. They did have Patrol shoulder knots of coloured wool, rather long according to our present usage: Wolves—blue; Bulls—green; Curlews—yellow; Ravens—red. Each Patrol Leader had a flag with the animal represented on it. There were also badges. Each boy was given a brass fleur-de-lis badge which was fastened on to his coat; when he had passed a few tests (knots, tracking, the Flag) he was given another brass badge to fasten below the first, a scroll with the words 'Be Prepared' on it. These two together are now the basis of the First Class badge in Great Britain; but this early badge had one difference—the scroll turned downwards and not upwards as to-day.

B.-P.'s uniform consisted of shorts, a shirt with braided sleeves, a shoulder knot, collar and tie, and a trilby hat. The braiding was after the pattern he designed for the South African Constabulary officers. The long shoulder knot is now in B.-P.'s Room at Imperial Headquarters, London. He wore the same badge in his hat as the boys wore. They were probably disappointed that he did not wear his famous cowboy hat!

The daily programme was as follows:

6 a.m.	Turn out. Air bedding. Milk and biscuits.
6.30 a.m.	Exercises.
7 a.m.	Notices as to day's activities with demonstrations.
7.30 a.m.	Clean camp.
7.55 a.m.	Parade. Flag break followed by Prayers. Breakfast.
9 a.m.	Scouting practices.
12 noon	Bathing.
12.30 p.m.	Lunch.
1–2.15 p.m.	Rest.
2.30 p.m.	Scouting practices.
5 p.m.	Tea.
6 p.m.	Camp games.
7.15 p.m.	Rub down and change.
8 p.m.	Supper.
8.15 p.m.	Camp-fire yarns. Short exercises (breathing, &c.).
9.15 p.m.	Prayers.
9.30 p.m.	Turn in. Lights out.

B.-P. used the koodoo horn (captured in Matabeleland in 1896) to rouse the camp and for signals; several short notes meant 'Rally'; a long call meant 'Ready'. This horn was later used to open the first Scoutmasters' Training Camp at Gilwell Park in 1919, and is still used there; it was also sounded by B.-P. at the opening of the Coming-of-Age Jamboree in 1929.

The exercises used morning and evening were simple ones rather on the lines of those given in *Scouting for Boys*. Many of the Scouting practices were in tracking and stalking, and also in observation training. Tracking-irons were used for laying some trails; in one photograph a boy is seen making a track on the sand strip. The chief officer of the coastguard gave instruction in knotting, life-saving, and resuscitation; he supervised practices in fire-drill when the boys jumped from the cottage windows into a sheet; he also talked about the flag and of naval traditions and customs.

Bathing included water games and the use of two boats; the most popular game was the whale hunt—a game that B.-P. adapted from a suggestion of Thompson Seton.

The rest after lunch was strictly enforced; the boys could chat together, but were not allowed any activity.

The evening camp games were mostly for fun. Basket-ball was

played with an improvised net. 'Bang the bear' was popular, and so, too, was cock-fighting. Such muscle-and-wind strengtheners as 'the struggle' were practised.

For the evening meal the boys had to be particularly smart and clean; they called this 'dressing for dinner'.

The camp-fire yarns were mostly of B.-P.'s own adventures, many of which were incorporated in *Scouting for Boys*. Often they had reference to the practical Scouting of the following day. No one recalls that they did any singing other than the Eengonyâma Zulu chant.

Sir Percy Everett has written down his memories of those camp fires.

> Round the camp fire at night the Chief told us thrilling yarns, himself led the Eengonyâma chorus, and in his inimitable way held the attention and won the hearts of all.
>
> I can see him still as he stands in the flickering light of the fire—an alert figure, full of the joy of life, now grave, now gay, answering all manner of questions, imitating the call of birds, showing how to stalk a wild animal, flashing out a little story, dancing and singing round the fire, pointing a moral, not in actual words but in such an elusive and yet convincing way that everyone present, boy or man, was ready to follow him wherever he might lead.

The Eengonyâma chorus is given in *Scouting for Boys*, and is perhaps not as well known as it used to be. B.-P. heard it in 1887; he then met Zulus for the first time and was greatly impressed with what he called 'a wonderful anthem'.

B.-P. was very keen on getting boys accustomed to night conditions; hence the night picket, when B.-P. himself might try to get into the camp from outside the boundaries. One day he told the boys that he was going to 'invade' the island and they were to stop him. By this time they had learnt a thing or two, so they posted a scout to keep an eye on his movements and send signals to the others as B.-P. crawled through the undergrowth. As he passed under a big tree, a command 'Halt' came from above, and there was Donald B.-P., who thus had the distinction of capturing his uncle. B.-P. used this incident as a good example of the wisdom of looking up as well as around.

There were various competitions, some between the Patrols and some for an individual prize. Thus a prize was given for the best collection of leaves of trees with their names. Another was given for observation tests; this was won by H. B. Emley. Trail following was done by Patrols as well as individually; trails were laid in various ways—the tracking-irons have already been mentioned—but some were laid with bits of coloured rag on branches and by Scout signs. Many different practices and competitions in observation were carried out, such as finding messages hidden in trees; indeed, B.-P. seems to have put most stress in the training on observation, tracking, stalking, and similar forms of Scouting.

On one whole day each Patrol went off on its own with uncooked rations, and had to look after itself, knowing that, at some time during the expedition, they would come under B.-P.'s observation. They had previously had practice in making fires and in making dampers.

The programme was a crowded one for such a short camp as B.-P. tried to deal with all the topics set out in his second leaflet. It is no wonder that some parents afterwards complained that their sons 'arrived home very tired'.

After hearing from the parents, B.-P. drafted a report; this was not published; some of the information is given in this account of the camp, and a few paragraphs of general impressions are worth quoting.

The Troop of boys was divided up into 'Patrols' of five, the senior boy in each being Patrol Leader. This organisation was the secret of our success. Each Patrol Leader was given full responsibility for the behaviour of his Patrol at all times, in camp and in the field. The Patrol was the unit for work or play, and each Patrol was camped in a separate spot. The boys were put 'on their honour' to carry out orders. Responsibility and competitive rivalry were thus at once established, and a good standard of development was ensured throughout the Troop from day to day. The Troop was trained progressively in the subjects of Scouting. Every night one Patrol went on duty as night picket—that is, drew rations of flour, meat, vegetables, tea, &c., and went out to some indicated spot to bivouac for the night. Each boy had his greatcoat and blankets, cooking-pot and matches. On arrival at the spot, fires were lit and suppers cooked, after which sentries were posted and bivouac formed. The picket was scouted by Patrol Leaders of other Patrols and myself, at some time before eleven p.m., after which the sentries were withdrawn and picket settled down for the night.

We found the best way of imparting theoretical instruction was to give it out in short instalments with ample illustrative examples when sitting round the camp fire or otherwise resting, and with demonstrations in the practice hour before breakfast. A formal lecture is apt to bore the boys.

The practice was then carried out in competitions and schemes.

For example, take one detail of the subject, 'Observation'—namely, tracking.

1. At the camp fire overnight we would tell the boys some interesting instance of the value of being able to track.

2. Next morning we would teach them to read tracks by making footmarks at different places, and showing how to read them and to deduce their meaning.

3. In the afternoon we would have a game, such as 'deer-stalking', in which one boy went off as the 'deer', with half a dozen tennis balls in his bag. Twenty minutes later four 'hunters' went off after him, following his tracks, each armed with a tennis ball. The deer, after going a mile or two, would hide and endeavour to ambush his hunters, and so get them within range; each hunter struck with his tennis ball was counted gored to death; if, on the other hand, the deer was hit by three of their balls he was killed.

This was our principle for teaching most of the items.

Discipline was very satisfactory indeed. A 'court of honour' was instituted to try any offenders against discipline, but it was never needed. In the first place the boys were put 'on their honour' to do their best; in the second place, the senior boys were made responsible for the behaviour of the boys forming their Patrol. And this worked perfectly well.

In his draft report he noted how easily boys of such contrasted social conditions had mixed. This experience impressed him deeply; out of it grew the basic idea of the fourth Scout Law.

After the Brownsea Camp, B.-P. could once more turn to the writing of *Scouting for Boys*; his experience with those twenty boys gave him more confidence in his scheme and had suggested to him a number of further ideas; perhaps the most valuable gain was that he had seen the effect of his camp-fire yarns and had a sounder notion of what appealed to the boys.

His diary gives no information on the progress of the book before 22 December when a note records that he 'worked all morning on *Scouting for Boys*' while staying at Middleton-in-Teesdale. Wherever he went he was quick to note any information or incident that could be used in the book. Thus at the beginning of September he was staying at Cloan in Perthshire as the guest of R. B. Haldane (later Viscount Haldane) then Secretary of State for War, to discuss Army reform. In the course of conversation Mrs. Haldane, the statesman's mother, gave B.-P. some information about the Elsdon Murder, or Winter's Stob, and recalled seeing the gibbet on which Winter was hanged at Stang's Cross. All that, with a sketch, went into *Scouting for Boys*.

Much of B.-P.'s time during November and December was taken up with a lecture tour which was part of the programme he had agreed upon with Pearson. The Y.M.C.A. proved helpful in organizing some of the meetings. The first was held at Hereford on 8 November 1907, and he told his audience that this was the opening of his 'crusade'. His purpose was twofold: first to arouse public opinion to the urgent need for providing some kind of guidance for the many thousands of boys who were not under good influence; secondly, to expound the ideas of Scouting as a means of attracting boys to existing organizations, or to a new formation—Boy Scouts. His own fame was an unfailing attraction, but he was an excellent lecturer, for his good humour and quick wit and his stores of exciting tales of real adventure held his hearers' attention. Sometimes he would use a blackboard to illustrate his points with sketches or diagrams. Later on, when the scheme was more developed, he would have a Boy Scout on the platform and explain the details of uniform and badges. During November and December he visited Swansea, Radcliffe (Lancs.), Exeter, Carlisle, Glasgow, Edinburgh, Scarborough, and London.

This left little time for concentrating on his writing, but he was able to send off additions to the manuscript to the typist. In order to be free from distractions he returned on 26 December to Mill House, Wimbledon Common, and there settled down to putting the book into shape for the printer.

A letter to his mother on 30 December says, 'All goes well here. I am working hard and enjoying frequent walks between whiles in this splendid air.'

It is interesting to note that this letter has on it the well-known Scout badge and the address of the 'offices' in Goschen Buildings—which consisted of a share of two rooms provided by Pearson.

P. W. Everett was at that time Pearson's literary manager, and it fell to his lot to supervise the publication of the handbook. He recalls that the author

was much more businesslike than most authors and artists, partly, perhaps, because he adopted that excellent labour-saving device of returning your own letter with appropriate comments against each paragraph. In this way I could always depend on a quick and satisfactory reply to any queries. Sometimes I would have to wait at Wimbledon while he finished a chapter. It was fascinating to watch him writing and sketching, now with the right hand, now with the left. He is an omnivorous reader of books and papers, and was quick to find and use any fact or incident which would be helpful. He was also most careful to check any statement made, and I can only remember one instance in which he was misled. He had sent to me the story of a boy who had shown great presence of mind in a case of poisoning. This was being set up for use when I received a characteristic note. 'Please delete the story I sent you for *Scouting for Boys* of the lad who saved his mother's life from poisoning. Subsequent inquiry shows he half killed her with the wrong remedies! R.S.S.B.-P.'

B.-P. left Mill House on 6 January 1908, and the first of the six fortnightly parts of *Scouting for Boys* was published that month. They won immediate popularity; four reprints were called for during that year.

On 29 March he received the proofs of the first issue of *The Scout* weekly paper; during that year it reached a circulation of 110,000.

These few facts are a sufficient indication of how quickly (indeed, startlingly quickly) the idea of the Boy Scouts captured the imaginations of the boys of Great Britain.

Whale hunt off Brownsea Island. Sketch by B.-P.

CHAPTER FOUR

'SCOUTING FOR BOYS'

MOST PEOPLE IF ASKED TO MAKE A LIST OF HALF A DOZEN BOOKS that had considerable influence during the first quarter of the twentieth century would not think of including *Scouting for Boys*. Yet that book created a world-wide movement, and its sales, both in the original and in translation, have been, and continue to be, enormous; it is, in fact, one of the world's best sellers.

It is an error to suppose that only boys seized on the book when it was first published; its value and interest were recognized in unexpected quarters. On 17 March 1908, for instance, a 3,000-word review appeared in *The Times*. The anonymous writer posed the question, 'How far can the faculty of observation, which is the necessary part of a Scout's intellectual equipment, be acquired by training?' He went on to refer to the work of Baden-Powell and 'E. Thompson-Seton, the Canadian naturalist and sportsman, and others experienced in the ways of the wilderness, who are attempting to establish Scouting as a schoolboy's sport'. This led him to a consideration of 'the parts of his *Scouting for Boys* which have already appeared'. From this it is clear that the reviewer had not waited for all the fortnightly parts to be published; this explains the limited view he took of the scheme. He noted how the booklets were being read 'with the keenest interest by those to whom they are addressed. . . . The author sees that it is useless for a boy to specialise on military scouting until he has had a general education in the many and manifold arts of open-air living.' The assumption that the aim of the scheme was military training was commonly made at that period, and is still occasionally brought forward in criticism. More must be said on this point on a later page.

The book was revised and reprinted in volume form in May 1908. It was reprinted five times during that year, and when a new edition was published in 1909, a review appeared in the

Spectator on 25 September. By then some 100,000 boys had already become Boy Scouts. It was now possible to get a wider view of the scheme than had been practicable for *The Times* reviewer writing before the book was complete. So the article begins: 'This book does not belie its sub-title. It is in every sense of the word a manual of sound citizenship.' The sub-title was 'A Handbook for Instruction in Good Citizenship'. One passage from this review illustrates how the larger conception of the underlying purpose had been realized.

The Boy Scout is always playing the game. He knows that he is following the rules of the brotherhood as much when he is doing his duty at his lessons, or, it may be, in some employment, as when he is out in camp; when he is keeping his body fit and clean and his mind active as when he is playing Scouts' games on a Saturday afternoon. In emphasising this side General Baden-Powell shows himself a man of real genius. Boys are uncompromising idealists, and they want a game which they can play all the time and give their whole mind to. 'Scouting' provides this complete absorption, and it is a beneficent absorption, since no element of wholesome training is omitted.

After noting some of the features of the training, the reviewer, like his *Times* contemporary, selects the subject of observation for special remark.

He learns to follow spoor, and to observe the smallest details, like a second Sherlock Holmes, and make proper deductions. This habit of close observation and a retentive memory seems to us one of the most valuable sides of the training, and it can be learned anywhere—among the shops of a London street as well as in the hills and fields.

What was it that made this book so attractive and persuasive? At first glance it may seem rather a hotchpotch of anecdotes and bits of instruction illustrated by the author's sketches. It was this patchwork style that suited the semi-literate boys of the early years of this century. In fact B.-P. was using the same method that Newnes, Pearson, and Harmsworth found so successful with a semi-literate public. A more solid text-book style of treatment would have made no appeal to the shop-boys and newspaper-boys that B.-P. wanted to capture.

There was, of course, the popularity of B.-P. as a national hero to ensure that the book would at once catch the eye, but that does not explain its continual appeal. The author had with uncanny skill touched those chords in boy-nature that remain through all the changes of exterior civilization.

An adventurous and romantic atmosphere is created from the beginning. Even the use of the term 'Camp Fire Yarn' for the divisions of the chapters helped to call up a picture to stir the imagination. The subjects dealt with were as thrilling—tracking, stalking, pioneering, camping, life in the open, path-finding, and so on. Above all there was the flow of suggestions for things to do—not merely read about—such as fire-lighting, cooking out of doors, making rafts, constructing shelters, and watching animals. So, too, there was a demand on the intelligence; this is a fact often overlooked by students of Scouting. B.-P. encouraged the boy not only to observe correctly but to draw correct conclusions by the use of his reason; the making of this into a kind of Sherlock Holmes game in no way lessens its value as mental training.

It should further be noted that throughout the book there is a strain of idealism that boys appreciate even if they do not always find expression for it; B.-P. showed how this idealism could be turned into action. He provided the practical means for developing those qualities of character that boys admire in their heroes, 'men accustomed to live on their own resources, taking their lives in their hands, brave and loyal to their employers, chivalrous and helpful to each other, unselfish and reliable; MEN, in fact, of the best type'. So he showed the boys how they, too, could become self-reliant, and how they could, by practice, learn to keep cool-headed and useful in time of sudden emergency. He pointed out that this requires training; so first aid, fire-fighting, life-saving, and other skills must be learned in order to BE PREPARED.

The method of training will be discussed in a later chapter; here it is sufficient to point out that the system of grouping the boys into small units or Patrols exactly meets that love of being a member of a gang that every boy experiences for good or ill.

When all these features of *Scouting for Boys* are taken into account, it is no longer surprising that boys read it with avidity and at once began forming Patrols. Many a Troop began in this fashion, and the boys looked for the Scoutmaster. Some men, after reading the book, were equally enthused and began looking for the boys. The fact that the initiative so often came from the boys themselves at once stamped Scouting as something unusual.

The book is primarily addressed to boys, but at the same time B.-P. wanted to help the men who would train those boys; he therefore included 'Hints to Instructors' at the beginnings and ends of the yarns. A final chapter was directed entirely to the instructor, and, judging from the portion of the manuscript that has survived, B.-P. evidently found this last part the most difficult to write, for there are three drafts.

He seems to have been greatly impressed by an anonymous pamphlet published in 1905 by Aldens of Oxford. The title sufficiently explains its tenor. 'The decline and fall of the British Empire. A brief account of those causes which resulted in the destruction of our late Ally, together with a comparison between the British and Roman Empires. Appointed for use in the National Schools of Japan. Tokio, 2005.'

This pamphlet gave B.-P. the text for his final words to Instructors (or Scouters, as we should now say). He drew a parallel between the Romans crowding to the circuses and 'the crowds now flocking to look on at paid players playing football'. In the first edition this theme was developed with some warmth, but in later editions he modified his attack. As an alternative to watching games, he offered practical Scouting.

It would be interesting to follow the modifications made in this last chapter from edition to edition, but this would not be to our immediate purpose. This chapter was published separately as a twopenny pamphlet in the autumn of 1907. It was in the last part of *Scouting for Boys* that B.-P. passed on to Scoutmasters the ideas that developed as a result of the growing experience of the Movement.

The main text of the book has undergone little change since 1908; an occasional paragraph has been added to meet new conditions. It should be remembered that it was first published a year before Blériot flew across the Channel, yet it still holds boys and its remarkable sales continue. During the Second World War exiled Scoutmasters urged the need for preparing supplies of *Scouting for Boys* in readiness for the liberation of their countries and the re-establishment of the Movement, and, as soon as the war was over, this ever-young book again provided the inspiration for training boys on the lines laid down by B.-P. in 1908. These facts indicate that B.-P.'s appeal is to those needs of boys that do not change however much external conditions of society may be transformed.

Before we consider the historical development of Scouting it is desirable that we should understand its enduring principles and methods.

⚜ ⚜ ⚜ ⚜ ⚜ ⚜ ⚜ ⚜ ⚜ ⚜ ⚜ ⚜ ⚜ ⚜ ⚜ ⚜ ⚜

CHAPTER FIVE

FIRST PRINCIPLES

B.-P. PREFACED LATER EDITIONS OF 'SCOUTING FOR BOYS' WITH the following statement:

> Scouting has been described by more than one enthusiast as a revolution in education.
>
> It is not that.
>
> It is merely a suggestion thrown out at a venture for a jolly outdoor recreation which has been found to form also a practical aid to education.
>
> It may be taken to be complementary to school training, and capable of filling up certain chinks unavoidable in the ordinary school curriculum. It is, in a word, a school of citizenship through woodcraft.
>
> The subjects of instruction with which it fills the chinks are individual efficiency through development of—
>
> Character,
> Health, and
> Handicraft in the individual, and in
> Citizenship through his employment of this efficiency in Service.

In refusing to make extravagant claims, B.-P. was following the policy he had formulated from the beginning of the Movement. Scouting is an aid to be used where helpful; it is not an attempt to supplant the more traditional methods of *compulsory* schooling; the free association of boy and man in a *voluntary* scheme is in itself an important element in that training of character which B.-P. always put first amongst the purposes of Scouting.

'Character' was a word he constantly used in expounding the aims of the Movement. What did he mean by it? The answer can be given in some words he used in 1913 when discussing the educational value of Scouting.

> . . . education in high ideals, in self-reliance, in sense of duty, in fortitude, in self-respect, and regard for others—in one word, in those attributes that go to make up *Character*.

He believed that it was possible to develop deliberately those qualities of character that are desirable, and by so doing prevent less desirable qualities from growing powerful. He was fond of setting out his ideas in the form of charts; he liked, as it were, to see the map of the route and then to lay his plans carefully for reaching the objective he had chosen. Here is one such chart.

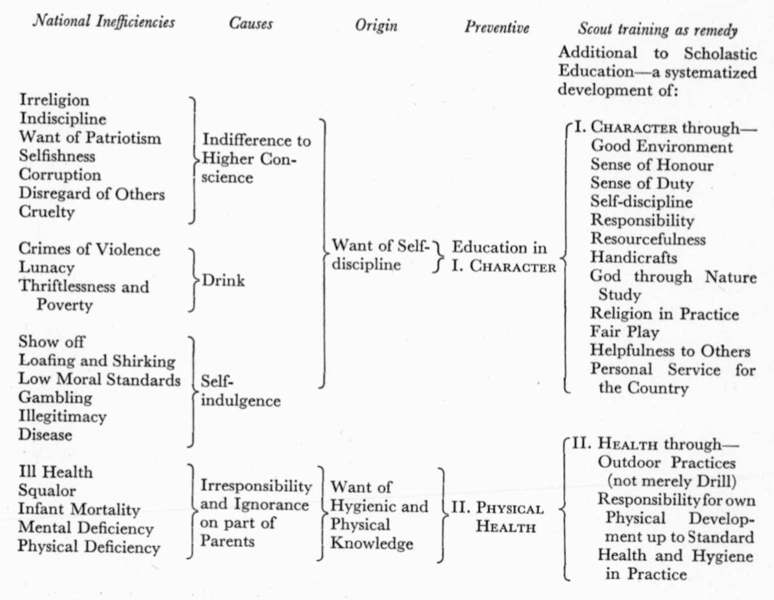

This method may seem strange to some who have followed the considerable extensions of the study of psychology since 1908; yet nearly forty years later, Sir Richard Livingstone, President of Corpus Christi College, Oxford, wrote:

Might we not devise a system of education which shall try to cure the weaknesses to which human beings are inclined and to encourage the virtues which they require? . . . How should we proceed? We should decide what virtues we require and the best way to develop them. We should note the merits and defects of our own and other nations and try to discover their origins. We should consider the special weaknesses of our own age, and peculiar temptations and dangers, moral and spiritual, to which it is exposed, and how to counteract them. We shall get increasing help from psychologists, indispensable though dangerous advisers, whose theories may be advantageously checked by common sense, by the practical knowledge of which a great store is locked up in the minds of active teachers, and by study of actual experiments in 'teaching men to behave as they do not behave', in the making of character.[1]

This is, in fact, a description of what B.-P. attempted in this chart. His main source of suggestion was his own observation of men and boys; he was not a student of psychology and, indeed, in 1907 he would not have derived much help from that science as it was then expounded. His was a practical knowledge and it was on this basis that he constructed his scheme for the training of character.

While he realized that the homily has little effect on a boy unless it is coupled with action, he saw the need for setting before him a reasonable ideal of conduct, and he knew that if a boy gives his word of honour, he will in nine cases out of ten keep his promise. So, as a foundation, B.-P. framed the Scout Law and the Promise the boy makes when initiated. It should be noted how skilfully use was made of a boy's love of joining a society of boys bound by oath.

The Scout Law now reads:

1. A Scout's honour is to be trusted.
2. A Scout is loyal to the King, his Country, his Scouters, his Parents, his Employers, and to those under him.
3. A Scout's duty is to be useful, and to help others.
4. A Scout is a friend to all, and a brother to every other Scout, no matter to what country, class or creed the other belongs.
5. A Scout is courteous.
6. A Scout is a friend to animals.
7. A Scout obeys orders of his Parents, Patrol Leader, or Scoutmaster, without question.
8. A Scout smiles and whistles under all difficulties.
9. A Scout is thrifty.
10. A Scout is clean in thought, word and deed.

The tenth Law was not included in the first edition of *Scouting for Boys*; it appears in the first official Rules of 1911. The Boy Scouts of America have added two laws:

A Scout is Brave, and
A Scout is Reverent.

[1] *Some Tasks for Education* (1946), pp. 37–8.

It should be noted that the laws are positive—'A Scout *is*' something or other. There are no 'nots' or 'don'ts'. B.-P. knew how provocative a 'don't' can be. He was often urged to add to the Laws such prohibitions as 'A Scout does not smoke'. These he always condemned. He preferred the way of self-control and moderation to the way of interdict. Here he differed from Thompson Seton who gave his Woodcraft Indians such laws as 'No smoking', and attached to each a penalty. The only penalties in Scouting are the withdrawal of the badge for a period or, in extreme cases, dismissal; both are so rare as to be almost unknown amongst the boys.

On becoming a Scout, the boy makes this Promise:

On my honour I promise that I will do my best—
To do my duty to God, and the King,
To help other people at all times,
To obey the Scout Law.

At first this was called the Oath, as indeed it still is in the United States.

The Promise is a voluntary undertaking. If any kind of pressure is brought upon the boy to join the Boy Scouts (as, for example, if the Movement became a compulsory Government organization) his Promise can have no binding moral force. The fact that he freely chooses so to bind himself puts upon him a personal responsibility that few boys are prepared to evade.

The words 'on my honour' are of first importance. B.-P. considered that one of our most urgent tasks is to develop the sense of honour and upright dealing in a boy. On it, he said, 'the whole of the Scout's future behaviour and discipline hangs'. This is not inculcated so much by precept as by treating the boy as a responsible being who can be trusted. Trust calls forth trust. The few failures are a small payment for the many successes.

The words 'I will do my best' again show B.-P.'s commonsense attitude. He realized how great a demand the Law makes on any boy, so he deliberately brought the obligation to a level at which the recruit can feel, hard as the job is, that if he does his best, he is still true to his Promise.

'Duty to God' is an obligation laid on every Scout. At the start of the Movement B.-P. consulted the leaders of the Churches

COMING-OF-AGE JAMBOREE, 1929

ST. GEORGE'S DAY SERVICE AT WINDSOR, 1937. B.-P. SPEAKING FROM THE STEPS

and, as a result, relations have always been friendly save for those inevitable misunderstandings that are part of human nature. A Group (consisting of Wolf Cubs, Boy Scouts, and Rovers, or one or more of these) can be sponsored by a Church and, if it is so wished, membership can be limited to its adherents. Other Groups can be open, that is, admit boys of any Church or of no Church; but in the case of boys with no Church connexion, the Movement hopes that by the influence of the Scouter, by simple prayers, by the service known as a Scouts' Own, and by the wonder of nature, the boy may be brought to a realization of the meaning of 'Duty to God'.

Every Scout is expected to be loyal to his own country and to serve it to the best of his ability. Just as Scouting does not prescribe any one form of religion, so it does not advocate any one political philosophy provided the Law and Promise are accepted; the training for good citizenship has nothing to do with political parties; it is for the adult citizen as such (and not as a Scout) to determine the form his duty to the community should take.

It may be asked, 'Is all this really effective? Does the boy really mean to carry out the Promise? Does he really understand the Law?' The answer is to be found amongst the many thousands, or rather millions, of men who were Boy Scouts. The Movement is no longer an experiment; fathers who themselves were Boy Scouts are now sending their sons to the Movement. Those of us who have many years' experience behind us have talked over this point with former Scouts who are now family men; again and again we are told how the Law and the Promise have proved steadying factors long after these men have left the Movement. This, of course, does not apply to all, but the number of known cases of this kind is so large that we can confidently claim that, whatever else of his training the boy may forget, he does not forget his Promise and its implication. As a boy, he understands with the mind of a boy, but as he grows older so the Law gains in significance.

This is no small claim to make, especially of a period when standards of conduct and of honour have been often derided; for many boys whose parents no longer go to Church or even own a Bible, the Scout Law has provided a code that, we may hope, at least fills a gap that modern civilization has created.

All this sounds rather portentous on paper; but the Promise and Law create the spirit in which Scouting lives. It is well to mark two other characteristics of that spirit. The first is cheerfulness; B.-P. once startled a meeting of Scouters by telling them not to take themselves 'too damn seriously'. He often said and wrote, 'Scouting is a game'. By that he meant it was not a heavy instructional process, but something to be enjoyed with plenty of fun and laughter. Not, let it be said, with that forced heartiness that is so nauseating, but the laughter that comes from enjoying what we are doing. And boys do enjoy being Boy Scouts—otherwise there would not be so many of them.

The second important element cannot be simply labelled; it is covered by B.-P.'s phrase, 'the fresh excitements of new adventures'. This love of the unexpected is a mark of the true Scout. 'I have little use', wrote B.-P., 'for a cut-and-dried system in a Scout Headquarters building.' That is why he stressed the importance of a lively imagination in the Scouter.

Let us turn to the active side of Scouting. The scheme of activities is based on the natural desires of the normal boy. The appeal is to that element of the vagabond, pioneer, and explorer which is part of boyhood. Hence the significance of the opening sentence of B.-P.'s 'Explanation of Scouting' in *Scouting for Boys*: 'By the term "scouting" is meant the work and attributes of backwoodsmen, explorers and frontiersmen.' This was an innovation in boy training. What little organized training existed in 1908 was more an indoor than an outdoor business. Scouting is an outdoors activity, and it owes much of its appeal to that fact. Camping, for instance, in those early days was not a popular pastime as it is to-day; indeed its present vogue is largely due to the influence of the Scout Movement which taught the boys the fun of camping, and they, as men, have continued to enjoy that kind of holiday.

To whatever degree conditions may force Scouts indoors, such as weather, darkness, or town-life, this is a second-best. Scouting did not begin in a building but in the streets, the parks, and the open country. If it gets too fond of its headquarters huts and other buildings, its spirit will quickly wilt.

This love of the open air is as much a principle of Scouting as the Promise or the Law.

CHAPTER SIX

THE PATROL SYSTEM

THE DISTINCTIVENESS OF SCOUTING LIES NOT SO MUCH IN ITS principles as in its methods; it was here that B.-P. was a pioneer. When he framed his scheme, the normal method for training boys was by set lessons or by some form of mass instruction. For this B.-P. substituted the small unit, or Patrol, under the leadership of one of its members, to ensure individual and personal training. This conception goes back to the beginning of his planning, for it will be recalled that his draft for his first pamphlet launching the scheme was headed 'Boy Patrols'. The idea was, and remains, the clue to his method and to the success of the Movement.

The very strangeness of the notion made it difficult for Scoutmasters at first, and for new-comers to-day, to grasp the significance of this Patrol System. It is even more difficult for onlookers to understand how Scouting works; that is why so few members of the general public appreciate what is being done. They see the surface characteristics—the open-air life, the happiness of the boys, and the benefits they derive—but they rarely penetrate below that surface.

B.-P. found it necessary to expound this new method again and again; as we shall see his institution of a training scheme for the Scoutmasters was largely directed to making it easier for the Patrol System to be understood.

One of the many explanations he gave will serve here to stress the main points. This extract comes from *Aids to Scoutmastership*, published in 1920.

The Patrol System is the one essential feature in which Scout training differs from that of all other organisations, and where the System is properly applied, it is absolutely bound to bring success. It cannot help itself!

The formation of the boys into Patrols of from six to eight and training them as separate units each under its own responsible leader is the key to a good Troop.

The Patrol is the unit of Scouting always, whether for work or for play, for discipline or for duty.

An invaluable step in character training is to put responsibility on to the individual. This is immediately gained in appointing a Patrol Leader to *responsible* command of his Patrol. It is up to him to take hold of and to develop the qualities of each boy in his Patrol. It sounds a big order, but in practice it works.

Then, through emulation and competition between Patrols, you produce a Patrol spirit which is eminently satisfactory, since it raises the tone among the boys and develops a higher standard of efficiency all round. Each boy in the Patrol realises that he is in himself a responsible unit and that the honour of his group depends in some degree on his own ability in playing the game. . . .

It is important that the Scoutmaster recognise the extraordinary value which he can get out of the Patrol System. It is the best guarantee for permanent vitality and success for the Troop. It takes a great deal of minor routine work off the shoulders of the Scoutmaster.

But first and foremost: THE PATROL IS THE CHARACTER SCHOOL FOR THE INDIVIDUAL. To the Patrol Leader it gives practice in Responsibility and in the qualities of Leadership. To the Scouts it gives subordination of self to the interests of the whole, the elements of self-denial and self-control involved in the team spirit of co-operation and good comradeship.

But to get first-class results from this system you have to give the boy leaders real free-handed responsibility—if you only give partial responsibility you will only get partial results. The main object is not so much saving the Scoutmaster trouble as to give responsibility to the boy, since this is the very best of all means for developing character.

The Scoutmaster who hopes for success must not only study what is written about the Patrol System and its methods, but must put into practice the suggestions he reads. It is the doing of things that is so important, and only by constant trial can experience be gained by his Patrol Leaders and Scouts. The more he gives them to do, the more will they respond, the more strength and character will they achieve.

It will be noted how frequently the word RESPONSIBILITY occurs in this passage; it is indeed the key-word in B.-P.'s thought. The Patrol is small enough for each Scout to feel that what he does is of importance, and he can reasonably look forward to being a Patrol Leader or Second. The Second was originally called a 'Corporal', but this term was dropped in 1912; he is chosen by the Patrol Leader as his assistant; in the United States of America the term 'Assistant Patrol Leader' is used. This sharing of responsibility is an important principle of organization.

The operation of the Patrol System can be briefly described. The Scoutmaster must, of course, train the first half-dozen or so recruits. From amongst them the first Patrol Leaders are chosen. It is then their responsibility to arrange for the training of later recruits through the early stages. This will not all be done by the Patrol Leader himself, for the more efficient Scouts will train the less efficient. The Scoutmaster will watch progress to make sure that there are no gaps in the training. He himself, with his assistants or with the help of friendly instructors, will provide instruction in the more advanced stages. Much of this will be given to the Patrol Leaders for them to pass on to the Scouts: the Scoutmaster becomes, as it were, the Patrol Leader of his Patrol Leaders.

The Patrol meeting together in council discusses its activities and makes its plans for its future progress. The regular Patrol training meeting is of the utmost importance; it is a boys' affair and they have to learn by experience to work and play together if they are to achieve anything.

Then comes the Court of Honour. This term is a little misleading to-day, but it has an interesting history. As we have seen, in B.-P.'s report on the Brownsea Island camp, he formed a Court of Honour for disciplinary purposes, 'but it was never needed'. His experience has proved typical; the occasions for serious disciplinary action are rare; the Court of Honour still has this function in reserve, but its main business now is to be a kind of management committee. In the United States of America the term 'Troop Leaders' Council' is used and this is what in effect the Court of Honour is. The members are the Patrol Leaders. In the early days of a Troop the Scoutmaster acts as chairman until the boys find their feet; then one of the Patrol Leaders becomes chairman and the regular presence of the Scoutmaster is no longer necessary. The Court plans the future activities of the Troop, its regular meetings, its day expeditions, its camps and hikes, and indeed its whole programme. It further controls the spending of the small weekly subscriptions paid by the Scouts.

From this it can be seen how in Scouting the boy is given the experience of self-government; he learns the need for give and take in the Patrol meeting in council, and later, as a Patrol Leader, he develops that experience on a wider scale in helping to run the Troop.

Thus as early as 1908 B.-P. was training boys in self-government through placing on them responsibility; this he regarded as an essential element in preparation for adult citizenship. We are now accustomed to this idea, for schools have found it useful, but at that early date it was an innovation in the training of boys.

This Patrol idea is carried into all parts of the scheme. Thus B.-P. preferred Scouts to move to a rallying-point by Patrols, unobtrusively, rather than in a mass as a Troop. So, too, in camp the unit remains the Patrol. As he wrote:

> Scouts' camps should be small—not more than one Troop camped together; and even then each Patrol should have its own separate tent, at some distance from the others. This latter is with a view to developing the responsibility of the Patrol Leader for his distinct unit.

B.-P. had little use for mass methods of instruction, and he discouraged any form of military drill apart from the minimum practice needed if a Troop *has* to march somewhere. Even then he preferred the Troop 'to move in single file along each side of the road'. On the subject of drill he was quite emphatic in his opinion.

> Military drill tends to destroy individuality, whereas we want, in the Scouts, to develop individual character; and when once drill has been learned it bores a boy who is longing to be tearing about on some enterprise or other; it blunts his keenness. Our aim is to make young backwoodsmen of our Scouts, not imitation soldiers.

Even for physical training he preferred to make the boy 'individually responsible for his own health and to carry out his physical development by personal exercises and practices "on his own" and in his spare time'. Mass physical jerks were not to his liking except as an occasional special piece of training for a display.

Apart from the short-lived term 'Corporal' (now 'Second') he avoided as far as possible military terms; thus instead of 'Attention!' or 'Shun!' he used 'Alert!' when giving orders.

In spite of such clearly expressed views on military drill, B.-P. was accused in 1908 of teaching boys to be military-minded; this charge has been made at intervals ever since. It was inevitable in the early days, for the launching of the scheme coincided with the campaign for conscription waged under the patronage of Lord Roberts. B.-P. did not support that cause, but he was known as a soldier, and as an admirer of Lord Roberts. The conclusion drawn was that his Boy Scouts were really a kind of cadet force in attractive disguise. B.-P.'s answer was that the qualities of character needed in a good citizen in peace and war were much the same—self-reliance, initiative, loyalty, and courage. His scheme he claimed was directed at training boys to be good citizens under all conditions, and that might mean joining in the defence of the country, but this was a subsidiary result and not his main purpose. Part of the difficulty was that his conception of a soldier was unusual at that period; we can appreciate it better after two world wars when such qualities have proved so valuable—particularly in the Second World War. It is curious that at a time when soldiering meant to most people drill—drill—drill, his deliberate rejection of drill as a method of training should not have prevented the charge of militarism being made. It may be hoped that it has now been laid to rest.

⚜ ⚜ ⚜ ⚜ ⚜ ⚜ ⚜ ⚜ ⚜ ⚜ ⚜ ⚜ ⚜ ⚜ ⚜ ⚜ ⚜

CHAPTER SEVEN

THE BADGE SYSTEM

THE BADGE SYSTEM IS AN INTEGRAL PART OF THE BOY SCOUT scheme. B.-P. had introduced a badge of efficiency in scouting when he was Colonel of the 5th Dragoon Guards—this was the first use of a special badge in the Army. As this had proved so successful in stimulating the men to reach good standards, he carried the idea into the Boy Scouts.

There are two groups of badges:

1. Badges of progress in general Scouting, and
2. Badges for hobbies, personal interests, and specialized Scout subjects, such as Gardener, Carpenter, Star Man, or Camper.

The first group, those for general Scouting, now includes Tenderfoot, Second Class, and First Class. In the original issue of *Scouting for Boys* there was no test for a Tenderfoot; he was described as 'a boy who is not yet a Scout'. The complete Scout badge consisted of two pieces; the fleur-de-lis from the north point of the compass, and the scroll underneath with the motto 'Be Prepared' (B.-P.'s initials). A small knot hangs from the bottom of the scroll; this is a reminder, like a knot in a handkerchief, that a Good Turn must be done each day. The scroll was awarded to the boy who passed the tests for Second Class; the fleur-de-lis was added on passing the First-Class tests. The tests as laid down were numbered consecutively, to make it clear that the Scout was expected to continue his training from test 1 to test 12 without a break. This arrangement was dropped later on, and it seems a pity that the old sequence was thus broken, for Scouts tended, and still tend, to rest at the end of the Second-Class tests.

Here are the original tests.

To become a *second-class scout* and gain the motto badge, a boy must satisfy his Scoutmaster in the following details:

1. Tie four of the following knots in less than thirty seconds each knot: Bowline, fisherman's bend, reef knot, clove hitch, sheet bend.
2. Track a deer's 'spoor' (made with tracking-irons) or a horse's track for a quarter of a mile in not more than fifteen minutes; or, in a town, to describe satisfactorily the contents of one shop window out of four observed for one minute each.
3. Go at scout's pace for one mile in not more than thirteen minutes. (Scout's pace is alternate walking and trotting.)
4. Know the scout's laws and signs.
5. Know the composition of the Union Jack, and the right way to fly it.

To become a *first-class scout* and gain the whole scout's badge, a boy must pass the following test—in addition to those for second-class—before a Court of Honour. (N.B. In the case of a new troop the Scoutmaster can act as the Court of Honour.)

6. Point out the direction of different points of the compass where he stands.
7. Make a journey alone of not less than fifteen miles from point to point by walking, riding, boat, or bicycle.
8. Describe or show the proper means for saving life in case of one (selected by the Court) of the following accidents: fire, drowning, runaway carriage, sewer gas, ice-breaking; or bandage an injured patient, or revive apparently drowned persons.
9. Be able to read and write.
10. Have at least sixpence in the savings bank.
11. Show that he has brought a recruit to the Boy Scouts, and has taught him to tie the six principal knots.
12. To lay and light a fire, using not more than two matches, and cook a quarter of a pound of flour and two potatoes without cooking utensils.

Two points will be of interest to present-day Scouts. In 1908 it seemed necessary to make sure that a First-Class Scout could read and write; this perhaps indicates the type of boy it was hoped to attract; and secondly, the cooking had to be done 'without utensils'.

These tests were revised after a few years' experience. In 1911 they took a form that was not substantially changed for some thirty years. A Tenderfoot test was added and an age-limit laid down. Here are the 1911 tests.

Tenderfoot.

A boy on joining the Boy Scouts must be between the ages of 11 and 18 and pass the following tests before making the promise:

Know the Scout's laws and signs, and salute.
Know the composition of the Union Jack and the right way to fly it.
Tie the following knots: Reef, sheet bend, clove hitch, bowline, fisherman's, sheepshank.

He is then enrolled as a Tenderfoot, and is entitled to wear the buttonhole badge.

Second-Class Scout.

Before being awarded the Second-Class Scout's Badge a Tenderfoot must

1. Have at least one month's service as a Tenderfoot.
2. Have a knowledge of elementary first aid and bandaging.
3. Know the Semaphore or Morse sign for every letter of the alphabet.
4. Follow a track half a mile in twenty minutes; or, if in a town, describe satisfactorily the contents of one shop window out of four, observed for one minute each, or Kim's Game, to remember sixteen out of twenty-four well-assorted small articles after one minute's observation.
5. Go a mile in twelve minutes at Scout's pace.
6. Lay and light a wood fire in the open using not more than two matches.
7. Cook a quarter of a pound of meat and two potatoes without cooking utensils other than the regulation billy, in the open, over camp fire if possible.
8. Have at least sixpence in a savings bank.
9. Know the sixteen principal points of the compass.

First-Class Scout.

Before being awarded a First-Class Badge a Second-Class Scout must

1. Swim fifty yards.
2. Have one shilling at least in the savings bank.

3. Send and receive a message either in Semaphore or Morse, sixteen letters per minute.
4. Go on foot or row a boat alone or with another Scout to a point seven miles away and return again, or if conveyed by any vehicle (railways not allowed) or animal, go a distance of fifteen miles and back. He must write a short report of the journey. It is preferable that he should take two days over the journey.
5. Describe the proper method of dealing with two of the following accidents (allotted by the examiners): Fire, drowning, runaway carriage, sewer gas, ice breaking, electric shock. Bandage an injured patient, or revive apparently drowned person.
6. Cook satisfactorily (over camp fire in the open, if possible) two out of the following dishes: porridge, bacon, hunter's stew; or skin and cook a rabbit, or pluck and cook a bird; also, make a damper of half a pound of flour, or a twist baked on a thick stick.
7. Read a map correctly, and draw an intelligible rough sketch map. Point out a compass direction without the aid of a compass.
8. Use an axe for felling or trimming light timber, or, as alternative, produce an article of carpentry or joinery, or metal work, made by himself.
9. Judge distance, area, size, numbers, height, and weight within 25 per cent. error.
10. Bring a Tenderfoot trained by himself in the points required for a Tenderfoot Badge.

It will be noticed that these tests are far more advanced than those originally devised. Probably B.-P. found that he had underestimated how much a boy will learn when he is engaged in things he likes doing. When these tests are considered as a whole it will be seen that they cover a variety of subjects and that a First-Class Scout has had a valuable all-round training. Moreover, the tests do necessitate concentration of mind while proving attractive to an open-air boy; each boy finds one or more of the tests troublesome, but to get the badge he must practise for these as seriously as for those he likes. This need for 'stickability' was constantly stressed by B.-P. as an essential element in character training.

In addition to these efficiency badges there are others

intended to encourage each Scout to develop his own particular interests or to specialize in some form of Scouting or of public service. This part of the scheme was developed during the early years from the modest three badges given in the first issue of *Scouting for Boys*; these were for Signalling, First Aid, and Stalking. By 1911 there were forty-one such badges available; the list was sufficiently up to date to include an Airman badge. Some of the badges are for public service, and the gaining of a selection of these leads to the award of the King's Scout badge—in 1909 King Edward VII permitted this name to be used. Such badges as Pathfinder, Ambulance, Cyclist, and Signaller were amongst the first group qualifying for the King's Scout badge.

A Scout who gained six proficiency badges (without any limitation of choice) was granted the All-round Cords, and a King's Scout (who had to be a First-Class Scout) who gained twenty-four badges was awarded the Silver Wolf. This award was open to all Scouts for achievement in this way until 1922 when it became an exclusively honorary award from the Chief Scout to adults rendering the Movement valuable service.

It is natural to wonder if this large assortment of badges is a desirable feature of Scouting. Boys have been seen in Scout uniform with their sleeves plastered with badges ranging from Basket Worker to Naturalist. And in the United States of America a Scout can wear a special band across the body to take numbers of badges.

The onlooker may well ask if any one boy can possibly have such versatility, and the assumption is made that the badges are given too easily. This is certainly so in some cases, but more rarely now than in the early days. The large number of badges is not an invitation to each Scout to see how many he can gain. The purpose is to provide such a range of interests that even the dullest boy can find at least one badge to stimulate him to increase his skill and knowledge.

B.-P.'s own comment on the system is important as it expresses a point of view typical of his way of thinking but not easily understood by more conventional people.

Our aim is merely to help the boys, especially the least scholarly ones, to become personally enthused in subjects that appeal to them individually, and that will be helpful to them.

We do this through the fun and jollity of Scouting; by progressive stages they can be led on, naturally and unconsciously, to develop for themselves their knowledge.

But if once we make it into a formal scheme of serious instruction for efficiency, we miss the whole point and value of the Scout training, and we trench on the work of the schools without the trained experts for carrying it out.

Our standard for Badge earning—as I have frequently said—is not the attainment of a certain level of quality of work (as in the school), but the AMOUNT OF EFFORT EXERCISED BY THE INDIVIDUAL CANDIDATE. This brings the most hopeless case on to a footing of equal possibility with his more brilliant or better-off brother.

We want to get them ALL along through cheery self-development from within and not through the imposition of formal instruction from without.

He knew that the system could be abused and that 'badge-hogging' was a weakness in some Troops, but he was not prepared to scrap the whole scheme because some misused it; he preferred to develop in the Movement a public spirit that would set the matter right, and this has been largely accomplished; the Scout with badge-measles is now a rare phenomenon.

CHAPTER EIGHT

1908

IT IS HOPED THAT THE LAST THREE CHAPTERS HAVE PROVIDED those who have no first-hand experience of the Boy Scouts with a sufficient understanding of its main principles and methods to make the story of the Movement's development more intelligible. Occasional reference has been necessary to later years; we must now return to 1908.

That must have been an exciting year. No one, certainly not B.-P., had foreseen the enthusiasm with which boys and men took up Scouting. The normal course of developing a new scheme was expected—a small beginning and a steady building up over a period of years. But this prospect was quickly shattered. Practical problems had to be settled as they arose, and during much of that first year B.-P. was in the north of England in command of the newly formed Northumberland Territorial Force; he was deeply interested in this and it had the merit of being the kind of pioneering work that called out his greatest powers.

The little office in Henrietta Street was overwhelmed with inquiries. B.-P. had persuaded an old army friend, Major Kenneth Maclaren, to be Manager (or Secretary), and he had as his assistant Miss Margaret Macdonald, who was later to be Secretary of the Girl Guides for many years. P. W. Everett gave constant help with *The Scout* and with other publications. The first issue of *The Scout* appeared on 14 April 1908, and in that year reached a weekly circulation of over 100,000 copies. It was in *The Scout* that B.-P. was able to guide the Movement before any other official ways were available, and for more than thirty years he contributed a weekly article with interruptions due to ill health. *The Scout* did much to bring boys into the Movement, for it appealed to boys of all types with its stories of adventure and instructional articles.

One of the early proposals in *The Scout* was a competition to select thirty boys to attend B.-P.'s second camp. In August he wrote to a friend:

My days, and often nights, have of late mostly been spent manœuvring with my 'Terriers'. Things are going very well both with the Territorials, and, especially, with the Boy Scouts: this fad really is going ahead to an unexpected extent. I signed an agreement last night granting copyright [i.e. of *Scouting for Boys*] in Germany, and it is already being translated into Russian and Norwegian. Two days ago I had a very appreciative letter from [Theodore] Roosevelt upon it; and my correspondence on it grows daily bigger. In the last four weeks 5,000 copies of the book were sold! I only wish I had more time to devote to it so that I could meet the development half way and 'make it hum'.

I do wish we were having our camp at Brownsea again but I am obliged to have it up in my own district this year so as to be available for my own work as well. So we go into camp next Saturday near Hexham on the Roman Wall, in a wild country teeming with romance—in fact our theme for two days and nights is 'The Quest of King Arthur' who lies asleep in some hidden cave in that neighbourhood. This will I hope make his story and chivalry very real to the boys.

He liked to link up local history or romance with the boys' training and the Roman Wall and King Arthur supplied both.

The site was at Humshaugh about five miles north of Hexham. The camp was from 22 August to 5 September 1908. One of the campers afterwards recorded the impression made on him by the camp-fires when B.-P. (or 'The General' as he was usually called at that period) would tell yarns of his adventures, or give talks about the next day's activities, or answer any questions the Scouts liked to fire at him on such subjects as natural history or astronomy.

The question of uniform had to be faced from the beginning. A note on this topic in the first chapter calls for some expansion. A more complete explanation by B.-P. adds details.

I knew from experience with boys of all sorts in our first experiments in Scouting that one fellow got his trousers all torn and wet going through a scrub, another wearing a small cap got his face—very nearly his eyes—badly scratched by thorns in going through the bush at night, others got too hot in their coats and waistcoats, another, going bareheaded, got sunstroke, and so on. So it became necessary to suggest some kind of dress that would suit all phases of Scouting and yet be healthy and inexpensive and comfortable. Then everybody would come to be dressed much the same as his neighbour—in fact, in uniform. So I thought out what would be the best patterns to adopt. Now—and here is a useful tip for you—whenever I went on an expedition of any kind I kept a diary and that diary included a list of the clothing and equipment I took with me, with a note of what I need not have taken and also of what I had omitted

B.-P.'s sketch of Scout uniform from the first edition of *Scouting for Boys*

to take. All this information came in useful when one was going on another expedition. Also I drew a sketch of myself showing what dress I found most convenient for the job I happened to be doing. At one time it was in India, another in South Africa, also Scotland, Canada, West Africa, Himalayas, etc., etc.

From these data I compiled what I thought would be a dress applicable to most countries. I had used it to some extent in dressing the South African Constabulary when I formed that Corps, and so a good deal of the idea came into the Boy Scout uniform when I devised that.

It is possible to trace the origins of one or two items. B.-P. had first used the cowboy hat in Ashanti in 1895 and so became known to the natives as 'Kantankye' (He of the Big Hat). This was in days when a good deal of freedom was allowed on active service as regards uniform. It was during the same campaign that the idea of the Scout staff was born. B.-P. noted how useful such a staff was to the officer in charge of the engineers in testing footings and making measurements when his men were laying the field telegraph. Apart from uniform B.-P. collected other ideas on his expeditions, for it was probably in West Africa that the left handshake was noticed; this was a mark of distinction between a chief and his most trusted followers. The Scout colours, green and yellow, were those of the South African Constabulary and were a combination of the colours of the Transvaal and the Orange Free State.

In 1908 the uniform was a striking innovation; the touches of colour given by the scarf and the Patrol shoulder-knot were a pleasant contrast to the normally drab and restrictive clothing of boys; shorts were almost revolutionary; they were worn (rather long) for football, but they were not ordinary wear. Scouting did something to forward the adoption of more comfortable dress for boys.

The problem of uniform for Scoutmasters was not easily solved; for some time B.-P. tried to avoid laying down firm rules, but at last he was forced to do something to curb the exuberant fancy of those who adopted aigulets, gauntlets, and even spurs. So Scoutmasters were advised to wear 'knicker breeches' with shirt and collar, puttees, or leather gaiters; if a jacket was worn, then a 'white linen collar' was necessary. Shorts were suggested for camp wear. It was not until after the First World War that Scoutmasters were recommended to wear shorts when in uniform. Some of us can recall the courage it took to appear in public so dressed.

Curious little problems arose in those early months. Soon there were complaints from park officials in London and elsewhere about boys practising Scouting to the annoyance of the respectable public. So a 'Passport' was devised to meet such objections. Applications for these were not always as amusing as the following specimen, 'Pleas will you send a dozen cards which will allow us to go into the fields without being persecuted at 4d a dozen.'

After the Humshaugh camp B.-P. decided that some kind of organization must be set up throughout the country to keep an eye on developments and ensure that Scoutmasters were men of integrity. So on 28 September 1908 he circulated the following letter:

Dear Sir,

As you may remember, I first promulgated the scheme of Scouting for Boys with the idea that any Boys' Leagues or Clubs who wished could adopt it as a means of providing additional wholesome attraction in their programme.

But now I find in practice that, in addition to its adoption by Leagues, young men, and even boys themselves, have started Patrols independently in all parts of the country. This, of course, is a very good sign of its being popular with them, but at the same time lays it open to failure or abuse.

It has been suggested to me from several quarters that these efforts should be recognised and directed locally, and in some centres the local advisory committee, composed of gentlemen representing the different boys' organisations, have taken up the organisation and the recognition of the various Patrols and Troops in the neighbourhood.

It has also been represented to me—and I fully recognise with justice—that the want of discriminating supervision in the appointment of Scoutmasters, and in the bestowal of Scout Badges, is leading to confusion and misunderstandings.

Duties of Local Committees. My proposal, therefore, is to extend the system of advisory committees to every city where gentlemen will be so good as to serve upon them.

The chief duties of such committees would then be:

1. To bring into touch with themselves all Patrols and Troops of Boy Scouts in their district and register them.
2. To have in their hands the appointment of Scoutmasters and bestowal of Badges and rewards, etc.
3. To encourage the Movement generally as they find best.

In addition to these there are secondary duties which already some committees have taken up with good results, such as:

1. The allotment of districts to respective Scoutmasters as their recruiting ground.
2. The acquirement of a store of camp and games equipment for issue on temporary loan to the various Patrols and Troops as they may require them.
3. The employment of Scouts at fêtes, etc., whereby funds can be obtained.
4. The institution of an employment bureau for deserving Scouts.
5. Supervision of demonstrations, etc.

Local Secretary. I would suggest that local committees, on taking up these duties, should forward to my Manager the name and address of the gentleman who will act as their Secretary, and be our means of mutual communication.

Travelling Inspector. I have appointed Mr. Eric Walker to act as Travelling Inspector, and he will be available, free of charge, to local committees for consultation, or for conducting examinations of Scoutmasters, and Scouts, and for lecturing locally should they desire it.

Scoutmasters. In the first place it seems desirable that Scoutmasters themselves should pass some sort of test that will guarantee their being fit and proper men to teach the lads.

With this in view, I have drawn up a short syllabus of desirable qualifications (attached).

A candidate could thus be examined in these, either by the Inspector or by three members of the Committee and be by them recommended for a certificate if considered fit. Or two certified Scoutmasters would be empowered to carry out the examination and recommend the candidate for his certificate.

There would thus be three ways by which a gentleman can pass his tests for Scoutmaster:

1. Through the Travelling Inspector.
2. Through three members of the Local Committee.
3. Through two qualified Scoutmasters.

It is particularly desirable that the Scoutmasters should not be made liable for sending returns or accounts or for subscriptions.

Scouts' Badges. Boys can join the organisation and receive their enrolment cards and button-hole badges without any test whatever. But to obtain the rank and badge of second or first-class Scout they must pass the prescribed tests at the hands of a qualified Scoutmaster, assisted by Patrol Leaders as directed in the handbook. This will enhance the value of the rank and induce boys to work for it.

Existing Scoutmasters and Scouts. I should like it to be understood that those who have been acting as Scoutmasters during the past few months and have borne the brunt of the work in the early days of the Movement will be entitled to rank as Scoutmasters without going through the regulation tests. These should take effect, say, from December 1st next.

To any of these gentlemen who may be recommended by the Local Committee, or who send me a satisfactory report of what they have done as Scoutmasters, I will award certificates as Scoutmasters.

In the case of boys who may be wearing first or second-class badges, it will be necessary for them to tell the Manager under what circumstances they obtained their badges if they wish to obtain a Scout's certificate, or such certificate will be forwarded on recommendation of the Local Committee.

Suggestions Invited. It is difficult to suggest any scheme that will suit all localities equally well, and I particularly desire to avoid clashing with any existing organisations for boys; I merely want to help them and, if possible, bring them into mutual touch through the common bond of Scouting, and at the same time to provide an organisation where the boys or Scoutmasters (as often happens) who desire it can be independent of existing leagues.

For these reasons, therefore, I merely offer these ideas as a basis for a solution of two or three difficult points which have arisen, and shall be very grateful for any amendments or alternative proposals that may be sent in to reach me not later than October 8th.

In conclusion, I should like to take this opportunity of thanking you for your very kind co-operation in starting the scheme which already promises, with such help, to become a widespread and self-supporting agency for good among the rising generation, not only at home, but also in our colonies and abroad.

I am,
Yours very truly,
R. S. S. Baden-Powell.

The attached 'Tests for Scoutmasters' read as follows:

1. A general knowledge of the handbook *Scouting for Boys*, especially the Scout Laws.
2. A full appreciation of the moral aim underlying the practical instruction all through the scheme of Scouting.
3. Personal character and standing such as will ensure his having a good moral influence over boys, and sufficient steadfastness of purpose to carry the venture over difficult and slack times.
4. Age not less than 18.
5. Ability to provide a clubroom of some sort for Scout meetings.

This document calls for careful study as it illustrates so well some of the principles of organization that B.-P. applied from the earliest days—principles that still guide the Movement in spite of its vast growth. Most important of all is the stress put on local, as contrasted with central, control. 'The man on the spot' was in B.-P.'s opinion more likely to come to a sensible decision than some unknown person in a distant head office. The relationship all through must be a personal one, not a paper one. This meant leaving considerable latitude for going wrong as well as for going right, but greater harmony would result as a consequence of that freedom. It is once more the principle of responsibility rather than that of direction. The same applies to the Scoutmaster; within wide limits he must be permitted to apply Scouting in the way he finds best suited to local conditions and not be too hampered by rules and regulations and set programmes of activities.

Inevitably this decentralization has meant occasional failures and an unevenness in the quality of the results; but these are outweighed by the gains in the sense of responsibility and a freedom to make the greatest use of local conditions. The advice 'that the Scoutmasters should not be made liable for sending returns', &c., should be noted. This repeats his statement in the 'Foreword For Instructors' in *Scouting for Boys*, 'I have no desire to trouble Instructors with red-tape returns, and so on.'

Attention should also be given to the 'Tests for Scoutmasters'. The word 'Tests' now seems hardly suitable for these very general suggestions, for we are accustomed to think in terms of training courses and certificates of efficiency. These general requirements have remained, substantially, the basis of appointment for Scoutmasters. No technical efficiency is required by these 'Tests'; a 'general knowledge' is all that is expected. This meant that no one need be deterred from undertaking the work for lack of skill in tracking or outdoor cooking or pioneering; such matters are learned with the boys. A test of practical efficiency would have debarred many young men from taking up Scouting, and B.-P. found it necessary in later years to remind Associations that would-be Scoutmasters need not be Admirable Crichtons; his view was that an understanding of the purpose of the training and an appreciation of the Scout Law are of far more importance than being able to tie a bowline or to cook kabobs.

This open invitation to become Scoutmasters resulted in men of all types and of varied experience taking up the work. Some were professional men, others were working men; some had colonial experience, others had not travelled beyond their own counties; some were well to do, others had small wages. The clergyman might find a railway porter as his colleague, and a doctor might be assistant to a village schoolmaster. So it has been ever since. Few movements have brought together such a diverse company of men to work for a common cause.

As a result of this circular a register of Scoutmasters was opened at Headquarters, and these men were known at first as 'Certificated Scoutmasters'. The register is not very informative for it consists merely of an index volume containing names and addresses with the date of registration. Most of the entries record names and addresses but not Troops. Men who had been running Troops before October 1908 were registered *en bloc* without any indication, unfortunately, of when they had begun their service. Some Troops were registered by the Local Committee and some with Headquarters, and it was not until 1919 that central registration was required. As a result it is impossible to say which was the first Troop formed. There were certainly some Patrols and Troops established before the end of 1907 as a result of B.-P.'s lecture tour in the autumn of that year. As guidance these pioneers had the scheme issued in May 1907, *Aids to Scouting*, and the twopenny pamphlet 'The Boy Scout Scheme' which became the last chapter of *Scouting for Boys*. Others no doubt waited for the publication of *Scouting for Boys*. Local Committees were not systematically established throughout the country until the autumn of 1908, so that until this was accomplished many Patrols and Troops were working without any supervision or written authority.

The hope expressed in the circular that Scouting might prove a 'common bond' between existing boys' organizations was frustrated. B.-P. argued that all would gain strength if they took counsel together and exchanged experiences. There was never the least desire on his part to dominate the field, and he was quite willing to join in with others for the common good. Only one close association was formed—with the Y.M.C.A. Boys' Department then under the guidance of W. B. Wakefield. In the autumn of 1907 B.-P. discussed the matter with the Y.M.C.A. leaders and as a result they organized the series of meetings already mentioned at which he could address the public on the subject of Scouting as a method of training boys.

The circular stated that Eric Walker had been appointed Travelling Inspector. W. B. Wakefield undertook to do the same work voluntarily in the north, leaving Eric Walker to concentrate on the south. When in 1910 the term 'Travelling Inspector' was changed to 'Organising Commissioner', W. B. Wakefield withdrew; twenty-six years later he presented a camping site in the Lake District to the Boy Scouts Association.

The close working with the Y.M.C.A. gradually loosened. This was inevitable. B.-P.'s notion of sharing Scouting with other organizations proved unworkable; the Movement had, in its own right, gained such a momentum that it became an entirely separate entity. B.-P. made one more attempt, in 1909, to form what he called a 'combine' of the heads of boys' organizations but met with no support. Friendly relations have, however, always been maintained with other bodies, but the attempt to dovetail one into the other created more problems than it solved.

So the idea of a general council of all the leaders did not develop as B.-P. hoped. It was not until 1936 that a Standing Conference of National Juvenile (now Youth) Organizations was set up; its purposes were not quite in line with B.-P.'s proposals but it represents some measure of his intentions.

CHAPTER NINE

EARLY DAYS

HOW WAS A TROOP CARRIED ON IN THE EARLY DAYS? HERE IS AN account of the 1st Newport (Isle of Wight) Troop by its founder, J. H. Burgess. He is now (1948) Group Scoutmaster and is typical of the many men who have carried on quietly all these years in a work that brings little public recognition, but has its award in the consciousness of having helped to train good citizens.

In 1907 the writer was a sergeant in a Territorial regiment, keenly interested in military scouting, and an earnest student of *Aids to Scouting*, the handbook for Army use written by Lieut.-General R. S. S. Baden-Powell, still the popular hero of the siege of Mafeking.

Towards the end of that year he decided to form a boys' organization in Newport, to be called the Vectis Juvenile Scouts, trained on purely military lines.

Passing a newspaper-shop early in January of 1908, the writer saw a fourpenny pamphlet in the window, entitled *Scouting for Boys*, and purchased it. Fascinated by its contents he altered his mind concerning the mooted Vectis Juvenile Scouts, and took steps to convert it into the system dealt with in the new book, his first recruit being his brother. Other boys were approached, and recruiting was soon in brisk progress.

As the fortnightly parts of *Scouting for Boys* were published they were purchased, and by the end of January the 1st Newport Troop was in being. It was registered at the provisional Headquarters in London, and on Saturday, 8 February 1908, the certificate of enrolment was received. Unfortunately, although the small registration card was carefully preserved for many years it was lost during one of the frequent removals to new headquarters.

Four Patrols were formed, Hounds, Wolves, Peewits, and Tigers.

Recruits now came in rapidly, anxious to take part in this new game of Scouting, fascinated by its kinship to the life of the backwoodsman.

The question of uniform or some sort of equipment now arose, the boys being anxious to wear the dress shown in the booklets *Scouting for Boys*, at the time reaching the last issue of the set of six. But Scouting was something new, and except for metal badges obtainable from Headquarters, it proved impossible to get Scout equipment, for the simple reason that manufacturers apparently did not exist.

To practise cooking the Scouts each bought a tin mug, a set of four one-gallon boiling cans of tin being purchased, and the boys enthusiastically boiled vast quantities of water, exultant to think that they could light fires to do it. Then tea appeared and the mugs were brought into better use than for the drinking of hot water. The writer's wife spent hours making semi-haversacks with wire hooks to replace the bags, thus freeing the boys' hands.

At last the writer's queries from various firms brought fruit, for Gamages wrote to say that although they had nothing in the form of Scout equipment or clothing, they had a number of hats for disposal which they thought would answer admirably to fill that need at any rate. The charge would be fourpence-halfpenny each.

So a postal order for nine shillings was sent off with a request for two dozen of these very-suitable-hats, which duly arrived.

The writer gasped with dismay when he opened the parcel, for the hats-very-suitable-for-Scouts were a weird mixture of ordinary felt hats of various types, colours, sizes, and shapes, no two alike. But there was one treasure—a real slouch hat, dark grey in colour, apparently the uniform hat of some Colonial police force, its side turned up in a very professional manner and clipped there by a metal fastening.

But the boys did not mind. They shared the hats with great glee. Thus, equipped with weird hats and mug-carrying sling straps of wide white tape, the 1st Newport wore its first uniform.

The next requirement was a tent, for the Troop intended to go to 'camp' at Easter, and again the writer's wife was called into service. A neat little square tent of unbleached calico resulted, which the Scouts greeted with great enthusiasm, and continually practised pitching.

By the end of March all Scouts had received the official enrolment card, which bore the Scout badge on one side, and on the reverse a lithographed message in the Chief Scout's handwriting, worded: 'You are now a Scout. I trust you—on your Honour, at all times to do your best to carry out your Duty; and to do a good turn to somebody every day. R. S. S. Baden-Powell, Lt.-Genl.'

Funds were non-existent in those days. The writer had newly married, and his pay was small; too small to leave a margin for Scout work. So it became necessary to cut expenditure rigorously. One result was a Union Jack, purchased for ninepence, to be the Troop flag. This poor little flag achieved fame and respect, for every Scout who took his Scout Promise (Scout Oath in those days) did so under it. One thing which caused it to be valued highly by the older Scouts as the years passed was the fact that every one of the eleven Scouts who died for his country during the First World War had taken his Scout Oath under it. Unfortunately, by accident, ten years later it became torn, and for some years three inches of it, fastened to its staff, hung in the Scout headquarters. Then came another hurried removal, and the poor little remnant was lost, despite frantic search by the old Scouts who knew and loved it so well. Probably some recruit, working hard in the removal, destroyed it, ignorant of its history and value.

In April a complete edition of *Scouting for Boys* was issued. The writer possesses his original first edition, a prized link with the early days. In this month the paper *The Scout* appeared, and a number of copies were bought by the Scouts in the Troop.

Easter duly arrived, and the Troop set out for a day on Bowcombe Down, proud in their possession of a 'trek-cart', a three-ply tea-box cut down, painted grey, and lettered, 'Lieut.-General Baden-Powell's League of Boy Scouts—1st Newport Troop'. A lid was fitted, and two broom handles threaded through rope loops in the side for carrying purposes, and in this 'trek-cart' the tent and four cooking-tins were placed.

A cyclist Patrol had been organized, and on the way practised moving through country reputedly that of hostile Indians, scouting up side roads, and covering the main party with its 'trek-cart'.

Tea-making, potato-cooking, signalling, and various other Scouty activities were practised, and at night the Troop went home after a good day, pleased with its first 'camp'.

A photograph taken at this 'camp' shows the flag mentioned, the tent, and the 'trek-cart'. The hats-suitable-for-Scouts can also be seen, the boys having turned most of them up on one side to try and copy the one police hat mentioned.

A few boys had left, but more were coming in, and the Troop steadily increased in strength. The lack of a headquarters was a handicap, for although all possible activities were practised outdoors, in bad weather it became necessary to assemble in the writer's house twenty or thirty boys at a time. In a comparatively small room twenty noisy boys, full of vitality and high spirits, were a tight fit; but all enjoyed it, for the spirit which prevailed among those early Scouts was wonderful, despite handicaps of all kinds and primitive equipment. There is no doubt that where the boys have to work for everything, to 'make-do', and to put up with inconveniences and shortages, it brings out the best in them. The spirit which prevailed in later years, when finance was not a problem, nor shortages met with, was often lacking in the essential keenness which characterized the pioneer Scouts of the Troop.

About midsummer we heard that a Troop had been formed in Sandown, and a Troop in Cowes was reported during the late autumn. These were followed by Troops at Shanklin and Ventnor. The latter was formed by a schoolmaster, and at first did not belong to the Baden-Powell organization. It wore different badges, and differed in other details, but during 1909 joined the B.-P. organization and amended its uniform accordingly, relinquishing its name of National Scouts.

At Whitsun the 1st Newport held another one-day 'camp', walking to Thorness, and practising cooking and Scouting on the beach. This was the last of the one-day camps, for the next one was on orthodox camp lines.

By autumn it was possible to obtain Scout hats, and shirts or jerseys, and it became obvious that the Troop could not go on in its primitive state as far as dress was concerned. This caused the first crisis in the Troop, now nearly fifty strong. Uniform was eminently desirable, but it was impossible to equip a boy fully at a cost of much less than fifteen shillings. The writer's wife offered to make the haversacks. A test showed that by using brown holland it was possible to provide them for sixpence, if the material were purchased in reasonable bulk. By eliminating other desirable but not strictly necessary items, it was found possible to get the cost down to an absolute minimum of ten shillings.

And so the die was cast. The Troop would go into uniform of the regulation type, voting being in favour of jerseys as opposed to shirts, on the ground that the former could be used after their use for Scout purposes had ceased. And then came the vital question. Who was to pay for it?

In those days the pound sterling was worth more in purchasing power than it is to-day, and wages were low, few boys getting more than about five shillings a week. Troop funds did not exist, and there were no known friends of the new organization whom we felt able to approach. The boys must, therefore, buy their own and for those who were unable to do so no help was possible.

Naturally boys did not care to attend meetings in the old-style primitive outfit, the immediate effect being a drop in the strength of the Troop to about eighteen boys. A few of the others did manage to save sufficient money to obtain uniform later, and returned to this Troop.

Towards the end of the year the writer was successful in obtaining permission to use the old Borough Hall, which older readers will remember. In after years it became a garage, which exists there to-day. Although only available for one evening a week this was a tremendous help, particularly in view of the approaching winter, when outdoor activities were inevitably restricted.

After about two months, before the end of the year, we met another of the numerous problems we had to face during the early days, for on appearing at the Hall for one of our weekly meetings we found it occupied by workmen, industriously engaged in laying down a special dance floor. Although our permission to use the Hall had not been cancelled it had evidently lapsed. So we wandered out into the cold of a December night, dejected and homeless once more.

However, a good friend appeared, for the father of one of the Scouts gave us the use of a small room forming the annexe to a derelict house at the back of his premises.

With what gratitude and satisfaction we received this kind act! At last we had a real Headquarters! The room was of unfaced brick and measured about eight feet by twelve, rather small when all the Scouts were assembled, but none the less welcome. It was choked with lumber, and being derelict was very dirty. But a week of hard work performed miracles, the room being cleared, whitewashed, and thoroughly scrubbed.

Then with intense satisfaction we commenced to make a club-room of it. At that time the old wooden barrack-rooms at Parkhurst Barracks were being demolished, to be replaced by the imposing brick structures visible to-day, and greatly emboldened by our need we went up to try and obtain something for a table. We were given one of the old doors, which relays of Scouts carried to our new headquarters. We had about three shillings in the funds, sufficient to buy some wood to make the legs of our intended table, and some American cloth to cover it. And the table duly appeared, much admired by everybody. Notice-boards, mantel ornaments, and even a form constructed of scrap timber were produced.

Then we formed a library, every boy bringing one or more books not needed at his home. Some, such as *How to Breed Canaries* and *Little Annie* and *History of Norman Architecture*, were received with doubtful enthusiasm, but some were more suitable, and a librarian was appointed, who performed his duties with great enthusiasm and much self-importance. Finally, a Scout brought a pair of old and torn lace curtains which his mother was about to throw away, and the fitting-up of this wonderful club-room and 'Headquarters of the 1st Newport Troop Baden-Powell Scouts' was complete.

Then somebody suggested a canteen, and the Patrol Leaders went into a huddle about it, various dark and secret meetings being held. As a result, a sixpenny kettle, three fourpenny cups and saucers, and a little sugar and tea were produced. Somebody brought an old 'Beatrice' stove, which stank abominably but did function. But a teapot! Funds did not admit the purchase of it, and no Scout's mother appeared to have one she did not need, so we made the tea in the kettle—charge, one halfpenny per cup, including sugar and a little Nestlé's milk from a tin which the writer brought.

The Troop had some marvellous times at this headquarters. Scouting of all kinds was practised, cooking in the yard, or open-air work out on the adjoining downland.

During the winter of 1908–9 preparations were made for our first regular camp. Funds were still to be counted in shillings rather than pounds, and the old system of improvisation had to be practised. Again the writer's wife was called into service, and another small tent of unbleached calico was made.

Then we were seized with the idea of making three tents in sections, four sections comprising one tent. Each section was tightly folded and fastened to the haversack of a Scout, the four sections being assembled and linked together by threading cord through holes at the edges. Again finance, or the lack of it, poked up its unwelcome head, and the Troop went into another pow-wow to think of a way to raise some money.

The result was a photographic mount, about eight inches by six, with the figure of a sitting kitten painted on it. By its side was a similar but larger figure, cut out from black emery paper, and stuck to the card at the side of the smaller one. A box of matches was glued to the card and the wording, 'Don't scratch me, scratch mother', painted on. A short length of cheap ribbon threaded through holes at the top completed the article.

For two or three weeks the club-room resembled a small factory, as Scouts worked hard making and assembling the cards. Then the boys took them out for sale at twopence each. Results were very good. Not only sufficient to buy the tent calico was earned, but a margin of fifteen shillings was left over. The Troop was now rich by its own standards of wealth, but the work went on until the demand appeared to be exhausted, by which time we had well over a pound saved.

Other Spartan-like essentials of camp equipment were made, and at last Easter arrived. Assembling on the morning of Good Friday the Troop marched out to Chillerton, the selected camp site consisting of a grassy pit on the southern slope of Chillerton Down. As became usual in after years, Scouts who had to work on Saturday walked into Newport very early in the morning, and as most worked in shops to 10 p.m. in those days they assembled in the market-square at 11 p.m., the writer having vivid memories of those midnight journeys back to camp.

This was their first experience of camp life as far as most of the Scouts were concerned, and the first night was very lively, for few could sleep under the new conditions. But on the Monday evening all marched back to Newport, thoroughly satisfied.

Experience at Chillerton camp had shown that the calico tents were unlikely to be very waterproof in case of heavy rain, so much trouble was taken in obtaining heavier tents at a price within our reach. At last we managed to secure a very serviceable Patrol tent made by sewing six Navy hammocks together, end pieces being added. The hammocks were obviously condemned stores, but for the twelve and sixpence paid the tent was of good value. It was used in various camps for three years. Intensive efforts to obtain some more money resulted in sufficient being earned to buy another tent at the same price. Furthermore, the calico tents were painted over with boiled linseed oil, and thus equipped we felt more confident of being able to face bad weather when we went to our next camp.

This was held at Whitsun in an old chalk pit at the foot of Garstons Down, Gatcombe. This became our favourite camping place, to which we went at every opportunity for the next three years.

CHAPTER TEN

1909

THE YEAR 1909 WAS A DECISIVE ONE IN THE HISTORY OF SCOUTING. It could have continued, as during 1908, as a very loosely organized association with B.-P., *Scouting for Boys*, and *The Scout* as the links between the scattered Patrols and Troops that had sprung up all over the country. The result would probably have been confusion, for all kinds of unscrupulous people were already making use of the name 'Boy Scout' and, by implication, that of B.-P., for methods and practices that were far from consonant with his ideas. Already, too, other 'Scout' associations were being formed each with its little head and each with its own brand of crankery—there were the British Boy Scouts, the National Peace Scouts, the Empire Scouts, and so on. Most of these soon disappeared though a few isolated groups of the British Boy Scouts lingered for many years. These had been formed by Sir Francis Vane who had been London Commissioner for Boy Scouts, but had quarrelled with the parent body on the vexed question of militarist tendencies. Sometimes the term 'B.-P. Boy Scouts' was used to distinguish the parent Movement, but its registered name of plain 'Boy Scouts' won the day.

The circular quoted in Chapter Eight shows that B.-P. was well aware of the dangers of complete licence, and he saw the necessity of some kind of central control but so organized as to leave the maximum amount of freedom to the local units.

At the beginning of 1909 Major Maclaren resigned owing to ill health, and J. A. Kyle was appointed Secretary, the name 'Manager' being dropped, but he had the additional and short-lived rank of 'Chief Scoutmaster'. New offices were taken at 112–18 Victoria St., Westminster, providing twelve rooms for a staff that had quickly grown to twenty-six. The Local Committees, soon renamed Associations, were being rapidly formed, and the first Report (1910) gives a list of 450 that had been constituted in Great Britain and Ireland by the end of 1909. County Presidents, County Commissioners, and District Commissioners had also been appointed, but in the same way that the Patrols preceded the Associations, so these in their turn were often constituted before the appointment of Commissioners—the organization was in effect constructed from the circumference inwards and not from the centre outwards.

Meanwhile B.-P. had been collecting round him a number of voluntary helpers and advisers at the new Headquarters. One of the features of B.-P.'s plan was to have some voluntary helpers, or Headquarters Commissioners, in charge of departments of the work, with a paid staff to manage the routine business. This combination of voluntary Commissioners with a permanent staff has worked well, but since 1945 it is not as easy as it was in 1909 to find men of means and leisure who can devote their thought and energy to directing the Movement.

Mention must be made of some members of that first group. Lt.-General Sir Edmund Elles became Chief Commissioner, a position he held until 1922, and to which he gave generously of his time and administrative abilities. Colonel Ulich de Burgh was Deputy Chief Commissioner and was later to fill other positions of importance until his death in 1922. P. W. Everett was in charge of literature and was to occupy a number of important positions in his long career in the Movement. Lt.-General Sir Herbert Plumer, an old comrade of South Africa, dealt with relations with other boys' organizations and was Vice-Chairman to B.-P. The Field-Marshal, as he afterwards became, remained an active supporter of Scouting whenever his military duties did not take him out of the country. He was in some ways a contrast to B.-P., and stories are still told of his firmness as Chairman of committees and his strict views on smoking and other frailties; he lacked B.-P.'s strong sense of fun, but the two together were an admirable combination. The Movement benefited greatly by Plumer's wise advice.

It will have been noticed that of the four names mentioned only one is that of a civilian, and a study of the first list of Commissioners shows that perhaps half had military or naval rank. This fact was frequently used to bolster up the criticism that the Boy Scouts were a military organization, but there is a simpler explanation. B.-P. was naturally inclined to seek help from the type of man with whom he had served for so long, and the retired officer had the leisure needed for the work.

The first issue of *The Headquarters Gazette* in July 1909 established an important channel of communication between B.-P. and the Scoutmasters. Each month in his 'Outlook' he expounded his ideas and gave his impressions of what he had seen of the Scouts in action. In this way he was able to check extravagances and bring men back again and again to the simple interpretation of *Scouting for Boys*.

As with all new organizations the problem of finance had to be faced; B.-P. took the hard way; the obvious method to cover Headquarters expenses would have been to exact a subscription of membership from all Scoutmasters and Scouts. But from the beginning he laid it down that each unit must be self-supporting from the Patrol or Troop up to Headquarters itself. Publications brought in some royalties and profits, and the equipment department became increasingly important as a source of income. The latter was started with some hesitation as to what the demand might be; badges could only be bought from Headquarters and the price of these was kept as low as possible; but uniform could be bought anywhere. The first Quartermaster, Henry Holt, felt that he was taking a serious risk when he laid in a stock of twelve Scout hats!

In addition to these sources, subscriptions and donations were received from many well-wishers, but care had to be taken that this did not mean depriving local Associations of funds. At the end of 1909 there was a sum of £45. 1*s.* 1*d.* in hand. The *Daily Telegraph*—always a good friend of Scouting—organized a fund in 1909 that brought in over £6,000, and a dinner to likely supporters in 1911 resulted in a further sum of £3,500.

Such dull but unavoidable matters as organization and finance do not paint the living picture of Scouting in its vigorous beginnings. The year 1909 was to see a number of events that once and for all established the new Movement as a recognized part of the national life, and indeed of the life of all British lands and of many foreign countries.

In April 1909 a party of Scouts from this country went to Germany at the invitation of the Wandervögel; this is the earliest recorded visit to the Continent by Scouts. The prominency

Punch, 1 Sept., 1909

Our Youngest Line of Defence

BOY SCOUT TO MRS. BRITANNIA: 'Fear not, Gran'ma; no danger can befall you now. Remember, *I* am with you!'

taken by army officers in welcoming the Scouts showed that the idea of the Movement had been misunderstood—and so it has been ever since in that country. The party visited amongst other places Heidelberg, Nuremberg, Munich, and Berlin. One of the Scouts reported: 'We went by train to Grünewald, while a battle Alt-Wandervögel v. Wandervögel and Boy Scouts was to take place. On the battlefield the crowd and photographers followed us so much that a hopeless muddle was made of the whole affair.'

Then in August B.-P. ran his third camp; this was organized in an unusual way. There was a land-site at Buckler's Hard near the mouth of the Beaulieu River, and a water-site, as it may be termed, on C. B. Fry's training-ship *The Mercury*. Two Troops were there and they took it in turn to be Scouts on land and Scouts on the water. This was the beginning of Sea Scouts, though they did not officially appear in the Regulations until 1912. B.-P.'s eldest brother, Warington, himself an expert sailor, wrote the handbook *Sea Scouting*.

September brought the first big public demonstration of the strength of the new Movement. On 4 September some 10,000 Boy Scouts gathered at the Crystal Palace. B.-P., in the full uniform of a Lt.-General, took the salute as Chief Scout. It was rather unfortunate that amongst the trophies presented by friends for competition was a small machine-gun; this became the text for many a discourse on the military tendencies of Scouting. Far less notice was taken of another phenomenon that was of lasting significance. As B.-P. went round the grounds to see the Scouts at close quarters he came across a small band of girls. They wore Scout hats and scarves with their feminine dress, and they carried 'poles' (in those days the staff was usually called a 'pole', or less politely, a 'broomstick'—as it often was!). B.-P. asked these girls who they were; the leader replied: 'Please, Sir, we are the Wolf Patrol of the Girl Scouts, and we want to do Scouting like the boys.' This public appearance hastened the organization of the Girl Guides. The problem had already arisen and it was announced in *The Headquarters Gazette* in the previous month that large numbers of 'Girl Scouts' were registered at Headquarters, and 'a scheme is being prepared for them'. B.-P.'s sister Agnes wrote a handbook called *How Girls Can Help to Build the Empire*; this was later followed by the more elaborate *Handbook for Girl Guides* published in 1912. The name 'Girl Scout' is still used in the United States of America.

The Crystal Palace Rally was also of great importance on account of the Conference of Commissioners and Scoutmasters that was then held. The chief subject of discussion was the religious policy of the Movement, and particularly the interpretation of the promise 'To do my duty to God'. Most boys' organizations of that period were attached to Churches, and the Bible class or some other form of religious instruction was an integral part of the activities. B.-P. wanted to cast the net wider; he had his eyes on boys who were outside all Church influence. There were a number of dangers to be faced; the Movement might be boycotted by the Churches as being non-religious, or at least of not being specifically religious; there was also the possibility of being charged with fostering some kind of vague pantheism or nature-worship. All these criticisms have been levelled at the Movement; they overlooked B.-P.'s desire to build a bridge between the complete paganism of the boys without any Church affiliation and the development of religious faith. He began, as it were, from outside with the wish to bring the boys to a knowledge of religion through their Scouting; this he felt was the thing needed most, rather than permanently to leave untouched those outside the Churches. The problem called for skilful handling.

Amongst those invited to the Conference was H. Geoffrey Elwes, a representative of the Church of England Men's Society. B.-P. invited him to express his views, and it was largely as a result of H. G. Elwes's clear exposition of the problem that a policy was worked out that received the approval of the leaders of the Churches. In the first issue of the Regulations (1911) that policy was stated as follows:

> It is expected that every Scout should belong to some religious denomination and attend its services. Where a troop is composed of members of one particular form of religion it is hoped that the Scoutmaster will arrange such denominational religious observances and instructions as he, in consultation with its Chaplain or other religious authority, may consider best. Where a troop consists of Scouts of various religions, they should be encouraged to attend the service of their own denomination, and in camp any form of daily prayer and of weekly Divine Service should be of the simplest character, attendance being voluntary.

The wording of the opening sentence should be noted. No 'must' is used, thereby leaving that freedom to meet special conditions that B.-P. liked his Scoutmasters to have; a 'must' would, of course, have at once defeated his purpose of getting together those who did not belong to any religious body. It was characteristic of his wisdom that the word 'must' was rarely used.

This statement of policy remained substantially unchanged for forty years, and where it has been loyally observed friction has been avoided, and all the Churches, Roman Catholic as well as Protestant, have actively supported the Boy Scouts. When one recalls the sectarian storms over education that raged during the first decade of this century, the measure of B.-P.'s skill in winning support can be better appreciated.

Shortly after the Crystal Palace Rally 6,000 Boy Scouts of Scotland met at Glasgow to be inspected by the Chief Scout; he was accompanied by Sir William Smith, the founder of the Boys' Brigade. It was an interesting reversal of the roles played by the two men in 1903 at a Boys' Brigade Rally at the same place. B.-P. had then told Sir William how much he envied him the honour of having brought together such a fine company of boys. Of the 1909 Rally B.-P. wrote:

> The numbers on parade were about equal to those of my former review of the Boys' Brigade. The force was too large to address directly, so I assembled the Patrol Leaders that they might hear what I had to say. . . . I turned to Sir William. His eyes were suffused as he said in a reminding way: 'Do you want to change places with me NOW?' A smaller man would naturally have resented or been jealous of a rival organisation coming up on his original invention and almost overshadowing him in his own sphere. But there was none of that in Sir William's great mind.

On 3 October B.-P. went to Balmoral to be knighted by the king. Edward VII was greatly interested in this new organization, and gladly allowed the term 'King's Scout' to be granted to those who gained special qualifications for public service; he gave instructions that the royal parks were to be open to the Scouts, and he promised to review them in the summer of 1910, but he died on 6 May of that year, and it was his successor who was to carry out the royal promise.

CHAPTER ELEVEN

1910–14

EARLY IN 1910 B.-P. HAD TO MAKE A DIFFICULT DECISION. THERE was a rapidly growing need for his personal direction of the Movement, and it was becoming clearer every week that appeals to him for visits and for consultation would be incessant. Invitations were also coming from overseas where the pioneers of Scouting urgently sought his advice and encouragement. During 1909 he had found it difficult to fit in such requests with his duties to the Territorials, and, by nature, he was a man who devoted himself completely to whatever he undertook. At the end of March 1910 he resigned from the command of the northern Territorial Division, but, though this eased the strain, it did not solve the major problem. Without his constant watchfulness the Movement might easily have developed along wrong lines, for its methods were original and so unusual that there was need for much educational work amongst the leaders to ensure that more traditional habits did not smother the new ideas. He put the problem to Edward VII, and also discussed it with Haldane. Both advised him to give his whole time to the Boy Scouts. Haldane wrote:

> I feel that the organization of the Boy Scouts has so important a bearing on the future that probably the greatest service you can render to the country is to devote yourself to it.

So on 7 May 1910 B.-P. resigned from the army at the age of 53 after a service of thirty-four years.

To-day, with our knowledge of the achievements of the Boy Scouts, we may feel that such a decision was inevitable, but in 1910 no one could be yet certain whether the new organization would collapse as quickly as it had risen, or become established in strength. Apart from this element of chance, there was the natural reluctance to break off a career that had meant so much to him, not merely in honours, but in the delight he took in work that called out his finest powers. He was deliberately cutting himself off from the prospects of further advancement such as came to seniors such as French and to contemporaries such as Plumer.

The Scout ran a competition during the first part of 1910 to select two Patrols, the Wolves and Beavers, to go to Canada with B.-P. in August. The boys were under the charge of Eric Walker and of Captain A. G. Wade who later become Organizing Secretary for the north. After crossing the Dominion the Scouts camped near the Rockies and had a wonderful time with Red Indians, ranchers, trappers, and backwoodsmen. On their return eastwards they made short halts at a number of centres to give displays and meet Canadian Scouts. Meanwhile B.-P. was touring the country, inspecting Scouts, addressing meetings, and discussing the Movement with leading citizens. He then went to New York for two days to meet the National Council that had been set up to organize the Boy Scouts of America.

The story of how Scouting was introduced to the United States is typical of how it reached other countries, for there was no deliberate propaganda from London; visitors saw what was happening and appreciated the possibilities and then, on returning home, started Scouts.

During an autumn fog in London in 1909 William D. Boyce, a Chicago publisher, lost his way, and a Boy Scout came to his rescue and took him to the address he was trying to find. When W. D. Boyce offered a tip he was surprised to be told that Boy Scouts (of whom he knew nothing) did not take money for doing a good turn. This unusual statement roused Mr. Boyce's curiosity, and he asked for further information about this new organization. As a result he returned to the States with a trunkful of pamphlets, copies of *Scouting for Boys*, and specimens of badges and uniform. He found that there were already a few Troops in his own country formed by men who had learned of the British Movement; there were also other organizations such as Thompson Seton's 'Woodcraft Indians' and Dan Beard's 'Sons of Daniel Boone' that were working on parallel lines. The leaders of these organizations were brought together and agreed to form the kind of 'combine' that B.-P. had dreamed of for Great Britain.

The Boy Scouts of America (strictly speaking of the U.S.A.)

was incorporated on 8 February 1910 with Ernest Thompson Seton as Chief Scout.

The Movement in the States was fortunate in securing as Secretary a young lawyer, James E. West, who had himself known the unhappiness of a friendless childhood. His position became that of Chief Scout Executive and in the course of thirty-two years of devoted service he built up a great organization inspired with his own idealism.

B.-P. was again in the States at the beginning of 1912; he was then able to visit a number of towns to address public meetings on Scouting. The Movement was faced with the same kind of criticism to which he had grown accustomed in England. Here is the local newspaper report of one meeting.

With James E. West of Washington D.C., the Chief Scout Executive of the Boy Scouts of America, Gen. Baden-Powell appeared on the platform to speak. He was greeted with mingled cheers from the Scouts and hoots and catcalls from a certain element of the local socialist organisation.

The General was not permitted to proceed far with his address before interruptions from the socialist group forced him to stop; he then invited some of the socialists to ask questions regarding the Movement.

Question after question was fired at the General, who promptly answered them all. It seemed to be the impression of the socialists, judging from the questions, that the Scout Movement was antagonistic to labour, and based on purely military principles and for military purposes.

At the conclusion of his address, General Baden-Powell called upon the socialists to send some of their speakers to the platform. After several had been heard, one of the socialist speakers volunteered the statement that Western socialists had misunderstood the purposes of the Boy Scout Movement, and expressed the opinion that the organisation would result in building up a better nation.

The spread of Scouting in the U.S.A. was almost as spectacular as it had been in the United Kingdom.

The census for 1910 gave the total membership ('so far as it has been possible to ascertain') in the United Kingdom as 107,986 with an average of 1 Scoutmaster or Assistant to every 14 boys. This was within the proportions desired by B.-P. whose standard was 1 Scoutmaster or Assistant to 16 boys, so that a Scoutmaster with 1 Assistant could run a Troop of 32

Scouts (4 Patrols) and give attention to each individual. As he wrote later:

> Men talk of having fine Troops of 60 or even 100—and their leaders tell me that their boys are equally well trained as in smaller Troops. I express admiration ('admiration' literally translated means 'surprise'), and I don't believe them. 'Why worry about individual training?' they ask. Because it is the only way by which you can educate. You can instruct any number of boys, a thousand at a time if you have a loud voice and attractive methods of disciplinary means. But that is not training—it is not education.

The number of Boy Scouts (apart from Scoutmasters) in the United Kingdom for the years before the First World War was as follows:

1910	100,298
1911	113,909
1912	126,431
1913	137,776

The number of Scoutmasters and Assistants had reached 14,557 in 1913.

During this period the Movement was expanding throughout the British Dominions and Colonies, but the numbers were not as yet considerable, the total for 1913 being 32,757. Possibly the earliest Troop established overseas was at Cape Town in March 1908. A series of articles in a boys' paper called *The Union Jack* attracted some boys who decided to become Scouts. They set out to find a Scoutmaster and so established the first South African Troop. At the end of the same month copies of the early parts of *Scouting for Boys* reached Sydney, New South Wales, Australia, and three boys formed Patrols. In 1912 B.-P. made a tour of the West Indies, Australia, New Zealand, and South Africa and was able to stimulate the development of Scouting in those countries.

More and more foreign countries were starting Boy Scouts. The importance of this was recognized by the appointment in 1911 of C. C. Branch as International Commissioner 'to promote friendly relations with kindred organisations abroad'. By 1913 there were some 300,000 Scouts in the U.S.A. A beginning was made in France with the Éclaireurs de France in 1910; this admitted boys of both Catholic and Protestant Churches or of no Church connexion; a Protestant body, Éclaireurs Unionistes, followed in 1911. Several Catholic groups united in 1920 to form the Scouts de France. Scouting started in Switzerland in 1911, and in the same year in Norway. By 1913 some fifteen countries, including Germany, had Boy Scout Associations; at first the position in Germany seemed much the same as elsewhere, but within a few years there were at least six rival pseudo-Scout organizations; the one thing they had in common was a tendency to regard Scouting as a preparation for military service.

Troops of British boys were also formed in foreign countries; the first Paris English Troop was formed in November 1909.

Boy Scouts were coming frequently before the public during these early years. They were on duty at the funeral of Edward VII in May 1910, and again at the Coronation of George V in June 1911, when the Scouts of this country were joined by a party of Boy Scouts from Canada. In the following month the king, who had just become Patron of the Association, carried out his father's intention and reviewed the Scouts in Windsor Great Park on 4 July. It was indeed a great occasion. Some 26,000 boys from all over the country and from overseas were there. Naturally the fact of seeing, and being seen by, the king was the outstanding fact of the day, but for most of the boys their first sight of the Chief Scout must have been an equally memorable event. The Windsor Rally was important for one of those innovations that B.-P. was fond of making. He had no wish for Scouts to be drilled for a ceremonial march-past, so he devised a method that became accepted as the Scout form of rally. The boys are scattered round a semicircle some distance from the base; where possible they are concealed by trees or shrubs, but even when they lie down the first impression given to the spectators is that they have vanished. At a signal all leap up and rush forward shouting Patrol cries and brandishing their staffs; at an arranged distance from the rallying-point they come to a halt in dead silence. The effect is always startling, and even alarming to those who see it for the first time and feel as if they were the objectives of the charge. It is a typical B.-P. device; it avoids keeping boys standing for long periods, and the physical and emotional release of the charge and the shouting predisposes the boys to listen quietly to the personage of the rally.

Later in that year at his investiture at Caernarvon the Prince of Wales accepted the office of Chief Scout of the Principality and received a staff from the Welsh Scouts. It may be noted that the first edition of *Scouting for Boys* was dedicated to Prince Edward and Prince Albert, the future Edward VIII and George VI.

An experiment of considerable possibilities began in 1911. A farm at Buckhurst Place, Wadhurst, Sussex, was put at the disposal of the Association for the training of Scouts in farming either for this country or overseas. The boys were allowed a large measure of self-government; each Patrol had its own homestead where the instruction received at the main farm could be applied. There were some difficulties about control as the property did not belong to the Association and the owner had his own ideas on management; but these problems were being overcome when the First World War resulted in such a drain on man-power that the experiment had to be brought to an end in 1916. It had been hoped that Buckhurst Place (another B.P.) would become the first link in a chain of such training farms throughout the Dominions and Colonies. This conception was in keeping with ideas that Kingsley Fairbridge was at that date working out; perhaps had chance brought him and B.-P. together some of the early struggles of that pioneer would have been avoided. A link, however, was made in later years by donations to the Fairbridge Memorial Homes, Rhodesia.

On 4 January 1912 the Royal Charter by which 'The Boy Scouts Association' became 'one body corporate and politic' was granted. In the main text B.-P. was referred to as 'Chairman of the Council' and not as Chief Scout, and provision was made for the nomination of his successor as Chairman. The bylaws refer to him as Chief Scout.

The control of the Association was vested in a Council of from thirty to seventy members. The management was in the hands of a Committee appointed by the Council from among its own members; a certain number of the Committee retired each year but were eligible for re-election.

B.-P.'s idea of the Council—the nearest approach he could get to his cherished 'combine'—was that it should be as representative as possible of the national life and of those concerned with the right training of boys. The Charter Council included representatives of the Churches, the Law, the Services, the universities and schools, the Dominions and Colonies, and a few of the existing boys' organizations. Such a Council serves two main purposes; it guarantees to the public the integrity of the Movement, and its broad membership ensures that expert advice is available on any problem of the relation between Scouts and the national life. The Council meets once a year, but its work is carried on by the Committee whose members are able to give the necessary time and thought for regular consultation.

The suggestion has been made from time to time that at least a proportion of the Council should be elected by members of the Movement itself. B.-P. was opposed to this, not because he objected to the principle of election, but because he could not see how it could be translated into practice, and for him 'Will it work?' was a more important question than any theorizing. He felt that it was most important that the members of the Committee should consist of men who could see a good deal of each other as heads of the departments at Headquarters, or in some other close association that would mean frequent opportunities for those informal exchanges of views that are often more fruitful than formal Committee meetings. Elected members, he felt, might not be able to get to London regularly, even for monthly meetings, and thus the close personal relation he desired would not be possible. There are frequent opportunities for discussion and consultation in the Local Associations where, again, the personal association of men known to each other by frequent intercourse is a channel for suggestions or criticisms. The adults who train the boys do, in fact, elect some representatives to the Local Association committees. In the Troop the boys in their Patrol Meetings, and the Patrol Leaders in their Court of Honour, are all the time gaining experience in running their own affairs and so are being prepared for citizenship. Like the British Constitution the Boy Scouts Association is a mixed affair. Other countries have other methods; in Norway, for instance, the Chief Scout and all Commissioners are elected.

Reference has already been made to B.-P.'s overseas tour of 1912. This had an unexpected significance, for on the voyage out to the West Indies he met Miss Olave St. Clair Soames, and in October of that year they were married. A wedding-present fund (limited to subscriptions of one penny from each Scout) resulted in the gift of a motor-car from the Movement.

Increasing demands on the services of Headquarters called for a reorganization of the staff in 1912; Ewen Cameron became Secretary with Captain A. G. Wade as Organizing Secretary. Eric Walker became Private Secretary to the Chief Scout.

The year 1913 was full of promise; there was no inclination, as the Annual Report expressed it, to 'rest and be thankful'. At the beginning of the year the Duke of Connaught became President, a position he was to hold until his death in 1942. As Governor-General of Canada he had been Chief Scout of the Dominion and had taken a personal interest in the development of Scouting there.

The great event of the year was the Imperial Scout Exhibition at Birmingham in July. It was a wise decision to hold this in the Midlands rather than in London; 20,000 Scouts were there including representatives of the Dominions and Colonies and of twelve foreign countries; it was in fact the precursor of the Jamborees. The most important aspect of the Exhibition was not the great Rally, but the series of practical demonstrations of crafts, hobbies, and useful handiwork. In this way the public realized that Scouting was something more than a club; as the visitors moved round the stalls they could see boys practising all kinds of hobbies that are not only useful but might well prove the beginning of a lifetime interest.

At the Rally on this occasion, as at Windsor, the King's Scouts and Life Savers were grouped together for special commendation. The latter were Scouts who had received one or other of the awards given for pluck and skill in giving immediate aid to those in peril. In the early years of the Movement the Chief Scout put a great value on this aspect of the work; such deeds showed better than anything else that Scouting promoted those qualities of initiative and cool-headedness that he desired to cultivate in the boys. Up to January 1914 the total of Gallantry Awards for Life Saving since the foundation was 792. Such awards are still given, but the former practice of emphasizing the record in public has fallen into disuse.

An appeal for a Permanent Endowment Fund was opened in September 1913. The response was most promising, but the coming of war in August 1914 meant the closing of the appeal; the total reached was just over £100,000.

The Annual Report of January 1914 included a reproduction of a coloured picture by John Hassall of a Red Indian with a Boy Scout looking towards a rising sun bearing the date 1914 with a large question mark. The answer was of a different character than the one expected—it was war.

CHAPTER TWELVE

THE EVE OF WAR

JANUARY 1914 SAW THE PUBLICATION OF *POLICY, ORGANISATION AND RULES* (P.O.R.). This had been preceded by four annual issues of *Regulations*; inside the cover of the new version B.-P. had the words printed, 'Rules on how to play the game of Scouting for Boys'. It was as if he feared the increasing number of regulations; his desire to avoid red-tape was strong, and he particularly wanted to keep Scoutmasters free from paper-work such as the making of returns and the filling up of forms. The 1914 P.O.R. contained seventy-four rules; the 1947 edition has 530. The increase is largely due to the development of new sections, and many of the rules refer to badges. None the less the Boy Scouts Association is no more immune than other human organizations from the disease of adding rule to rule. Each can be defended, but in the aggregate the effect is daunting to a newcomer. Fortunately B.-P.'s idea of Scouting as a game has become part of the spirit of the Movement and this tends to defeat over-organization. Constant vigilance is necessary to ensure that freedom to the Scoutmaster which B.-P. regarded as essential.

The Annual Report published at the beginning of 1914 contained a list of seven lines of development along which B.-P. hoped progress could be made. They were:

1. Training of Scoutmasters.
2. Organization of Senior Scouts.
3. Organization of Junior Scouts.
4. Organization of Scouting among poor boys in slums.
5. Development of Sea Scouts branch.
6. Development of the Farm School branch.
7. Provision of adequate national Headquarters.

The order of urgency is interesting, but the First World War

LORD SOMERS (*right*), THE SECOND CHIEF SCOUT, WITH HIS SUCCESSOR, LORD ROWALLAN (*left*), THE THIRD CHIEF SCOUT. 1939

WAR SERVICE, 1939–45. EVACUEES

upset the programme. As we have already seen, the farm had to be abandoned as a result of the call on man-power.

The need for a scheme of training for Scoutmasters had long been in B.-P.'s mind. He encouraged Commissioners and successful Scoutmasters to organize experimental courses, and such camps were held for London in 1910 and in Yorkshire in 1911; courses of lectures were also given; thus in London in 1911 a course of three evenings weekly for three weeks had been attended by thirty-two Scoutmasters; but from the beginning B.-P.'s notion was that the main training should be done in camp. He studied the methods used and watched these experiments with close interest before drawing up a scheme of his own. This was his usual procedure; he liked practice and theory to go hand in hand and preferred a few tentative ideas to be tried out before setting down on paper anything definite. Thus after visiting one of these camps in 1913 he wrote,

I think we want to arrive, first, at what are the *essential* points for a Scoutmaster to know, and to set out to teach these—all others must be subsidiary. Now, I take it the essentials are what we find laid down in *Scouting for Boys*. Therefore my idea would be to take that book as the programme of work, dividing it off into the number of days available, and then going through it as practically as circumstances will allow. The book is arranged on that idea. The second point about the training camp would be I think to give Scoutmasters practical instruction as to how a camp should be run. For this purpose I should be inclined to pitch the camp as it should be done for a Scout camp—each Patrol tent on its own ground in a wide circle round the central (Scoutmaster's) tent. The Scoutmasters should of course be in Patrols for the course, under their own Patrol Leaders and so learn Patrol discipline.

As far as possible they should run the camp—taking it in roster and be camp commandant for the day, quartermaster, and so on, so as to learn practically the work and requirements of these offices.

The whole principle of the Scout Movement should be impressed in the training, viz.—*Backwoodsmanship*, with life-saving as an important adjunct.

Later that year he amplified these suggestions and drew up a detailed syllabus. His suggestions included the following:

The Scoutmasters would be divided into Patrols of five; each Patrol having its own tent; each Scoutmaster taking it in turn to be Patrol Leader for 24 hours. Each Patrol in turn would supply for

24 hours a Scoutmaster to manage each of the following departments in Camp:

Routine duties and discipline.
Equipment, stores and issue.
Purchase and issue of food supplies.
Cook and serve meals.
Sanitation, medical and ambulance arrangements.

Early in 1914 a correspondence course entitled 'Scouting for Scoutmasters' was started in the pages of *The Headquarters Gazette*; each month B.-P. outlined a theme and set a number of questions for the candidates to answer. A Board of Examiners at Headquarters dealt with the replies; at first three members were thought sufficient; they were Colonel de Burgh, P. W. Everett, and Captain A. G. Wade, one of the Secretaries. The demand, however, was so great (some 800 entered) that the services of H. G. Elwes and of Ernest Young (then Headmaster and Scoutmaster at the Harrow County School) were also needed. Before a certificate could be issued the examiners had to satisfy themselves that a candidate was doing efficient work in running a Troop. The syllabus was as follows:

1. Character Training.
2. Self-improvement for making a Career.
3. Physical Health and Development.
4. Service for others as a Basis of Religion.
5. Boy Training, Methods, and National Importance.
6. Citizenhood.

The series of notes B.-P. wrote for this course were afterwards expanded in book form under the title *Aids to Scoutmastership* (1919).

The outbreak of war brought this correspondence course to an end.

During the Easter week-end of 1914 an open Conference was held at the Manchester Grammar School. Amongst those who took an important part must be mentioned Arthur Gaddum, another of that band of men of forceful character that B.-P. drew into the service of Scouting. This was not a Conference of the resolution-passing kind but more of a training occasion, such subjects as the following being discussed:

Scouting and education.
Senior Scouts.
The Patrol system.
Religious and moral basis.
The Court of Honour.

The Report of the proceedings proved of great help to those who were unable to be present. It was by such means that opinion in the Movement was educated and men brought gradually to realize the possibilities of the work.

The second of B.-P.'s lines of development, Senior Scouts, was to occupy his mind for some years. He set out his purposes in the following words:

1. To keep Boy Scouts in touch with each other and with the Movement when they have to leave their Troops and go out to battle with the world.
2. To preserve the ideals of good citizenship which they have been taught as Scouts.
3. To attract to the Movement young men who have not been Scouts, and to give them the opportunity for doing a service to their country.

The first practical step was of a kind that may seem surprising to-day. The National Health Insurance scheme was started in 1912 and the Friendly Societies were associated with its working. This suggested the formation of a Society for young men who had been Scouts; this could comply with the needs of the Insurance Act and at the same time provide a link for these former Scouts. So the Scouts Friendly Society was established in March 1914. It should be remembered that the Friendly Societies had for the past century been something more than mutual-benefit organizations; the meetings of the local groups, usually called lodges, were social as well as business occasions and men learned to manage their affairs by discussion and through the machinery of elected committees, thus providing an important training ground for local self-government. B.-P. saw here the framework into which could be fitted the picture, as he then saw it, of Senior and Old Scouts. The Scouts Friendly Society was organized in 'camps', not 'lodges', and the first was established at Toynbee Hall in the East End of London with

Dr. T. S. Lukis as Head Man. The outbreak of war hindered this development, but the Friendly Society has continued with the more restricted functions of a mutual-benefit organization. We shall see later how the idea of Senior Scouts was to pass through another phase before the end of the war.

The third line of development, Junior Scouts, was as inevitable as Girl Guides. From early days very young boys had been admitted to Troops mainly because they clamoured to share the fun their elder brothers were having, and sometimes because mother said that Jack could not become a Scout unless little Bobby also joined. There were also some Scoutmasters who accepted small boys to swell numbers. Such Troops B.-P. described as 'ridiculous', being 'largely composed of little chaps in big hats and baggy shorts grasping staffs twice as tall as themselves'. He therefore sanctioned experiments with Junior Scouts, as at first they were called. Most of these attempts were in the nature of a watered-down Scouting and lacked anything clearly distinctive. After this period of experiment B.-P. asked P. W. Everett to study what was being done and to draw up a provisional scheme. One of the first points was to settle on a name. B.-P. wrote:

The name 'Junior Scouts' will never do as a permanent one. I never thought of keeping it—but it does for preliminary use as explaining the Movement. We must invent a name that will appeal to the small boys. One S.M. called his 'Beavers'. Not a bad idea. Another man suggested to me 'Nippers'.

I had originally in my mind 'Wolf Cubs', or 'Cubs', or 'Colts', or 'Young Scouts'. 'Trappers' might be an attractive name if explained that a 'trapper' is assistant to a hunter or Scout.

The first scheme as published in *The Headquarters Gazette* in January 1914 was indeed a modified form of the Scout training and still lacked the needed distinctiveness. It was perhaps fortunate that B.-P. had not sufficient leisure during the war to produce the handbook that, as was stated in January 1914, was 'shortly to be published'. This gave more time for seeing how things were going, and it brought into the Movement many young women who were delighted to have the chance of training these 'nippers'. Their ideas and experiences were a valuable aid in elucidating the special problems of training young boys. At last B.-P. found what he wanted in Kipling's *Jungle Books*.

Here was a world of fantasy in which these small boys could play in company with Mowgli and the Wolves. It was not, however, until 1916 that *The Wolf Cub's Handbook* was published. Further consideration must be given later to the principles and methods of the new section.

The spread of 'Scouting among poor boys in slums' was one of B.-P.'s most cherished hopes. His first suggestion was that a fund should be started to help Troops in such areas; a beginning was made in 1911, but the amount received never reached a substantial sum. Experience showed that the main problem was not lack of money—that could be earned in many ways; the real need was for men to take up this special kind of work. From the early days of the Movement such men have been available; most of them have been men of few resources and of little social prestige. The work they do is, in some respects, the finest service the Scout Movement renders; it means bringing colour and enjoyment and a touch of romance into the drabbest surroundings, but more important is the personal guidance and friendship given to these boys. Many Scoutmasters of this type carry on such work quietly and almost unobserved; there is many a Troop in the crowded parts of our big towns that can claim a continuous history back to 1908 or 1909. Some of these Scoutmasters were men of social standing. The name of one, Dr. T. S. Lukis, has already been mentioned. More detailed notice must be given of another, Roland Philipps, a son of Lord St. Davids. He early became an enthusiastic follower of B.-P., and quickly grasped the significance of the unusual methods of Scouting. His chosen sphere of action was Stepney; he there bought a house as a centre of Scouting in east London where he was a District Commissioner. One of his great services to the Movement arose directly out of his experience as Scoutmaster and Commissioner. He found that boys had a difficulty in seeing the possibilities and application of the Patrol System, so he organized the Hackney Patrol Leaders' Parliament in November 1913 as a means of training them for their work. The plain talks he gave to these Leaders proved so helpful that he published them as a small book called *The Patrol System*, which, both in the original and in many translations, has played an important part in educating Scoutmasters as well as Scouts in this fundamental method.

The 'Development of the Sea Scout branch' proceeded steadily. There were unfortunately two fatal accidents, one at Leysdown in 1912, and the other on the Thames in 1913, which, though not directly connected with Sea Scouting, were setbacks; as a result more stringent safety rules were laid down. The greatest hindrance to the wider expansion of this branch has always been expense; but, making every allowance for this handicap, it is surprising that Sea Scouting has not proved as popular as might be expected. The coming of war, as we shall see, brought a great opportunity for national service by the Sea Scouts; this called out the finest qualities of this small but important branch of the Movement.

The last of B.-P.'s seven lines of development, 'Provision of adequate national Headquarters' was realized in 1917, when on 20 June the Duke of Connaught opened the new Headquarters at 25 Buckingham Palace Road. This had been made possible by the generosity of Dr. J. J. Acworth. In 1918 the term 'Imperial Headquarters' (commonly abbreviated to 'I.H.Q.') came into use. This, in a sense, is misleading as the Boy Scout Associations in the Dominions and Colonies are not run from Buckingham Palace Road though the relation is close; each of the Overseas Associations has its own constitution with its own Chief Scout and organization. There are variations in details to suit local conditions, but there is a common pattern throughout.

⚜ ⚜ ⚜ ⚜ ⚜ ⚜ ⚜ ⚜ ⚜ ⚜ ⚜ ⚜ ⚜ ⚜ ⚜ ⚜ ⚜

CHAPTER THIRTEEN

1914–18

THE WAR YEARS PUT A SEVERE STRAIN ON A VERY YOUNG MOVEment; it had still to be proved that the popularity of Scouting was something more than a temporary enthusiasm of high-spirited boys. This period was, in fact, the adolescence of Scouting; by the end of the war the Movement had grown up.

On 4 August 1914 Great Britain declared war on Germany. Three days before that B.-P. telegraphed to the War Office putting the Boy Scouts at the disposal of the Government. He himself offered to raise an irregular corps of Scoutmasters and old Scouts, but though the first offer was immediately accepted, the second did not meet with Lord Kitchener's approval. He thought it better that old Scouts should be distributed amongst the units of the New Army as leaven. Here it may be noted that when Kitchener was urged to make use of B.-P. in the army, he replied, as his secretary Sir George Arthur has recorded, that 'he could lay his hand on several competent Divisional Generals, but could find no one who could carry on the invaluable work of the Boy Scouts'. It may also again be categorically stated that B.-P. did not do any secret-service work during the war.

Most of the Scouts were in camp during those early August days. B.-P.'s plans were ready before then, and this meant that immediately the need arose the services of the Movement were available. Brief instructions were telegraphed to Commissioners and Secretaries, and were followed by a detailed list of possible duties for Scouts to undertake. Here is the list:

(*a*) Guarding and patrolling bridges, culverts, telegraph lines, &c., against damage by spies.

(*b*) Collecting information as to supplies, transport, &c., available.

(*c*) Handing out notices to inhabitants, and other duties connected with billeting, commandeering, warning, &c.

(*d*) Carrying out organized relief measures amongst inhabitants.

(*e*) Carrying out communications by means of dispatch riders, signallers, wireless, &c.

(*f*) Helping families of men employed in defence duties, or sick or wounded, &c.

(*g*) Establishing first-aid, dressing or nursing stations, refuges, dispensaries, soup-kitchens, &c., in their clubrooms.

(*h*) Acting as guides, orderlies, &c.

Sea Scouts. Watching estuaries and ports, guiding vessels in unbuoyed channels, or showing lights to friendly vessels, &c., and assisting coastguards.

Nearly every item on that list was, at one period or another, carried out. B.-P.'s foresight had again proved prophetic. It should be remembered that there was no previous experience to go upon as was to be the case in 1939; moreover, up to 1916 all services were of a voluntary nature nor were there in existence trained organized units to carry out innumerable tasks of an auxiliary character.

There were two large-scale demands on Scouts in addition to many smaller needs. One was for Scouts to watch bridges and telegraph lines; they were on duty within a few hours of the call. The Chief Post Office Engineer provided maps showing the positions of the secret-service lines, and 5,000 Scouts were stationed along these routes. Inevitably there were amusing contretemps; thus one harmless bug-hunter was taken to the police station for chasing his prey under a railway bridge. This work did not last long, but it filled a gap at a most critical period before the man-power of the country could be organized. The second duty, and one that lasted beyond the war, was undertaken at the urgent request of Lord Kitchener. This was an appeal for Sea Scouts to replace coastguardsmen who were needed at sea. Between 5 August 1914 and 7 March 1920 some 23,000 Scouts shared in this important duty of coast-watching. Lieut. W. R. Stanton, R.N.V.R., who was in charge of this service wrote:

When one details the duties which are being performed by these lads one is amazed by the pluck, endurance and readiness of mind which they show. The boys have to patrol the beach, three miles out and three miles back, in all weathers. Rain and sun, hail, storm and snow are all alike to them, and clad in their sou' westers and overalls, they might challenge comparison with the most seasoned mariner. They have to watch out for fishing boats that work by unauthorised hours at night, and to examine all boats coming in to the shore to see that the men have their permits in order. . . . The Scouts have to answer all Naval calls on the telephone, and report all vessels passing up and down. . . . Despatch-carrying is one of the most essential and arduous of the Sea Scout's tasks. He has to pass on from hand to hand the daily log kept by his own Patrol and by the Patrol next to him until it reaches the Naval Base Commander. Every night throughout the war have these lads carried their despatches along the coast.

Space will allow mention of only a few of the services rendered by the Boy Scouts—orderly and messenger work in Government offices, hospitals, and Red Cross centres, collection of waste paper, of blankets for the wounded, of metal waste, and of chestnuts and of the other things that suddenly become valuable in war-time, farm work, flax harvesting, distribution of official leaflets, and, perhaps most popular in the ears of the public, the sounding of the 'All Clear' bugle after air raids.

The value of the work already done was acknowledged a year before the end of the war in a message from the Prime Minister.

I do not think I am exaggerating when I say that the young boyhood of the country, represented by the Boy Scouts Association, shares the laurels for having Been Prepared with the old and trusted and tried British Army and Navy. For both proved their title to make the claim when the Great War broke upon us like a thief in the night.

It is no small matter to be proud of that the Association was able within a month of the outbreak of war to give the most intelligent and energetic help in all kinds of service.

When the boyhood of a nation can give such practical proofs of its honour, straightness and loyalty, there is not much danger of that nation going under, for those boys are in training to render service to their country as leaders in all walks of life in the future.

I can only say to all sections of the Movement, old Scouts and new Scouts, Scout Officers and Patrol Leaders, go forward, stick it to the end.

D. LLOYD GEORGE.

A War Service badge was instituted in 1914; it was awarded to Scouts doing at least twenty-eight days of service of three hours a day; some 70,000 of these badges were earned by 1918. There was also a special 100 Days' badge. A Scouts Defence Corps was formed for those under military age; training in drill and marksmanship was undertaken by these boys and their distinctive badge was a red feather worn in the hat. This formation was in part an answer to the possibility of national cadet training being established; the Movement did not feel able to support this suggestion which, had it been carried out, would have been contrary to the methods and ideals of Scouting. Critics naturally saw in the Defence Corps yet another proof of the covert militarism of Scouting, but, in fact, the Corps was not widely established, and with the coming of peace it faded away.

The Boy Scouts also raised funds, chiefly by earning money by odd jobs, for Huts and motor ambulances. Four Huts were established. Both the Chief Scout and Lady Baden-Powell took an active part as workers in the Huts at Calais and Étaples; the latter, in charge of the Rev. C. Butterworth, was partly destroyed by bombing. Six motor ambulances were also presented to the War Office. A special 'Save our Scouts' (S.O.S.) Fund was started during the war to give help to Scouts of other countries where the fighting had caused devastation. This became a permanent fund and by its means much-needed help has been given to foreign Scouts in distress.

As far as can be ascertained, 150,000 former Scouts served in the Forces; of these some 10,000 lost their lives. Unhappily amongst these were many young men who had been doing invaluable service to Scouting before 1914. A few names out of so many may be mentioned: Roland Philipps, Anthony Slingsby (Organizing Secretary, North), Maurice Gamon (Lambeth), T. S. Lukis (East London), J. L. Lawrence (Organizing Secretary, Scotland), and Oswald Williams (Organizing Secretary, Wales). It was to such young men that the Movement had naturally looked for guidance and leadership in the years to come. As in other spheres of the national life, so Scouting was to feel the loss of its young leaders.

The many awards and decorations received in the Forces included eleven Victoria Crosses. The devotion to duty during the Battle of Jutland shown by Boy Jack Cornwell, V.C., made a strong impression on Scouts, and a special award, the Cornwell Scout badge, was instituted to commemorate his heroism; this is granted for 'devotion to duty, together with great courage, endurance or gallantry'.

Even this brief record is sufficient to show how the Boy Scouts gave themselves without stint to national service during the First World War. The astonishing fact is that, in spite of all the time and energy so used, the Movement at home did not collapse but flourished. The census for 1913 gave a total for the United Kingdom of 137,776 boys, and that for 1917 of 152,175 but with 3,000 fewer Scoutmasters; the number of Troops remained almost unchanged. It was inevitable that with the enlistment or calling-up of so many Scoutmasters some Troops were left in the air, and a small number faded out. Older men came forward to help keep things going, and some women became Scoutmasters; they did excellent work, but the more mannish of them were a little terrifying. A few carried on after the war, and it is still possible for a woman to be a Scoutmaster 'in exceptional circumstances' (Rule 232).

These welcome war-time Scoutmasters could meet only part of the need. Scouting as a system of training, apart from national service, was kept going to a great extent by the Patrol Leaders, sometimes under the direction of a Senior Patrol Leader, a rank recognized in January 1917. This title was changed to Troop Leader in 1920. Sometimes there would be in the background a friendly grown-up who, feeling unable to be an active Scoutmaster, was willing to keep a kindly eye on the Troop. The war brought the Patrol Leader into his own and demonstrated once and for all the value of the Patrol System. Up to 1914 the importance of this method had not been fully realized—it was so contrary to traditional ways of training and of instruction. Some have seen a parallel between the Patrol Leader and the Prefect in a school, but there are few similarities; there is indeed a closer affinity with the monitorial methods of Bell and Lancaster, but no mention of their names is made in any of B.-P.'s writings or papers. A distinctive feature of this system is the smallness of the Patrol of six to eight boys; this meant in war-time that a Troop could maintain its existence and do valuable work with a small nucleus well within the capacity of a boy of character to control.

In January 1916 B.-P. wrote:

The Patrol System, with its leaders forming a strong and earnest Court of Honour in each Troop, has amply vindicated its existence and shown that when up against it boys can be relied upon to carry a thing through.

He encouraged the Patrol Leaders with the following personal message:

I always considered the Patrol as the important body in the Scout Movement, but since the war it has shown more than ever that it is the unit that can be relied upon to do its duty well.

I want you Patrol Leaders to go on and train your Patrols in future entirely yourselves, because it is possible for you to get hold of each boy in your Patrol and make a good fellow of him. It is no use having one or two brilliant boys and the rest no good at all. You should try to make them all fairly good. The most important step to this is your own example, because what you do yourself your Scouts will do also. Show them that you can obey orders whether they are given by word of mouth or merely rules that are printed or written, and that you carry them out whether your Scoutmaster is present or not.

Another indication of the increasing sense of responsibility amongst these young leaders was the development of Patrol Leaders' conferences. These were conducted entirely by the Scouts themselves, no adult being present except when they were lucky enough to have the Chief Scout himself at their discussions. These conferences were of considerable value in promoting an intelligent understanding of Scouting—though occasionally an exaggerated sense of self-importance was also developed. Many of these Patrol Leaders were to become the post-war Scoutmasters, and this experience of discussing problems was a useful preparation.

While war conditions compelled greater recognition of the value of the Patrol Leader, it also helped to emphasize the true function of the Scoutmaster. The need was realized for the steadying influence and guidance of an adult. There is a limit to the foresight of a boy; he can see immediate needs but he is unlikely to grasp the equal necessity of long-term training. Moreover, he cannot appreciate problems of conduct and character although he is often shrewd in his estimate of persons; it is here that the Scoutmaster can do his best work in studying the needs of each boy as an individual and in making sure that the training given leads on to all-round development of character and ability. The more he can leave day-to-day matters to his Patrol Leaders, the better can he concentrate on these other more permanent aspects of Scouting.

Headquarters staff was also greatly depleted on the outbreak of war. Both the Secretaries, Major Ewen Cameron and Captain A. G. Wade, were called up, and so also was Eric Walker, the Chief Scout's Private Secretary; this latter place was taken by Miss E. K. Nugent (later Mrs. A. G. Wade) who retained that position until 1941. C. H. West became Acting-Secretary in September 1915. In 1917 C. Dymoke Green was appointed his Assistant and succeeded to the position of Secretary in 1918. For twenty-one years C. Dymoke Green exercised in his undemonstrative manner a valued influence at Headquarters and throughout the Movement. He could speak as a Scoutmaster to Scoutmasters, and as a Commissioner to Commissioners, and this personal experience of running a Troop and of organizing a district gave a solidity to his advice that inspired confidence. D. Francis Morgan joined the staff in 1918; he became Assistant Secretary and, later, Legal Secretary.

The new premises occupied in 1917 made it possible to extend the Scout Club which had started on a small scale in the old buildings; this, at first, was chiefly of value to members of the services on leave, and it was hoped that it would develop into a permanent institution. Under the chairmanship of N. D. Power the Club continued to flourish for several years. The main problem was that of suitable accommodation, and in 1921 special rooms were built on the roof of Headquarters; these provided for a canteen, a Scoutmasters' Den, a Club Room, and a Library. Membership, however, declined. There was a temporary recovery during 1924 when many overseas Scouts were in London for the Wembley Jamboree. Various attempts to encourage membership were unsuccessful and after some ten years of activity the Club was closed.

In the last chapter it was mentioned that it was during the war years that the Wolf Cubs were established and that projects were formed for the development of Senior Scouts. We must now consider these in greater detail in the next chapters.

⚜ ⚜ ⚜ ⚜ ⚜ ⚜ ⚜ ⚜ ⚜ ⚜ ⚜ ⚜ ⚜ ⚜ ⚜ ⚜ ⚜

CHAPTER FOURTEEN

WOLF CUBS

WE HAVE ALREADY SEEN HOW THE WOLF CUB SECTION GREW OUT of an inevitable need. Three phases can be distinguished. In the first Scoutmasters were encouraged to experiment in methods of training young boys below Boy Scout age; the chief value of this period was that it brought out clearly the differences between the needs of very young boys and those old enough to be Boy Scouts. The second phase began in January 1914 with the publication of a few rules and tests. War conditions hampered the development of the scheme, but this proved valuable in showing that something more was needed than these simplified Scout tests. The third phase began in 1916 with the publication of *The Wolf Cub's Handbook*; the use made there of the Mowgli stories from *The Jungle Books* created an entirely new atmosphere—indeed it revolutionized the whole scheme.

The possibilities of the Mowgli saga were not at once realized, and for several years many Cubmasters failed to make full use of the opportunities B.-P. had put before them. It is significant that it was not until January 1923 that the full rules for Wolf Cubs were incorporated in the Rules. The year 1916 may, however, be regarded as the foundation year of this section. At an important Cub Conference in London in that year B.-P. outlined the ideas he was publishing in the Handbook; a special Wolf Cub department was set up at Headquarters, and, what proved of the greatest importance, the services of Miss Vera Barclay were secured as Assistant Secretary for Wolf Cubs. She brought to the work not only enthusiasm and imagination, but a sound understanding of the nature of the young boy; she saw clearly the need for keeping the substance as well as the method of training as distinctive as possible. The position was further strengthened by the appointment of N. D. Power as Headquarters Commissioner for Wolf Cubs, a post he held until

1927; he gave generously of his time and energy to developing the new section along sound lines.

The numbers of boys joining the Wolf Cubs steadily increased, as may be seen from the following figures:

1916 .	estimated 6,000
1917 . . .	28,450
1918 . . .	38,513
1919 . . .	46,172
1920 . . .	55,347

In 1938 the number was 156,657.

The greatest problem in the first years of the Wolf Cub scheme was to convince Cubmasters that they must avoid making the Pack a kind of baby Troop. During the first phase nearly all the experiments were in trying to teach Cubs elementary Scouting, and some Cubmasters boasted that their boys could beat the Scouts in their own job. Some even urged that when a Cub became a Scout he should be excused taking the Tenderfoot and Second Class tests and jump at once to training for the First Class badge. Quite apart from the serious misunderstanding this showed of a small boy's nature, there was the objection that the freshness and appeal of the Troop would be lost and that leaving the Pack would prove a disappointment instead of a new adventure. So, as with the principles of the Patrol System, the men and women who took up Cub work had to be educated in the new ideas.

The Wolf Cub scheme takes full advantage of the imitative and play-acting instincts of the small boy. B.-P. saw that, just as the love of the gang could be utilized in training boys of Boy Scout age, so the love of 'let's pretend' could be turned to good account in training the younger boy. The story of Mowgli's life in the jungle provides just the imaginative setting to capture the young boy's love of pretence as well as his love of animals. He can see himself as Mowgli; the Pack takes on a new meaning; the Jungle becomes his world of fantasy. All that is not surprising, and it would be what we should expect after telling any small boy a good tale about animals. What is surprising is how these particular stories seem an inexhaustible mine of ideas and suggestions. The obvious use of the tales is as material for play-acting, but some incidents lend themselves to formalized performance as dances that provide disciplined movement and natural physical exercise. They suggest, too, some of the simple ceremonies of the Pack, such as the Howl. B.-P. was alive to the love of ceremony that boys of all ages show, and both in the Pack and the Troop scope is given for this to good purpose. For the Cub learning to do things becomes a reproduction of Mowgli's training by Bagheera and Baloo under the leadership of Akela 'the great, gray, lone wolf'. So, too, innumerable games and other plays can be enjoyed in this jungle land.

Here then is something quite distinctive from the pioneer's world of the Boy Scout, and it at once gives the Wolf Cubs a life of their own without the risk of staling them for the Troop. The jungle has, however, its dangers. It is sometimes objected that an over-sentimentalized idea of animals is encouraged, but this is outweighed by the fostering of a more humane attitude towards animals, and the next time Johnny thinks of pulling the cat's tail he may stop to think again. A more serious danger is that of trying to transform every action into a jungle form of life. Wise Cubmasters know that there is a whole world of romance which can supply endless material for Cub activities outside the jungle.

At first B.-P. suggested that there should be a Cub Promise but no Cub Law. His original suggestion for the Promise reads:

1. Honour God and the King.
2. Do a Good Turn to somebody every day.

The present wording is:

I promise to do my best—
To do my duty to God, and the King,
To keep the Law of the Wolf Cub Pack, and to do a good turn to somebody every day.

Eventually, however, it was decided that a very simple Law would be as helpful to the Cub as to the Boy Scout. This reads:

The Law of the Wolf Cub Pack is:

1. The Cub gives in to the Old Wolf;
2. The Cub does not give in to himself.

A Pack is divided into Sixes each under a Sixer, but this is not intended as a faint reflection of the Patrol System. A Six is a convenient team for games, but the Sixer is not expected to

ONE OF THE BOYS WHO CAMPED AT BROWNSEA ISLAND, AUGUST 1907

It will be noted that the only 'uniform' he wore was a long Patrol shoulder-knot and a haversack. He was making a track on the sand strip

B.-P. TELLING A YARN ROUND THE CAMP FIRE AT THE HUMSHAUGH CAMP, 1908

exercise responsibility as a Patrol Leader does. The unit of the Wolf Cubs is the Pack, not the Six. It follows that the Cubmaster (usually known as 'Akela') has far more to do in working out programmes and in training than a Scoutmaster has to do. Young women have found this Cub work attractive, and those with the right abilities have had great success. About half the Cubmasters and Assistants are women—this proportion has remained fairly constant over a long period. Sometimes one of the Patrol Leaders of the Troop has a flair for helping with the Pack; and many Girl Guides have come into Cub work after their own training is finished.

One of the noticeable facts about the Cub scheme is that, once it had got established, it called for little revision. Small changes have been made in tests and new proficiency badges have been added from time to time, but substantially the scheme remains that set out in the Handbook of 1916. This success is in part due to the long period of trial and error that preceded the formulation of the rules, but there can be no question that the major contribution in that success was B.-P.'s adoption of the Mowgli stories as the right setting for the training.

⚜ ⚜ ⚜ ⚜ ⚜ ⚜ ⚜ ⚜ ⚜ ⚜ ⚜ ⚜ ⚜ ⚜ ⚜ ⚜ ⚜

CHAPTER FIFTEEN

THE FIRST SENIOR SCOUTS

THE WOLF CUB SCHEME SOLVED THE PROBLEM OF WHAT TO DO with boys under eleven years of age who wanted to be Scouts. The problem of retaining the older boy was far more difficult. There was a tendency for boys to leave their Troops when they went to work. It was not until the passing of the Education Act of 1918 that the school-leaving age was fixed at 14 without exceptions. Up to that year boys could get permission to leave school before the age of 14 if they had jobs to go to, and permission was rarely refused.

During the first ten years of the Movement Scouting had not spread widely amongst boys of the Secondary Schools. Since that period there has been a considerable increase in the number of Scouts in Secondary Schools either in their own Troops or in local Troops, so much so that the criticism has been made that the Movement has become a bourgeois affair. A visit to a few typical Troops in our larger towns soon shows that there is little foundation for this charge. The fact is that Scouting has considerably widened its appeal since 1908 and it now covers all sections of the boy population. Certainly no boy in one of the big Public Schools before 1920 would have thought of being a member of the Boy Scouts, though he might take a kindly interest in the village Troop at home.

The Scout who goes to a Secondary School will probably remain in his Troop until the age of sixteen, but the Primary School-boy who goes to work at fourteen or fifteen is pulled away from the Scouts because he feels grown-up and no longer wants to associate with 'kids'. If he is a Patrol Leader he will probably remain in the Troop as the responsibility he exercises gives him a special interest. Some exceptionally good Scoutmasters have always held many of these older boys, but the Movement is chiefly manned by ordinary folk, and while successful with younger Scouts they often prove unable to capture the enthusiasm of the older ones.

B.-P. puzzled over this problem for some time; he sought the advice of Scoutmasters, of schoolmasters, of Board of Education officials, and indeed of all who had useful experience in training the older boys. During the First World War there was a strong national urge towards an improved educational system; this resulted in the famous, but unhappily abortive, Fisher Act of 1918. B.-P. was consulted by H. A. L. Fisher, the President of the Board of Education, and there is no doubt that the first Senior Scout scheme owed something to these conversations, for B.-P. tried to frame it in such a way that it would fit into the new plan. There was another urgent reason for tackling this question. War inevitably brought an increase in juvenile crime. Magistrates recognized the steadying influence of membership of an organization such as the Boy Scouts, and the Home Office discussed the problem with B.-P. He was naturally anxious to increase the attractiveness and holding-power of Scouting so that greater numbers of older boys would find in it a legitimate outlet for their high spirits and adventurousness.

A scheme was at length published in the middle of 1917. An examination of this reveals the several lines of thought that went to its making. The reluctance of the older boy to associate with younger ones was met, it was hoped, by the fact that 'the recent institution of the Junior Branch, The Wolf Cubs, . . . clears the Scout Movement proper in the eyes of the bigger boy from the charge of being a "kid's game"'. This proved a partial remedy only, for to the boy of 15 or 16 a younger boy of 11 or 12 is still a 'kid'. The need for recognizing the changed needs of the older boy was clearly stated. 'What is wanted is a definite status and attraction for the senior boy.' Or, to quote B.-P. again: 'The necessity for them [i.e. Senior Scouts] arises in the need for extended and separate training for the older boy.'

It was also decided to link up Scouting with the boy's work by instituting a series of 'Studies' that would increase the boy's knowledge of his trade or business. There were two ideas behind this proposal; one was to give the boy a chance of obtaining better qualifications in his job, and the other to link Scouting and work in his mind and so prevent, it was hoped, the development of the idea that going to work meant breaking away from all previous associations.

Here are the main provisions of the scheme:

1. Senior Scouts would be First-Class Scouts over 15½. They would form Senior Patrols in connexion with their own Troops.

In certain cases it might be advisable to form Lone Patrols or special Troops under the District Commissioner.

The power of promoting elder Scouts to these Patrols would stimulate promotion in the Troop which is often very slow where elder Scouts remain members.

Scouts in the Senior Patrol would hold rank between a Patrol Leader and Assistant Scoutmaster but would have no executive power over the Troop, unless specially authorized by the Scoutmaster.

2. Senior Patrols could be started where the want is felt of some scheme to interest and retain the older boy, or to encourage specialization.

3. Special activities, games, and studies would be open to these, entitling them to Proficiency Badges of a higher standard than that of the Scouts.

4. Each Patrol would constitute a squad for Public Service duties, a class for studies, and a team for games and competitions.

5. Scout uniform would be worn and a special cockade in the hat.

6. The Leader would be elected by the Patrol, and might hold the rank of Assistant Scoutmaster. He would be its Captain in games, club arrangements, athletics, and also in its public activities, studies, &c.

7. The studies would be carried out through correspondence classes, and technical schools where possible.

8. The Badges would be awarded on tests such as would serve the holders as certificates of promising efficiency in the eyes of employers. For this purpose diplomas would be awarded.

9. The Patrols would incidentally form training centres for Assistant Scoutmasters; and could also be of assistance to the Scoutmaster in administering the Troop.

10. Where possible Local Associations should find premises for social purposes for these Patrols and should open Employment Bureaux where help and advice can be obtained.

It was decided that examinations in the 'Studies' would be held twice a year at Headquarters and that the standard would be high enough to give the certificate gained a real value in the eyes of employers. A note at the end of the scheme reads:

> Scoutmasters must remember that unless an elementary schoolboy continues his education, after leaving School at 14, by means of evening classes or correspondence schools, he will not likely be capable of taking on the higher training required for these badges or for Technical School classes when he attains the age of 16. It is hoped, therefore, that Scoutmasters will encourage their boys to make every use of the opportunities given by the various Educational Authorities.

It must at once be admitted that this scheme fell flat. Several reasons may be suggested. The time of its launching, 1917, was unpropitious; the war situation was at its most critical stage and there was no man-power available to carry through such an elaborate scheme. A more serious, and probably decisive weakness, was that on the 'Studies' side the scheme was too ambitious for a voluntary organization and the collapse of the Fisher Act left the Senior Scouts in the air. Few Scoutmasters felt competent to advise boys on this kind of work—that, they felt, was the job of the Education Authorities. Moreover, an employer would naturally regard a certificate issued by one of these Authorities after the boy had attended a recognized course of instruction as far more reliable than one issued by anyone else. The note quoted above shows that B.-P. intended the scheme as a means of encouraging boys to go to evening classes, but this was already being done by many Scoutmasters. There was, too, the unfamiliar idea of examinations at Headquarters; this was so contrary to Scout practice that Scoutmasters rather shied away from the whole suggestion.

The unfortunate result of this failure was that the need for 'definite status and attraction for the senior boy' was not met, and it was not until another war broke out that this problem was resolutely faced again.

The term 'Senior Scout' was in use for about a year; it then gave way to 'Rover Scout', though for a time the Senior Scout badge was worn. The original scheme was gradually transformed, or rather transmuted, into a plan for training a higher age-group than that for which this first Senior Scout scheme was intended.

CHAPTER SIXTEEN

WOODCRAFT AND TRAINING

THE PREVIOUS THREE CHAPTERS HAVE SHOWN THAT THE SCOUT Movement did not stand still during the First World War, but developed in several important directions. Preparations had been made for further advances. An indication of the spirit in which the future was being faced is given by the special form of the Tenth Annual Report issued in January 1919. The greater part of this consists of a vigorous article 'Scouting Towards Reconstruction' by the Chief Scout illustrated by a number of his liveliest sketches. The word 'reconstruction' was the shibboleth of the period, and, as B.-P. pointed out, 'there is no better and no more important work at this moment than that of ensuring an improved citizenhood in our oncoming generation'.

Another article brings us to an interesting episode in the history of the Movement; it is entitled 'Woodcraft and Camping' and was by John Hargrave, the recently appointed Commissioner for Woodcraft and Camping. Under his pseudonym of 'White Fox', he had published an attractive book called *Lonecraft*; this was followed by others of the same genre. He was a disciple of Ernest Thompson Seton and took over many of the ideas of *The Book of Woodcraft* and *The Birchbark Roll*. All this was attractive and did good so far as it persuaded Scouts to get out of doors and practise the skills of the backwoodsman. There was, however, a serious flaw. Both B.-P. and Seton wrote out of a wealth of practical experience, and it was a shock to discover that some of Hargrave's suggestions were impracticable in this country. One example will suffice. Had he spent half an hour trying to make camp utensils out of birch bark, he would have found that the birch as it grows on this side of the Atlantic does not yield large sheets of bark that can be manipulated as on the other side. This defect was not at first apparent; the appeal of Red Indianism (his narrow interpretation of 'woodcraft') found a quick response amongst the young Scouts. So in this Report he could write:

> One London Troop has been run on woodcraft lines for years with great success, and their camp fire ritual and council costumes are most elaborate and picturesque. Names such as 'Fleetfoot', 'Thunder Bird', 'Hawkeye', etc., have to be won by passing a stiff Initiation Test, and at the great annual naming ceremony the Scout thus honoured is given his woodcraft name at the Council Fire with due solemnity.

Here it may be noted that the appeal was not only to the romance of the Red Indian, but to the love of ritual that some boys and men have; B.-P. recognized this when he devised a simple investiture ceremony, but he also recognized that many boys and men are rather shy of anything elaborate and are just as likely to giggle when someone announces himself as 'Little Owl' as to regard him with awe. We shall find this conflict again between the ritualists and the plain-ceremonialists in the development of the Rover branch.

A more serious criticism was the tendency for the Red Indian enthusiasts to talk a woolly kind of pantheism about the Great Spirit (borrowed from *Hiawatha*); this was at variance with the declared principles of Scouting and naturally caused concern to the religious bodies that had so far given their support to the Movement.

B.-P. did not object to this so-called Woodcraft cult at first; he knew its dangers and limitations; after all he had himself carefully studied the scheme and had discussed it with Seton, but had rejected it as providing too narrow a foundation for his intentions. In his diary under the date 28 June 1918 B.-P. wrote: 'Saw Hargrave—no objection to his getting names of Troops doing Seton Woodcraft in Scouting, but don't make it a branch of the Movement.' Hargrave and his disciples failed to see that this Red Indianism is only a passing phase in a boy's life of which he quickly tires. There can be no doubt that this new stunt did have a rejuvenating effect on some Troops which, through lack of young Scoutmasters during the war, had become sluggish and in-doorish. It was all good fun while it lasted, and there were some Peter Pans who continued for years to call themselves by Red Indian names and to greet others with a 'How!'

Unfortunately Hargrave was not satisfied with the legitimate and limited use of Red Indianism; he wanted it to become an integral part of Scouting; he wanted the part to become the whole. He quickly became a centre of discontent. Every Movement has to face its 'candid friends', and they have a valuable function provided they are not the victims of mental jaundice and can recognize when they reach the dividing-line between loyalty to the principles they have voluntarily accepted and disruption. Scouting has always had such critics and has thus avoided the slough of complacency. Just after the war the critics, amongst whom was Hargrave, found an outlet for their grievances in a monthly journal called *The Trail* issued at first under the authority of the London Scout Office, but later repudiated. The general line was a familiar one: the Movement was being hindered by men who were too fixed in their ways to welcome new ideas. It was, of course, made clear that this was not an attack on the Chief Scout; the assumption was that he was the victim of a clique—a suggestion that showed little appreciation of his character. It was inevitable that a break would come. Hargrave left the Boy Scouts and formed an organization called the Kibbo Kift.

In 1920 B.-P. made a statement on Red Indianism that showed his usual balance of judgement.

I see that I have been quoted as advocating woodcraft as 'the key activity for true Scouting.' That is correct. But, then, the term 'woodcraft' has been explained as meaning to dress up like Red Indians, and that, therefore, I advocate the adoption of 'scalp locks and wampum, teepees and feathers.' This is not correct.

I know a little about the Red Indian, and he is not (and was not in his prime) all he is pictured by some who write about him only on his sunny side.

Still, I am not hostile to him. If we pick the plums out of the pudding, we find his romantic story, picturesque dress and customs appeal, in some cases, to the boy, and he can thus be useful to us. So can his African brother, the Zulu, the Haussa, the Somali and the Arab—all of whom I know. . . . But woodcraft goes a great deal deeper than the surface attraction or imitation of one or other of the more primitive tribes of men. . . .

Although it may be merely make-believe, yet, as a variation to the ordinary Scout training, Red Indianism can take hold, and can well be applied, *for a period*, in a Scout Troop.

By the time those words were written the woodcraft note, in the proper sense of the word, was being sounded in a permanent training centre near London. We have seen how B.-P. had for some years been longing to establish a training scheme for Scoutmasters, and at the end of the war the opportunity at last came when a Scottish District Commissioner, W. F. de Bois Maclaren, expressed a wish to buy a suitable site for camping for the Scouts of the East End of London. He was fortunately quite willing to combine this with a training centre for Scoutmasters, but his main intention was to provide a Scout camping ground.

It was not easy to find an accessible site near East London. Eventually the District Commissioner for Woodford, Essex, heard that Gilwell Park, Chingford, was in the market. It had a number of advantages; it was on the edge of Epping Forest and away from building areas yet within comfortable reach of Chingford station, the terminus of the line running through Bethnal Green, Hackney, and Walthamstow. After careful inspection, this estate of fifty-five acres was recommended to Maclaren and he presented it to the Association.

On hearing the news B.-P. wrote:

> This is good news indeed. . . . It sounds ideal—except I presume it will want some doing up—drains looking to, etc., to make it fit for habitation. I should like to see it, but since you all agree on it, I feel sure it is what we want. . . . But I am awfully checked by Ernest Young not being able to accept the directorship of the school. I can't think of another man, can you? His personality is all important to the Movement just now.

Not only drains called for attention! The house, of a most curious construction, was in a deplorable condition, and it would probably have been wiser in the long run to have pulled it down and to have built something more suitable, but it was decided to repair the late-eighteenth-century house with its small central earlier portion.

A pioneer party of Rovers under P. B. Nevill camped in the old orchard (using the shed known as the Pigsty) at Easter 1919. The formal opening was on 19 July. Parties of local Scouts and others from London spent week-ends clearing the grounds that had become a wilderness. Maclaren was a frequent visitor and he took great delight in watching the gradual realization of his hopes.

B.-P.'s letter quoted above refers to the problem of 'the directorship of the school'. Ernest Young had been a successful Scoutmaster and for some years had been a member of the Committee of the Council; few had a better grasp than he of the principles and practice of Scouting. At last another name was suggested—that of Francis Gidney who had formed a Scout Troop at Lichfield Grammar School in 1908 and had led it until going up to Cambridge in 1911. The choice proved a happy one, for he had a gay, pioneering spirit that found its greatest satisfaction in exploring a new field and in experimenting with new ways of putting *Scouting for Boys* into practice.

The new Camp Chief (a more suitable name than 'Director') had three guides; first the Chief Scout himself who very closely followed the progress of the training and was an unfailing source of ideas and of encouragement, secondly, *Scouting for Boys*, and thirdly, the scheme B.-P. had drawn up in readiness.

Here is the outline scheme handed to Gidney.

GILWELL PARK

DIPLOMA COURSE FOR THE WOOD BADGE

Open to all warranted Officers of the Boy Scouts Association

I. THEORETICAL: *Aims and Methods of the Scout Training* as defined in *Aids to Scoutmastership*, *Scouting for Boys*, and *Rules* in such subjects as Organization according to ages. Four lines of training: Nature lore for soul health and sex knowledge; National need and possibilities of the training.

A course of four studies either by correspondence in the *Headquarters Gazette*, or by week-end attendances at Gilwell Park as desired by candidate. This will form a Winter course.

II. PRACTICAL: In four groups of subjects:

1. Troop ceremonies and Campcraft.
2. Field work and Pioneering.
3. Woodcraft and Scout games.
4. Signcraft and Pathfinding.

The training will be at Gilwell Park in four week-end courses or eight days in camp as most convenient to candidate.

III. Administration: The practical administration of his Troop or District as shown by results of 18 months' work.

Awards: *One Bead on button hole*—for passing Nos. I and II satisfactorily. *One Bead on Hat String* and Diploma—for passing all three satisfactorily.

Two Beads on Hat String and Diploma—for passing with special qualifications for becoming a Camp Chief.

Approved District Schools or study circles under Camp Chiefs will be eventually carried out on similar principles but the *double beads* will only be awarded at Gilwell Park.

B.-P. left the Camp Chief to expand the suggested syllabus and to fill in the details.

There are several personal associations with B.-P.'s own experiences that should be noted. The beads were those on a necklace he had captured from Dinuzulu, the Zulu Chief, in 1888; at first the Wood badge was made up from original beads, but it soon became clear that the supply would be quickly exhausted, so replicas had to be made. The badge was not worn for long on the hat cord; instead it was strung on a leather thong or bootlace and worn round the neck. This thong was another link with B.-P.'s past. Early one morning during the last weeks of the siege of Mafeking, he was returning from one of his dawn tours of the defences and for once was looking a bit downcast. An old native came up to him and asked him why he was not whistling as usual. B.-P. admitted that he was rather worried. The native at once took off a leather thong he was wearing round his neck and gave it to B.-P. saying, 'Wear this; my mother put it on me for luck; now it will bring you luck.'

Yet another link was the Koodoo horn which he gave to Gilwell; this he had captured in 1896 during the Matabele Campaign. The horn is used for rousing the camp.

These personal associations indicate the importance the Chief Scout set on this new venture of training Scoutmasters.

The newly appointed Camp Chief was busy during the summer of 1919 in organizing camping for the boys and in working out a detailed syllabus for the practical part of the training course. The result is worth putting on record.

1. *Troop.*—Ceremonies; Form Patrols; Give Calls; Drill with staffs; Troop drill; Engonyama chorus; Patrol formation; Scout's pace; Investiture; Breaking the flag; Six exercises from *Scouting for Boys*.

2. *Campcraft.*—(i) Camp Sites—selection, sanitation, pitching, types of tents.

(ii) Camp Expedients—illumination, kitchen implements, beds, personal comforts, tidiness, &c.

(iii) Camp Cooking—quantities, utensils, fires and ovens.

(iv) First Aid—kit, hygiene, &c.

3. *Fieldwork.*—(i) Measurements—personal, distances, heights, areas, river widths.

(ii) Mapping—how to teach, sketch-maps, prismatic compass, panoramic drawing, reports.

(iii) Stars—how to recognize, telling time, night marching.

4. *Pioneering.*—(i) Axemanship—felling, crosscut, wedges, grindstone, care of knife.

(ii) Construction—rope and trestle bridges, derricks, huts and shelters.

5. *Games.*—Scouting and camp games.

6. *Woodcraft.*—(i) Observation and deduction—nature note book, &c.

(ii) Birds and Animals—found in locality, habits and uses, visit to Natural History Museum.

(iii) Trees—how to identify, how to interest Scout.

(iv) Herbs—food, medicine, poisonous.

(v) Soul development through Woodcraft, sex questions, realization of God.

7. *Signcraft.*—(i) Signalling—hand, whistle, smoke, semaphore and morse, pitfalls to avoid.

(ii) Nature Trails.

(iii) Sand-tracking.

(iv) Weather Lore—clouds, signs, home-made instruments.

8. *Pathfinding.*—By Patrols with sealed orders for ten-hour journey in Epping Forest; leaf collecting; report; sketch-map; panoramic drawing, &c.

Study circle work on *Aids to Scoutmastership*.

Visit to Imperial Headquarters; method of administration; Scoutmasters' Den; Scout Shop; Club Lunch.

Every Scoutmaster will have an opportunity of becoming acquainted with the Chief Scout.

The first practical course was held in September 1919 with nineteen Scoutmasters. They were divided into Patrols as B.-P. had laid down in his 1913 scheme; each Scoutmaster took it in turn to be Patrol Leader for twenty-four hours and to carry out the duties of Second and of other positions in the Patrol. This was the most original feature of the course and proved to be one of the secrets of its success. For the time being the Scoutmasters became Scouts under the Camp Chief as Scoutmaster. In this vice versa manner they were able to appreciate more fully the working and implications of the Patrol System. A not unimportant result of this method is that men of varied stations in life are mixed up in the same Patrol, and the bank manager or the landowner shares the daily life and chores with the shop assistant or gardener.

This unique method of training calls for further examination. B.-P.'s main intention was not to impart knowledge; the list of subjects given above is sufficient to make this clear. The short period most men can afford—less than a fortnight—precludes exact study of any subject apart from practical camping; this last activity goes on all the time and the daily inspections are an aid to improved camping. The course provides a series of appetizers and demonstrates at the same time the scope of Scouting and suggests to Scoutmasters many topics that they could bring within the reach of their boys. The main purpose of the course is twofold; to bring out the meaning and value of the Patrol System as a method of training in character, and to let Scoutmasters experience for themselves what is meant by the Scout spirit—one of those indescribable emanations that are the mark of any community working and playing with a common purpose and a common ideal. The astonishing thing is that in such a brief period this spirit is evoked—this is no longer a matter of theory but an experience that has been repeated year after year since 1919 not only at Gilwell but at the similar camps that have since been derived from that first training course both in this country and in many other countries. Gidney's own infectious enthusiasm and gaiety of mind helped to achieve this, but the main factor then and now is the genius of the method devised by B.-P.

Not the least valuable part of such a course is the exchange of experience and the discussions that go on in the Patrol camps;

the Scoutmasters talk shop all the time—that is one reason for getting them together. So the man working in the midst of an industrial town gets to understand the different problems of his neighbour who may have a Troop in a small country town, or in Australia, or Sweden.

The lecture type of training course is a familiar and customary affair. This method had been tried for Scoutmasters before 1914 and B.-P. had not been happy about it. On a Wood-badge course some lectures or talks are inevitably part of the scheme, but most of them are immediately translated into some form of activity—a competition or a game between Patrols. The journey in Epping Forest, now an over-night hike, comes at the end of the course, and, like the hike a First Class Scout has to make, is a summing up of what has been demonstrated during the previous days.

It should be remembered that the theoretical part is an essential preliminary of the practical part. This is based on the study of basic books; the candidate sends his answers to an unknown reader who adds comments and suggestions. This is not an examination in the usual sense of the term, but rather a means of ensuring that the candidate has grasped the main principles.

This important development of training for Scoutmasters did not pass uncriticized. One school of thought felt that too much attention was being given to practical Scouting and not enough to the spirit—they failed to realize how skilfully B.-P. had interwoven the two so that practical Scouting of the right kind done in the right manner inevitably develops the right spirit; the two are inseparable. Others resented the airs put on by some of the early trained Scoutmasters and their frequent use of such expressions as 'At Gilwell we did so and so'. Both objections died down as more and more Scoutmasters, including some of the critics, went to Gilwell and experienced the course for themselves. They were rightly warned that ten days there gave them no right to criticize men who had years of good Scouting to their credit.

There is, however, one criticism that must continue to concern all those engaged in this training work. It is difficult to prevent the rather humdrum Scoutmaster from using what he does on a course as a stereotyped programme to be followed meticulously; all are urged to use their own inventiveness to adapt the material to their local conditions and to remember that a ten days' course can do little more than provide specimens of the kind of things that can be done in a Troop. This is a danger, but it is not easy to provide protection from it since it is wrapped up with the personality of the individual.

Meanwhile the boys' camping field attracted more and more Scouts each week-end; some became 'regulars' and grew from boyhood to young manhood at Gilwell—from being Tenderfoot Scouts to being Scoutmasters. The unit of camping was generally a Patrol under its Patrol Leader without a Scoutmaster. There were even some older Scouts who camped at Gilwell throughout the summer, going up to London to work each morning. During 1920 some 5,000 boys camped at Gilwell, and since then many, many thousands have spent healthy and happy days there.

The almost accidental combination of a Boy Scout camping field with a Scoutmasters' training camp was most fortunate. It has meant that the staff has always had close touch with boys as well as with men. Had the training camp been a thing of itself there would have been the danger of the staff getting more and more out of touch with boy life, but, as it is, a stroll amongst the boys' camps quickly brings the theorist down to earth.

The majority of the Scout campers at Gilwell come from London and especially from parts east of the Mansion House. East London Scouting has also derived great benefit from the house bequeathed by Roland Philipps. Just before 1914 he had bought a house on Stepney Green as a centre for his Scout work. This became Roland House, which, with subsequent extensions, has become a settlement for Scouters wishing to help the movement in that area, and also an International Hostel for visiting Scouters of other countries.

CHAPTER SEVENTEEN

THE FIRST JAMBOREE

A GLANCE AT THE LIST OF MEMBERS OF THE COMMITTEE OF THE Council at the beginning of 1920 gives us the names of the team that the Chief Scout had formed to guide the development of the Movement. Here it may be pointed out that he gave this Committee and the Commissioners at Headquarters the same freedom of action that he wanted all Scoutmasters to enjoy. Naturally his own expressed wishes were generally accepted gladly, but there were occasions on which the Committee differed from him, and he was always ready to discuss such differences and to find agreement. He certainly did not impose his own wishes on the men who were responsible for the day-to-day running of affairs.

Some of those on the 1920 Committee have already been mentioned—Sir Edmond Elles, P. W. Everett, A. Gaddum, Colonel de Burgh, C. C. Branch, N. D. Power, Ernest Young, and H. G. Elwes. Mention should also be made of F. W. Pixley the Treasurer who was succeeded in the following year by Colonel A. D. Acland; the Earl of Meath who, in spite of his age, went through a training course at Gilwell in 1920; Captain B. S. Thesiger (later Admiral Sir Bertram Thesiger) who for many years rendered enthusiastic service to Scouting and especially to the Sea Scout section; Percy Armitage, another unswerving supporter; and Hubert S. Martin who became International Commissioner in 1918 at a period when the services of a man of his calibre proved of the greatest importance. To these should be added Major J. A. Dane who became Commissioner for the Training of Officers and as such had considerable responsibility for the extension of the work begun at Gilwell Park. His *Practical Hints for Commissioners* had been a useful guide for several years. It was later developed into the *Scout Commissioners' Handbook*.

Major A. G. Wade returned from military service to become Travelling Organizing Secretary for England. His abilities were soon in full use in organizing the first Jamboree.

It had been hoped to have some kind of celebration of the tenth anniversary of the start of Scouting in 1917, but the continuation of the war made this impossible. The date had in fact to be postponed until 1920. An early problem was to find a suitable name. B.-P.'s flair for attractive names led him to suggest 'Jamboree'. He could never recall where he had first come across the word, but it had stuck in his memory. When asked why he called a gathering of Scouts a 'Jamboree' he replied: 'What else could you call it?' Later he wrote:

Different people assign different derivations to the word, but whatever its derivation, it will have a quite distinct meaning for most people after this year [1920]. It will be associated with the greatest gathering of boys that has ever been held. 'Jamboree' to them implies a joyful, cheery gathering of boys with broad-brimmed hats and broad grins—complete in their workmanlike kit of shirt, shorts, staff, and scarf. They are the important part of the Jamboree.

B.-P.'s desire to make the Jamboree a gathering of Scouts from all over the world was not welcomed by some leaders of the Movement. To us the idea of Scouting as a link between countries seems an axiom, but in 1918 it was still unfamiliar to many. Some who shook their heads at the Chief Scout's optimism even went so far as to say that his plans were too bold and idealist, and one said that Scouting might 'totter to its fall' if such ambitious schemes were attempted. To which B.-P. replied: 'Don't be frightened. You take too serious a view of the whole matter. If the Movement is tottering, let it totter. As a matter of fact, it has plenty of vitality under the surface, and is quite capable of doing a very big thing in promoting international amity—and, what is more, it is going to do it.'

This first Jamboree was unlike those that followed. It was an indoor affair at Olympia, London, and the arrangements were discussed in detail by B.-P. whose fertile brain suggested many attractive forms of display. The Jamborees that followed were outdoor camps, and B.-P. was then content to leave the major work of organization to others while keeping a watchful eye on the general scheme.

A camp for 5,000 Scouts was established in the Old Deer Park, Richmond, for visiting Scouts and Scoutmasters.

Olympia itself provided two kinds of opportunity: first a vast arena (325 feet by 85 feet) for displays; and second, annexes where small exhibitions could be held. Both these were used to the full. A great back scene was painted showing a rocky coast with a ship at anchor, and to the right of this a forest scene with huts and other structures for the displays. A specially made drop-curtain, 120 yards long, shut off this scene. The concrete floor had to be covered with a foot of earth and tan for competitions, tent-pitching, and so on. These few facts will illustrate more than any description how different this first Jamboree was from the ones which evolved from it. It was more of a display and exhibition than a camp.

The display side included such items as trek-cart work, fire-fighting, tumbling, Morris dancing, physical training, gymnastics, ambulance work, bridge-building, camp-pitching, signalling, wrestling, and musical drill.

Special displays included country life and industries, colliery life, life of St. Patrick, the Red Hand of Ulster, a Highland gathering, the life of a Chevalier, customs of the Arawak Indians, African native life.

A pageant written by B.-P., called 'The Genesis of Scouting', told the story of Captain John Smith in Virginia and of Princess Pocahontas.

There was also a series of competitions, including tug-of-war, obstacle trek-cart race, relay dispatch-carrying, and band and bugling. A marathon long-distance ride was done by cycle over a distance of 100 miles from many points in England, the Scouts starting on 2 August and finishing in the arena two days later.

Exhibits were also judged; these included woodwork, metal-work, other handcrafts (models, bookbinding, toys, &c.), bridges, posters, scrapbooks (diaries, wild life, sketches), stamps, working models.

In the side halls there were a number of special exhibitions which attracted much attention. Most of these were in connexion with the competitions just mentioned, but there was one which, had the spectator been gifted with a sight into the future, would have been very closely inspected; this was the woodcraft section. This was represented by the Gilwell Park booth and the tracking strip. Gilwell was still a mystery, or even unknown, to the majority of Scouters. Hike tents and equipment, rafts, and other outdoor Scouting objects were the chief exhibits. They seemed novel to most people, and indeed they suggested new ideas for real outdoor Scouting to a degree it is now impossible to recall, for these have now become part of our normal Scout practice. The most popular item, however, was the tracking strip; here each day a story was set out as a challenge to the Sherlock Holmeses of the Movement; it particularly attracted the Scouts themselves, who spent long periods arguing about the clues and tracks.

On Sunday, 1 August, a special service was held in the arena, when some 8,000 Scouts were present. The Archbishop of York (Cosmo Gordon Lang) preached the sermon. One extract may be given:

> I am almost awed by the huge power of the boys assembled here. How is such a solemn trust as is implied in this Movement to be used? There is only one answer—to make a new and better world. You are out not to claim rights, but to do your duty; not to care for yourselves, but for others; not to work for the class, but for the commonwealth; not to suspect and fight other nations, but to make comrades and brothers.

There were also services at Westminster Abbey and at Westminster Cathedral.

By this time Jamboree weather had set in! At the Richmond camp on that Sunday evening there was a probability of the whole site being flooded; the Thames overflowed and part of the camp was under water, but the inhabitants and authorities of Richmond rose to the occasion and Scouts were soon quartered in schools and private houses. Olympia was also flooded on Monday, 2 August, but by people! Any doubts as to whether the public was interested in this new kind of exhibition were soon ended. At the opening of the afternoon performance on the Monday 14,000 spectators were in the seats.

There is no point in trying to record here the daily programme, or to describe in detail even a fraction of all that happened during that momentous week. More and more, as the days went by, the significance of the Jamboree became clear. What had started as a rally of Scouts to celebrate the tenth year of the Movement developed into a great demonstration of international good will. The Movement had come into its own, and the public recognized it for what it really meant—a new citizenship of youth knowing no boundaries of race or geography.

When invitations had been sent out to other countries to send Scouts to the Jamboree, few thought that the response would be anything like what actually happened. Twenty-one foreign countries sent parties of Scouts.

The last two days of the Jamboree must be recorded in greater detail, for they are milestones in the history of the Movement.

On 6 August B.-P. was acclaimed Chief Scout of the World. This tribute was spontaneous; it had not been planned as part of the programme when the Jamboree was being organized, but as the days passed it became more and more evident how strong a hold this one man had on the hearts and loyalties of those thousands of boys from so many lands. The unrehearsed ceremony took place in the arena on the Friday evening. With the flags of the nations unfurled, and the Scout flag flying, he accepted from the boys a title which no king or government could confer; and of all the honours showered upon him, this was to him the most precious.

On the following evening, the time had come to separate. At the final rally B.-P. gave his parting message.

> Brother Scouts. I ask you to make a solemn choice. Differences exist between the peoples of the world in thought and sentiment, just as they do in language and physique. The war has taught us that if one nation tries to impose its particular will upon others, cruel reaction is bound to follow. The Jamboree has taught us that if we exercise mutual forbearance and give and take, then there is sympathy and harmony. If it be your will, let us go forth from here fully determined that we will develop among ourselves and our boys that comradeship, through the world-wide spirit of the Scout Brotherhood, so that we may help to develop peace and happiness in the world and good will among men. Brother Scouts, answer me. Will you join in this endeavour?

There was no doubt of the great cry of 'Yes!' which followed.

'God speed you in your work, and fare you well.'

The Last Post was sounded in memory of Scouts who had fallen in the war. For a few moments there was a hush, then all joined in singing 'Auld Lang Syne'. After that the boys took charge; B.-P. was lifted shoulder high and carried across the arena amidst tumultuous cheering.

In summing up his impressions of that first Jamboree, the Chief Scout of the World wrote:

> The Jamboree, carefully planned though it had been, had not foreshadowed the development of the international brotherhood on a basis already so strong and so advanced as it proved, nor had it reckoned on so varied an expression of that wonderful Scout spirit, an exhibition that took onlookers by the throat as they had never been taken before. . . .
>
> To bring impressions into their proper perspective after the shock of such revelation requires time and reflection, but there cannot have been one among us under that great dome who did not feel that here in these times of anxiety and doubt was unfolded a prospect full of promise and hope, where men and future men of all nations were gathered as brothers in mutual happy comradeship under a common ideal for the weal of the world.

So the first World Jamboree ended.

A less spectacular part of the Jamboree calls for special mention. Leaders of the various contingents from all countries came together for informal talks about the future of Scouting as an international Movement. It was decided to set up a permanent organization—an International Bureau with Hubert Martin as its first Director, an honorary appointment he filled with outstanding success until his death in 1938. Funds to establish the bureau were provided by F. F. Peabody of the United States of America. Another strong supporter from across the Atlantic was Mortimer L. Schiff. It was also decided to call the full Conference together every two years, and Paris was chosen as the place for the one due in 1922. The national Scout Associations represented at Olympia became foundation members of the Conference.

⚜ ⚜ ⚜ ⚜ ⚜ ⚜ ⚜ ⚜ ⚜ ⚜ ⚜ ⚜ ⚜ ⚜ ⚜ ⚜ ⚜

CHAPTER EIGHTEEN

ADJUSTMENT

THE YEARS BETWEEN 1920 AND 1925 WERE A PERIOD OF ADJUSTment; the Jamboree of 1920 had been a striking demonstration of the vitality of the Movement and during the immediate post-war years all energy and thought had been concentrated on making that event a success. B.-P. was never in danger of becoming complacent; he enjoyed the pauses marked by such celebrations as a Jamboree, but to him they were occasions for stock-taking and for planning future progress. Some problems called for attention, notably Rover Scouts and the training of Scoutmasters. The Cub section and the Scouts up to the age of 15 have steadily gone on with their work through the years and have never caused serious concern. Indeed it has been said with a considerable degree of truth that a Scout Troop can carry on happily without being troubled by Headquarters or by Commissioners. This is still true to some extent, though Scouting has not proved an exception to the rule that an increase in the size and complexity of the central organization brings more and more interference with the activities of the members.

The year 1921 opened more auspiciously than could be then realized; it brought B.-P. into contact with two men who were to take leading parts in the future of the Movement. With Lady Baden-Powell he went to India at the invitation of the Viceroy. Several separate Scout organizations had been formed in that country, and B.-P.'s visit helped to bring them together. During the tour he met Sir Alfred Pickford who was then Chief Commissioner for India. Later, in July, Sir Alfred came to England and went through a training course at Gilwell in company with J. S. Wilson who was District Commissioner of the 1st Calcutta Association. Both were made Deputy Camp Chiefs, and on their return to India they ran the first Scoutmasters' Training Course in Bengal. Sir Alfred settled in England and became

Commissioner for Oversea Scouts. For a quarter of a century he was to exercise a great influence in the Scout world; his large and cheerful presence was combined with a sound judgement, and he quickly became an outstanding leader. Indeed his authority was so widely recognized that, in 1926, B.-P., when considering the problem of his own successor, could note in his diary 'Pickie as Chief Scout'. Unfortunately Sir Alfred had to return to business in later years and so was no longer able to devote his whole time to Scouting.

Under the guidance of Colonel de Burgh, the Rover Scouts had gradually been taking shape. The long illness that preceded his death in November 1921 was a serious handicap to this still young section. He had gained the confidence of the young men who were to shape the Rover Scout scheme. Unfortunately he was too unwell to attend a crucial conference on Rovers held in October 1921. This was a meeting of men of special experience invited by B.-P. to discuss with him the future of the new section. The points discussed included the following:

1. What is the object of the Rovers—
   (*a*) to retain the older Scouts as part of the Troop, or
   (*b*) to form a separate section to train as Scout workers?
   What should be the age-limit?
   Should Rovers obtaining warrants remain as Rovers?
2. Is it desirable to have Clubs for old Scouts in addition to Rovers?
3. What is the definition of Rovers?
4. Uniform.
5. Training and badges.

The main decisions were:

1. Objects—to retain older boys in Troops in Rover Patrols; to provide training for older boys in works and clubs; to train those over 18 to be Scout officers.
   Age—17 and over.
   Warrant—a Rover obtaining a warrant can remain a Rover.
2. It is desirable to encourage old Scout clubs of which Rovers can be members; minimum age for clubs—18.
3. A Rover Scout is a Senior Scout of 17 or over; he takes the same Promise as a Boy Scout, and there must be an enrolment ceremony.

4. No change in uniform desired.
5. (*a*) The initial Rover tests will combine the Tenderfoot and Second Class badge tests of the Boy Scouts.
   (*b*) First Class Rover—tests on same lines as Boy Scout. First Class badge but with stiffer requirements.
   (*c*) One special badge to be obtainable in some Scouting subject.
   (*d*) Rovers can take the King's Scout Badge with a higher standard than that required of Boy Scouts.

It was unfortunate that the question of an upper age-limit was not threshed out; as a result some confusion of thought bedevilled this section during the ensuing years; men holding warrants became Rovers and the attempts to combine training of the 17 to 21 age-group with the needs of mature men led to vagueness and uncertainty. Had the suggestion of Old Scout Clubs been vigorously put into effect, some of the resulting difficulties might have been avoided. The greatest set-back, however, to immediate progress was undoubtedly the failure to find someone to replace Colonel de Burgh to guide the Rover Scouts during the formative period. The publication of *Rovering to Success* in 1922 helped to bridge the gap, but it was not a training handbook on the lines of *Scouting for Boys*; it was a book of wise advice to young men. In December 1923 P. B. Nevill was appointed Acting Chief Rover Commissioner; he had been Commissioner for Kindred Societies since 1921 in succession to Arthur Gaddum, and this position he was to occupy for many years with considerable success. He was also closely associated with the work of Roland House, the Wardenship of which he resigned in 1925. The term 'Acting' implied a temporary position and recognized that he could give only part of his time to the Rovers. In effect he remained Acting Commissioner until February 1929 when for just over a year he became Commissioner for Rovers.

By the decision to raise the age of entry of Rovers to 17, the problem of the older Scout of 15 years or more was left unsolved. So for some years the Movement was disturbed with arguments about Rover Scouts and attempts to deal with the loss of boys at the age of 15 or 16. More must be said about these problems.

The outstanding event of 1922 was the Posse of Welcome to

the Prince of Wales (Edward VIII) on his return from his tour in the East. It was at the suggestion of King George V that some term other than 'Guard of Honour' was used on this occasion, and B.-P. chose 'Posse' as a suitable word. Some 60,000 Cubs, Scouts, and Rovers gathered at the Alexandra Palace to greet the Prince. He was presented with the Silver Wolf by his uncle the Duke of Connaught, President of the Association. It was a most delightful occasion and the Prince's obvious interest in the many sides of Scouting that were demonstrated added considerably to the success of the afternoon. One incident may be described in the words of Sidney Dark.

> Then the Prince mounted the platform. Here again was an intensely human scene—this one, slim, boyish figure standing conspicuous and alone with tens of thousands of boys in front of him. . . . At a signal the Scouts at the bottom of the hill gave a mighty yell and with waving flags and pennons charged up to the front line. It was a terrific rush at full speed and up hill, and it was not surprising that a few of the weaker brethren were left behind. After the rush, and a ripple of uncontrollable cheers, discipline and silence were again enforced, and the Prince made his speech.

Two years earlier the Prince had sponsored an appeal for funds for the Movement; the central organization has never asked for subscriptions from members who support their local organizations, but has always relied on direct donations and the profits from its shop; from time to time it has therefore been necessary to appeal for money from the public in order to meet growing needs. The Prince of Wales's appeal came just before a difficult economic period and the result was therefore disappointing; just over £30,000 was received.

The International Conference met in Paris at the Sorbonne in July 1922. Perhaps the place of meeting was partly responsible for the somewhat erudite discourses given. These were in the nature of a revelation to the British delegates; they had found that Scouting 'worked' and had not greatly bothered about its theoretic justification or its psychological foundations. An International Committee was elected consisting of: Count Mario di Carpegna (Italy), Lord Hampton (Great Britain), Frank Presbrey (U.S.A.), Sir Alfred Pickford (British Empire), Mortimer L. Schiff (U.S.A.), Dr. A. B. Svojsik (Czechoslovakia), Emmerich Teuber (Austria).

The Director of the Bureau reported that the number of registered Scouts in the world was 1,344,360.

One important outcome of this Conference was the recognition of the part Gilwell Park could play in promoting a true interpretation of Scouting throughout the Scout world. It was agreed that the Wood badge would be available for non-British Scoutmasters and that Deputy Camp Chiefs could be appointed to carry the training to their own countries.

Gilwell itself, however, was passing through a difficult period. The friction was due not to the training work but to the administration. There were, it is true, still some who decried the work at Gilwell on the grounds that good Scoutmasters are born and not made, and that too much emphasis on practical Scouting meant a loss of the spirit of the Movement. They were rightly irritated by the folly of some who propagated a kind of Gilwell cult. This opposition gradually declined as more and more men of long experience went through the courses and reported enthusiastically in favour of the scheme. Training was expanded in 1922 to cover the work of Cubmasters, and the extension of the scheme to other countries considerably raised the status of Gilwell. All this inevitably brought to the front problems of finance and control, and it was unfortunate that just when these difficulties became acute, Gidney, the Camp Chief, was absent in the United States doing valuable work in demonstrating how B.-P. wanted his ideas interpreted. The Movement in the States was developing rapidly under the energetic leadership of James E. West, the Chief Scout Executive, and this first-hand contact with the Camp Chief from Gilwell was of great importance. Gidney's American tour meant that it was impossible to discuss with him the administrative problems that were accentuated by his absence. The resignation in 1922 of Major Dane from the position of Commissioner for the Training of Officers was the first public sign of the growing tension. The Chief Scout himself took over these duties with P. W. Everett to assist him. In 1923 Dr. F. R. Lucas was appointed Assistant Camp Chief in charge of administration and of the boys' camping field; during his years at Gilwell, 'Lukie' endeared himself to all, and his influence in the camping fields was an important part of the informal training that Gilwell provides outside the training courses.

In what many regarded as mistaken loyalty to an Assistant, Gidney resigned, and it is not too much to say that those who had come under his influence were apprehensive as to the future of Gilwell. In November 1923 J. S. Wilson was appointed Camp Chief. He had resigned from the Indian Police and during that summer had helped at Gilwell. In some ways he was the complement of Gidney. The first Camp Chief was a man of restless imagination who infused into the training just the spirit of adventure, even of recklessness, that it needed in its early days. He was perfectly fitted to the task of pioneering a work for which there was no precedent, and the foundations he laid have not been disturbed. He had no gift for administration and his attempts at organization were frustrated by his own eager spirit. Wilson shared Gidney's understanding of Scouting to the full, but he brought to his task administrative ability of a high order that had stood some severe tests in India, particularly during the war years. The first full season under his direction convinced the most sceptical that B.-P. had chosen the right man to be the second Camp Chief.

It was as well that these difficulties had been overcome before 1924 as that year was marked by two outstanding events—the Empire Jamboree at Wembley and the World Jamboree in Denmark. The way for the first had been prepared by tours made by the Chief Scout in Canada and by Sir Alfred Pickford in Australia and New Zealand. When the suggestion was made that the Scouts should hold an Imperial Jamboree, there was a ready response. Over 1,000 Scouts from twenty-five parts of the Commonwealth and Empire outside the United Kingdom accepted the invitation; 10,000 other Scouts joined them in camp in Wembley Paddocks. The Prince of Wales (Edward VIII) witnessed the displays, joined the camp fire, and spent the night in camp. Amongst other visitors was the Duke of York (George VI), and Rudyard Kipling who saw his Mowgli stories in a new setting.

From Wembley many of the Scouts set off for Denmark. This, the second World Jamboree, was the pioneer of the now-accepted all-camp Jamborees in contrast with the indoor affair at Olympia in 1920. It was primarily a Boy Scout camp.

The camp dates were 10 to 17 August. To this period was added the novel idea of a further week of Danish hospitality during which Scouts would live in the homes of their Danish comrades and have an opportunity of seeing something of the country and of Copenhagen.

The programme of the Jamboree was built round the contests for the World Scout Championship. In these the following countries took part: America, Austria, Chile, Denmark, Finland, France, Great Britain, Holland, Hungary, Italy, Luxembourg, Norway, Poland, and Switzerland. 'Great Britain' in this connexion covers also parties of Scouts from the Dominions of Australia, New Zealand, South Africa, and from many other parts of the British Commonwealth and Empire. Other countries represented in camp, but not competing, were: Argentine, Belgium, Brazil, Bulgaria, China, Czechoslovakia, Egypt, Estonia, Japan, Latvia, Lithuania, Panama, Portugal, Roumania, Russia (Emigré), Siam, Spain, Sweden, and Yugoslavia.

The subjects judged were Turn-out (including camp equipment), Camp Craft, Camp Routine (i.e. discipline, punctuality, good behaviour), Songs and Yells, Folk Dancing, Camp Fire Entertainment, Swimming, two separate Scout contests, Patrol Obstacle Race, and twenty-four-hour Patrol Hike. It was a good all-over test of Scout ability and training, and—as a demonstration—of great value, particularly at this period of Scouting's life. It was wisely decided, however, not to continue such an all-embracing competition, as it carried with it the danger of emphasizing nationality at the expense of the spirit of brotherhood. The Boy Scouts of America gained the championship and gave a most spectacular Red Indian display.

Ermelunden gave the first idea of the great variety of camping methods and national activities which the Movement as a whole had the chance to realize visually. Each country had its camping area, and within that could organize itself along its own lines. A contingent would consist of a representative Troop together with a visiting group of Scouts. They soon settled down on their sites, and it was not long before Scouts were mixing together, examining each other's uniform (and swapping parts), taking note of different kinds of cooking places, discussing the merits of various types of tents, and then quickly going on to exchange invitations to tea-parties and other combined enjoyments.

The representative Troops were busy for much of each day taking part in the contests; their (more fortunate?) fellow

Scouts who had no such responsibilities were able to wander about, making friends and picking up ideas when they were not watching how their teams were progressing.

One of the biggest problems was the public. Day after day they came in their thousands to walk about amongst the camps, or to see the displays in the open-air arena. At times they almost seemed to swamp the camps and circulation became difficult. Then each evening came the camp fire. Here is an impression from a Swiss Scout:

> One cannot speak of the camp fires without referring to the great impression made one evening by a demonstration of languages originated by the leader Sven Knudsen. He invited one Scout from each country to say in his own language, *I trust you to do a good turn every day*. Thirty-two times these words were spoken, each time in a different language!
>
> The return to the camp along the dark roads of the forest was something specially fraternal. The Scouts, arm in arm, walked in parties of eight to ten without distinction of nationality. It was nothing unusual to see in the same group boys of five or six nations.
>
> It is nearly eleven o'clock. The groups break up. *Good night*, *God nat*, *buona note*. . . . A quarter of an hour afterwards the silence is such that a latecomer walks on tiptoe for fear of disturbing the calm of the night.

On the Sunday morning the Scouts were inspected by the King of Denmark. Rain poured down and everyone was drenched. As B.-P. said when later distributing the awards for the contests, 'I have seen great numbers of Scouts in my life, but I have never seen any as wet as you!'

The week following the Jamboree itself was, in some ways, no less notable. Denmark became one vast host to all these boy visitors. The organization of this hospitality was perfect. Each Scout received a coloured card at camp. This gave the clue to where he would find his host—it might be in the home of a working-man, or in the home of a banker; the result was the same—warm friendliness and a desire to make the boy at home. Excursions were arranged to places of interest in Copenhagen and the surrounding country. No Scout could leave Denmark without having got a good idea of the country, and, more important, of its people. It was an amazing week, and put the final touches on a Jamboree of genuine good will and comradeship.

The Jamboree was followed by the Third International Conference. One item on the agenda calls for mention here. Dr. Walter de Bonstetten, President of the Federation of Swiss Scouts, presented the first report of the International Scout Chalet at Kandersteg; it had been at his prompting that this had been bought in 1923 as a centre for camping and climbing to which all Scouts from all countries could go. Since then it has been increasingly used by Scouts of a multitude of nations. The institution of a Scouts Alpine Club in association with the Chalet has added to its value.

The need was felt for some time for an omnibus term that could cover all the varieties of warranted ranks. The Chief Scout wrote this comment on the proof of a pamphlet entitled *The Training of Scout Officers* in 1922:

> I don't like the term 'Scout Officers' at the head of this pamphlet because the word 'officer' gives an entirely wrong notion of the standing and duties of the man in charge of Scouts. His standing is that of elder brother; his duties are mainly those of a patent combined steering wheel and accelerator to give the direction and the incentive to the boys' activities.

Before long the term 'Scouter' became accepted as meaning any adult holding a warrant. This use was confirmed when *The Headquarters Gazette* changed its name to *The Scouter* with the issue of January 1923. The semi-official London journal *The Trail* was bought up in 1922 and incorporated in *The Scouter*.

H. G. Elwes had continued as editor up to that date, but his increasing physical disabilities led him to share the work with Ernest Young when the name *The Scouter* was adopted. For all practical purposes Ernest Young was editor, a position he occupied alone from 1926 to 1929. Under the sole editorship of H. G. Elwes the 'Gazette' had become a well-established part of the organization. His own monthly contributions did much to stress the spiritual implications of Scouting and thus continued the work he began at the Crystal Palace Conference in 1909. Some felt that his later notes tended to become rather mawkish; there was some truth in this and it may well have been a reflection of his own infirmity; certainly there was a feeling by 1923 that a more virile exposition of Scouting was needed.

⚜ ⚜ ⚜ ⚜ ⚜ ⚜ ⚜ ⚜ ⚜ ⚜ ⚜ ⚜ ⚜ ⚜ ⚜ ⚜ ⚜

CHAPTER NINETEEN

1925–8

THE TRUTH OF B.-P.'S DICTUM THAT 'SCOUTING IS A MOVEMENT AND not an Organization' is shown by the ease with which it can expand to cover new activities. Thus a growing interest in music led to the first Musical Festival in December 1925 under the direction of S. H. Nicholson (later Sir Sydney Nicholson) the organist and master of the choristers of Westminster Abbey. He had accepted the position of Commissioner of Music to the Association, and was anxious to extend the range, and raise the standard, of singing at camp-fires and to promote the enjoyment of good music. In the following year, the first Folk Dance Festival was held at Gilwell Park with the encouragement of the English Folk Dance Society, and for some years folk-dancing had a strong band of devotees in the Movement.

A further development came in 1927 with the organization of Scouting as a means of helping boys who suffered from physical or mental defects. The way in this direction had been pioneered by the Girl Guides in their Extension branch. For some years many Scouts had been visiting these unfortunate boys and had done much to brighten their lives. Doctors found that such visits brought a most marked improvement in the outlook of the children; they no longer felt cut off from the world and they discovered that there were many things they could do like other boys. When the time came to consolidate this work there was a difficulty in finding a suitable name; it was undesirable to label the work in a manner that would stress the plight of these boys. For a time it went under the title of the Department for Disabled Scouts, but this was too crude and was changed to the Special Tests Department; this was adequate as part of the organizing work was to modify existing Scout tests to meet various disabilities. Later the name of 'Handicapped Scouts' was adopted. The happiest title, however, is the Swiss—

Scouts malgré tout—this aptly describes the significance of this remedial form of Scouting. In this country the name of Sir Montagu Burrows was for long associated with the aid given to these handicapped boys.

In 1927 Mrs. Colebrook presented to the Association a house at Herne Bay as a Convalescent Home. Rosemary Home, as it was called, proved a great boon to a host of Cubs and Scouts up to the outbreak of war in 1939. The warden, J. R. Stanley, made Rosemary a place of happy memories for all the sick boys who there found health and strength.

Reference should also be made to the expanding work of the Public and Preparatory Schools Department. Troops were formed in many of the ancient Grammar Schools in the early years of the Movement, and some Preparatory Schools had welcomed Scouting, but the greater Public Schools held aloof for some years. It was felt that if boys in these schools were themselves Boy Scouts, some of them might become Scoutmasters in future years; they would at least have learned something of the principles of the Movement. With this end in view a special Commissioner was appointed to encourage the formation of Preparatory and Public School Troops. H. F. Stallard held this position for five years and during that period the number of Public School Groups increased by twenty-six. He was assisted and then followed in this work by Piers D. Power who was also Commissioner for Scouts. There was at first a little soreness amongst Scoutmasters of other schools who had been content to carry on their Troops without special nursing, but when the position was explained to them, they accepted the new development and helped where they could. An annual training camp for schoolmasters of Public Schools became a recognized institution and did valuable work in attracting men who otherwise would not have thought of Scouting. An attempt to establish a special certificate for Public School Scouts was soon given up as it was felt that this carried differentiation too far. Allied with this was the rise of Scout Clubs or Rover Crews at the universities; these have had varying fortunes, but those at Oxford and Cambridge have now a long record of good work not only in introducing undergraduates and, indeed, Heads and Tutors of colleges to the Movement, but in carrying out special duties at Jamborees and other gatherings.

AN EARLY SCOUT TROOP, *c.* 1910

WAR SERVICE, 1914–18. SEA SCOUTS ON COASTGUARD DUTY

During his term of office as Secretary of State for the Dominions and Colonies, the Rt. Hon. L. C. M. S. Amery suggested in 1923 that the Association should consider the possibility of encouraging emigration amongst Scouts. This idea was readily adopted, for it was completely in harmony with B.-P.'s wishes. Under the scheme Boy Scouts who were recommended by their local Commissioners and approved by Headquarters were given introductions to the Scout authorities in the Dominions to which they went. Each boy was looked after on his departure, at ports of call, and on arrival by members of the Scout Associations. So successful was this scheme that during the years 1927–8 over 2,000 Scouts between 15 and 19 years of age settled overseas. Later records showed beyond doubt that young fellows with a Scout background soon found their feet and became good citizens of their new countries.

The Movement was steadily expanding throughout the Commonwealth and Empire. Relations were maintained with the parent Association through the Commissioner for Overseas Scouts; Sir Alfred Pickford held this position until 1929 when for a year Colonel G. Walton took his place before becoming Commissioner for Rovers; he was succeeded by Harold Legat who, until 1948, carried on this friendly association in a quiet, effective manner that gave encouragement and won confidence. During most of this period the Rev. Cyril Butterworth was the capable and loyal secretary of this Department. Each Association overseas is autonomous and there has never been any suggestion of direction from London, but Headquarters in this country has proved a happy meeting-place and a useful clearing-house. Many thousands of Scouts and Scouters from these overseas parts have made their first visits to this country and to Europe as members of the contingents that have been sent to each Jamboree.

The Rover section had a Moot at the Albert Hall in London at Easter 1926; the main meeting was presided over by Lord Jellicoe, the Commissioner for London. The most impressive item was a King Arthur pageant which was to have unexpected results. Two years earlier a Conference at Headquarters revealed a divergence of opinion on the purpose of Rovering. One speaker claimed that Rovers did not primarily exist for training but were a brotherhood of service which 'all men in this country should join'. He wanted the age of entry raised to eighteen. His exposition of his ideas made it clear that he was thinking of what may be described as a lay religious order based on the Scout Promise. The implications of this point of view were not realized at the conference; one speaker asked for a definition of 'Service' and had this request been thoroughly discussed, the divided purposes that subsequently developed might have been avoided. The division of opinion was between those who regarded Rovering as a continuation of Scout training for those over 17 years of age, and those who visualized a brotherhood of men bound together by the obligation of service to the community.

B.-P.'s own view was stated in his 'Explanation of Scouting' prefaced to *Scouting for Boys*.

Rover Scouts are Scouts over 17 and in exceptional cases younger. They are organized in Rover Crews in their Group.

The object of their institution is to complete the sequence of the training from boyhood to manhood, through the progressive grades of Wolf Cub, Scout, and Rover.

The training of the Cubs and Scouts is largely a preparation for rendering Service which is consummated in practice by the Rover. Such Service in most cases takes the form of helping in the administration and training of the group. Thus the progressive cycle becomes complete from Cub to Scoutmaster. In this way the Scoutmaster, while retaining the young man under good influence at the critical time of his life, gains valuable help for himself in his work, and, in such cases as are fit for it, he turns out further recruits for the ranks of the Scoutmasters, while for the nation he supplies young men trained and qualified for making good useful citizens.

The King Arthur theme stressed at the Albert Hall Moot in 1926 captured the imaginations of many, both young and mature, and there developed from it a tendency to force the Rover programme into an Arthurian framework. B.-P. himself used the legend of Arthur and the Knights of the Round Table as a helpful symbolism, but some of the Rover leaders wanted to press too far. One of them persuaded the Chief Scout to visit the centre of a modern Arthurian cult in the West Country; he was far from impressed and thought the conception too artificial. One of the first results of this Arthurian phase was the elaboration of the ceremony of enrolment of a Rover Scout. Simple ceremonies have always had a part in Scouting as they do serve to mark for the boy the importance of the stages of his Scout progress. The ceremony of knighthood approved by the Church 'when chivalry was in flower' was adapted for the use of Rover Crews. The aspirant kept an overnight vigil, sometimes in a church, and the actual ceremony included a symbolical laving. The basic idea of a self-examination was sound and was recommended by the Chief Scout, but the extremes to which some went in elaborate ritual roused adverse comment. Some over-earnest leaders failed to see that this ceremonial development frightened off many young men who were not susceptible to the influence of ritual, or were shy of such elaborate proceedings. It must also be said, hard as it may sound, that for some this ceremonial verged on play-acting, though, unquestionably, it did exert a good influence over others.

A further development of this Arthurian theme was the use made of the apocryphal Quest of the Holy Grail. The suggestion was put forward by Dr. F. W. W. Griffin at a conference at York in 1928 that Rovers should organize themselves in Round Tables, and each member should undertake a definite Quest in the manner of the knights of the legend. It must, of course, be remembered that in talking of Arthur and the Round Table and the Holy Grail, the advocates of this approach to Rovering were thinking of the bowdlerized versions of the legends popularized by Tennyson and the Pre-Raphaelites; a reading of Malory's *Morte d'Arthur* is apt to shock readers of tender consciences. This idea of Quests was ingeniously worked out, and was doubtless of help in canalizing the vague longings of some young men attracted by this particular presentation. Others felt it was all rather too seriously applied and that perhaps a Quest of a Sense of Humour might well be added to the list. Parallel with this esoteric form of Rovering, there were still many of the over-17's who carried on with outdoor Scouting, and, while getting all the delights of camping and hiking, were developing into useful citizens. The pity was that one school of thought had, at least temporarily, attracted the limelight.

References have been made to several conferences; it would be tedious to record in these pages the proceedings at all of them. They were of great value in bringing together Scouters of many localities and the Headquarters Commissioners;

discussion on the chosen themes helped to ventilate opinions and grievances, but no formal resolutions were passed; it was the business of the Committee of the Council to consider the views put forward and to take whatever action they deemed desirable. There were conferences of many kinds: an annual one for County Commissioners and Secretaries, open conferences at which any holder of a warrant could attend as at Bristol in 1925, special ones for schoolmasters (1924) or with representatives of universities in 1925, or for Cubmasters in 1926. More detailed reference will be made to those that led to changes in policy, such as the Bournemouth Conference of 1927.

That Conference was held twenty years after the Brownsea Island camp, and it was fitting that this anniversary should be commemorated. The one thing lacking was the presence of the Chief Scout who was then touring South Africa. On 2 April 500 members of the Conference went to the Island where they were joined by four of the original campers. On the site of the first Scout camp an Act of Thanksgiving was made. The following special prayer was used:

O Lord, in Whose Son the perfection of Childhood, Youth and Man's estate was made manifest, and given unto us as a pattern and example of our own lives, we, assembled on this spot, give Thee thanks for the gift of Scouting. We thank Thee for the wisdom and foresight of our Chief, whose first camp here on Brownsea was the forerunner of our Brotherhood. We thank Thee for the enthusiasm and self-sacrifice of those, his immediate followers, to whom the early guidance of our Movement was entrusted. Above all, O Lord, we thank Thee for that Thou hast permitted us, Thy servants, to take our share in the service of the boyhood of our country; and for all the inspiration and happiness that Scouting has brought into our own lives. We ask for Thy blessing upon our Chief, upon the boys whom we are privileged to lead, and upon the Brotherhood of Scouts throughout the world. May we go forward from this spot rededicated to this Thy service, and in humble gratitude for Thy manifold mercies.

The Bournemouth Conference was notable for a paper 'The Position of Rover Leaders' by J. F. Colquhoun who, in 1927, became Chief Wolf Cub Commissioner. The title did not suggest anything exciting, but an important question was raised and solutions suggested that led to notable decisions. We have seen how each of the sections, Scouts, Cubs, Rovers, in that order, developed separately as needs arose; the problem calling for solution was how to secure co-ordination between the three sections. The position of Rover Leaders could not be considered in isolation, and it inevitably raised the problem of the relations between all the Scouters concerned in the three stages of training. The paper at the Bournemouth Conference suggested that the key lay in the right use of the Troop Council consisting of all the Scouters. Various alternative proposals were discussed by the speaker; that there should be an elected chairman, or that a new rank should be instituted of a Troopmaster, or that either the Scoutmaster or Rover Leader should be given seniority. No recommendation was decided upon by the Conference, but the problem had been clearly set out and ideas had been stimulated. The outcome was that the Committee of the Council devised the Group System. By this the unit is the Group consisting of one or more of the three sections, the aim being to have a complete Group with all three. The Scouter in charge is called the Group Scoutmaster and harmony of working is possible through the Group Council consisting of all the Scouters.

During this period the influence of Gilwell was rapidly extending; an outward sign of this was the increasing number of Gilwell scarves to be seen at meetings of Scouters. When Gilwell opened the staff wore a scarf of Maclaren tartan in compliment to the donor; this proved an expensive item of uniform, so when it was decided that all those who passed the practical course should wear the Gilwell scarf, a grey cloth was chosen and a patch of Maclaren tartan sewn on the point. In 1924 the use of the scarf was restricted to those who had gained the Wood badge. From 1922 to 1927 a special badge—a wolf's fang instead of the beads—was worn by those who had passed the Cub Course; this was called the Akela Badge, but in 1927 it was decided to have one badge, the Wood badge, for all trained Scouters.

The number of subsidiary training-camps recognized by Gilwell gradually increased both here and in other British countries as well as in foreign countries. The total number of Wood badges issued during Gilwell's first decade was as follows:

Cub	1,247
Scout	3,205
Rover	58

Many passed Part I (by correspondence) who were unable to attend Part II (in camp); this is shown by the following figures for Part I for the same period:

Cub . . .	2,160
Scout . . .	4,782
Rover . . .	221

The course for Rover Leaders and one for Sea Scouters were introduced in 1927, and in the following year the first course for Commissioners was held. The last has proved of great value in helping Commissioners to carry out their duties. An advanced Scout Course was an experiment but it did not become part of the main programme.

The Deputy Camp Chiefs were given stronger status by being appointed Assistant County (or District) Commissioners for training. All had been trained at Gilwell and were given the aid of notes on the syllabus for their private use. They were encouraged to help on courses at Gilwell from time to time. The Camp Chief visited as many of the subsidiary camps as possible and thus linked this important auxiliary work with the main camp at Gilwell and at the same time emphasized that all those concerned with the training of Scouters formed one team engaged on a common task. The appointment of Brig.-General E. G. Godfrey-Faussett as Commissioner for the Training of Officers in 1927 brought another energetic leader into the training team, and his visits to camps and to local conferences gave further impetus to this important work.

The institution of preliminary or district training in 1924 was a useful extension of the scheme. Courses of this kind could be conducted by District Commissioners or by Scouters chosen by them. A series of notes issued from Gilwell provided the material for this elementary training. In this way the busiest Scouter had some training brought to his own centre and was given a sound grounding for his work. Another important development was heralded in 1926 when Sir Arthur Evans, the distinguished archaeologist, presented some land at his home at Youlbury, near Oxford, as a training- and camping-ground for the neighbouring counties. He provided a Warden's house and a headquarters building, the foundation-stone of which was laid by the Chief Scout in February 1926.

American Independence Day 1926 was the occasion of an interesting ceremony at Gilwell. The Boy Scouts of America (U.S.A.) presented to the Boy Scouts of the United Kingdom a bronze statuette of a buffalo inscribed to

> *The Unknown Scout whose faithfulness in the performance of his Daily Good Turn to William D. Boyce in 1909 brought the Boy Scout Movement to the United States of America.*

The presentation was made by the American Ambassador in the presence of the Prince of Wales (Edward VIII) who accepted the gift on behalf of the Boy Scouts Association. Not the least pleasant part of the ceremony was the presence of Francis Gidney for the first time since his resignation. His health was already causing anxiety to his friends, and on his death two years later it was felt that his work should be permanently commemorated at Gilwell. It was decided that a log cabin would be a fitting memorial. This was constructed in the main by Don Potter who had been on the staff from the earliest days; his skill as a carver in wood resulted in many notable structures at Gilwell, such as the main gates and the totem at the boys' camp-fire circle. The Gidney Log Cabin was opened by the Chief Scout on Easter Day 1930.

The Fourth International Conference was held at Kandersteg in August 1926. In his opening speech, B.-P. said:

> Since the war there have been numbers of International Conferences of many kinds, but I think that we can justly claim that ours is unique in at least two particulars.
>
> First, we aim to teach, in a definite and practical way, brotherhood between the oncoming citizens of the different countries.
>
> Secondly, we teach not so much by precept and instruction as by personal leadership and example.
>
> People tell us that character and behaviour are entirely matters of heredity. But experience tells some of us that this is not altogether the case and that boys also largely follow the lead given them by their elders. In one country they watch with admiration the prowess of their fathers and elder brothers in the ball game, and in their turn they become ball players. In another, if they see their fathers adept in thieving or brave as soldiers, they will themselves shape their careers in similar directions. We are told 'they have it in their blood', but I think they gain the example equally through the eye. And that is why and where we make our success with Scouts. What the Scouter does his boys will do. The Scouter is reflected in his Scouts.

Let us, therefore, be careful how we go. As a first step let us be clear in our mind as to what exactly is our aim and what we are here for.

We are gathered here to consider ways and means of developing our movement on the most practical lines. It is incumbent on us, therefore, in our deliberations ourselves to extend that mutual good will and consideration towards one another which we would wish our Scouters and Scouts in their turn to practise.

The Scout in his Promise undertakes to do his duty to his King or Country only in the second place. His first duty is to God. It is with this idea before us, and reckoning that God is the one Father of us all, that we Scouts count ourselves a brotherhood, despite the differences among us of country, creed, or class. We realize that in addition to the interests of our own particular country there is a higher mission before us, namely the promotion of the Kingdom of God—that is the rule of Peace and Goodwill upon Earth. In the Scouts each form of religion is respected and its active practice encouraged, and through the spread of our brotherhood in all countries we have the opportunity of developing the spirit of mutual good will and understanding. . . . With these noble mountains around us, standing high and looking unmoved over centuries of men's petty affairs, they warn us with a new sense of proportion to aim high and to look wide.

The Conference decided to break the rule of having World Jamborees at four-year intervals each time in a fresh country; by this rule 1928 would have been the date for the next, but it was felt that there should be a special celebration of the Coming-of-age of the Movement in 1929 and that this should most appropriately be in the country of its origin, England.

After the Conference, the Camp Chief of Gilwell ran the 50th Gilwell Scout Course on the Kandersteg camp site; he was assisted by Deputy Camp Chiefs from France and Holland; of the forty Scouters on the course only two were British; the others came from fourteen different countries.

CHAPTER TWENTY

COMING-OF-AGE

THE COMING-OF-AGE JAMBOREE IS THE OUTSTANDING EVENT IN THE history of Scouting. Not even the centenary of the founder's birth in 1957, nor the Jubilee of Scouting, will have greater significance, for, in 1929, all eyes were on B.-P. himself. Strongly as he would have deprecated the suggestion, the Jamboree was his personal triumph. The Boy Scout scheme he had first planned as an aid to existing organizations had spread in its own right to most countries. To that Jamboree came representatives from the British Dominions and Colonies and from some thirty other countries; those boys and men were there to pay tribute to the Chief Scout of the World, and the peerage conferred upon him by King George V was the national recognition of a great citizen.

The census of the Scout world for that year was as follows:

United Kingdom	397,648
British Dominions and Colonies	290,977
British Scouts in other countries	1,961
British total	690,586
Scouts in other countries	1,180,730
World total	1,871,316

An interesting prelude to the Jamboree was a reunion at Pax Hill, B.-P.'s home in Hampshire, in July 1929, of twelve of those who had camped on Brownsea Island in 1907.

The question of place (always a crucial problem for a Jamboree) was settled when the Mayor and Corporation of Birkenhead offered the use of Arrowe Park—450 acres, with a Hall for conferences, excellent travelling facilities, and a port for those coming by sea. The happy chance that the place was named 'Arrowe' gave B.-P. an idea which was to mature as a symbol, 'The Golden Arrow'—a reminder of that great occasion.

The main events were as follows:

31 July. H.R.H. The Duke of Connaught opened the Jamboree.
1 August. H.R.H. The Prince of Wales arrived in camp.
B.-P. raised to the peerage.
2 August. H.R.H. The Prince of Wales took the salute at the Pageant of the Nations.
3 August. Wolf Cub Rally. Sea Scout display.
4 August. The Archbishop of Canterbury at Thanksgiving Service.
Cardinal Bourne at High Mass.
5 August. 40,000 people visited Jamboree.
7 August. Opening of three-day International Conference (the fifth).
10 August. Presentation to Chief Scout of the World.
13 August. Close of Jamboree.

Those who were at the Jamboree will always speak of the mud, as it seemed to play such a part in everything! It was no joke, and yet it was a joke; for, curiously enough, annoying and disconcerting as it could be at times, it never managed to spread depression. The good will and good humour of those 50,000 Scouts was unbeatable. As B.-P. said: 'Any ass can camp in fine weather; the rain reveals the true Scout.' And at Arrowe Park the rain certainly put all to the test!

Let a leading English journalist give his impressions—a man who has seen most of the great events of his time and put them on record. This is what Sir Philip Gibbs wrote:

It was a beautiful and unforgettable sight when this legion of boys swung by under thousands of flags. The grandstand and the whole arena were packed by dense crowds of the public, and the parade-ground was a great lawn with a background of noble trees. Far away on either side stretched the white tents, like the dream picture of a medieval tourney with pavilions of princes and knights under banners with many heraldic devices. But it was not the picture, it was the spirit of the scene that stirred one.

The hundred pipers of the young Scots played on this procession of boys, and troop after troop of Scouts, endlessly as it seemed, came at quick step past the saluting point in a marvellous pageant of young manhood from all those forty-two nations. They advanced in alphabetical order, with America leading under the Stars and Stripes,

B.-P.'s sketch to commemorate the twenty-first anniversary of the Brownsea Island camp

followed by Australia with a strong body of lads carrying their own flag and emblems. It was the Youth of the World that passed. They were of many nations, creeds, and colours.

There were South African negroes in grey shirts, Arabs from Palestine, Morocco, and Algeria in white robes, Indians in green turbans, black boys from the Gold Coast and Nigeria, natives of Jamaica, Kenya, Barbados, Ceylon, and other far countries of the British Empire. Latin America was there, with splendid contingents from Brazil and Chile. The old countries of Europe—Spain, France, Holland, Denmark, Norway, Germany—had sent their young manhoods, and new nations like Czechoslovakia, Esthonia, Latvia, and Lithuania were strongly represented.

I saw the glory and the splendour of the world's boyhood in that English park—all the world in miniature—and tried to peer into the unknown future toward which they go, so keen, so gay, so gallant, so humorous, without fear.

A grey, lean old man, with a tanned, leathery face and twinkling eyes under his Scout's hat, watched this living pageant of an idea that had come into his head. The world is moved by ideas, and this one of Baden-Powell's has in it the eternal spirit of boyhood and some touch of magic which is helping to exorcise old ghosts and demons and to draw the human family closer together in comradeship and service.

As I write, I still hear the storms of cheers which are rising up to the Chief Scout as the homage of the young knights of all nations to the veteran who knew their secret, their passwords, and the game of life. To-night, round the camp fires, they will sing their national songs and dance their old folk dances. It is a fairy-tale come true.

A French Scouter was greatly impressed by the discipline shown during these great rallies. So he recalls:

The irresistible rush at the end of the third day of the excited crowd of more than 35,000 Scouts towards the Prince of Wales's tribune. The charge, delirious with joyous enthusiasm, was stopped dead some yards from the royal box by a cordon of Rovers who had got there somehow. Not a single Scout tried to push through: discipline—but the cheering went on—Youth and Scouting. In appearance, the contingents were all higgledy-piggledy—in a picturesque and most unmilitary disarray. After the Prince's speech, and the final cheers, they broke up. I looked at my watch. In three and a half minutes, the enormous area was almost empty; in five not a soul; the 35,000 had all gone, without any signals or signposts. There was no scuffling, no blocks, no one was knocked over or crushed. This almost instantaneous dispersal was most impressive, and bore eloquent testimony to the self-discipline displayed by the Scouts of every nation.

This discipline was not the result of force; it was born of the Spirit. As I watched the march-past of the Canadians with their green and yellow jerseys, the silver-plumed Hungarians, the Sierra Leone negroes, or the Palestine contingent with their white veils encircled with the red and gold aghal, I could not help saying to myself: 'To think that they had all made the same Promise.'

Doubtless, in such a multitude, there must be differences in the value of that Promise, and the way it is kept; everyone acts according to his lights, natural or supernatural, and means of grace vary. But anyhow there was everywhere the same loyal efforts towards the best. That was the secret of the success.

Such spectacular events as pageants do not tell the real story of the Jamboree. That could be heard if we could talk to those who were there; many of them, alas, have fallen in the service of home and country; but those who survive would not talk so much of the big things which catch the public attention, but of incidents and minor happenings—a tea-party with Scouts from other countries, swapping badges, getting rations, the camp-fires, the minor mishaps of camping or of taking part in a display or show, and so on. It is the sum of all these little things which makes up the picture a boy takes away with him and chats about afterwards.

The visit of the Prince of Wales (Edward VIII) was the highlight of the Jamboree. The fact that he was in Scout uniform and camped at Arrowe Park gave added interest to his presence. At the Pageant of the Nations he took the salute, and made the announcement that his father, King George V, had raised B.-P. to the peerage. The message the Prince read out said: 'It has given me great pleasure to mark this signal event in your history by conferring a Peerage on the Chief Scout. Ever since its inception he has been the mainspring of this Great Adventure.' B.-P. took as his title the name of Gilwell; this recognition of the place it held in his estimation was warmly appreciated by all.

The Thanksgiving Service on 4 August was held in a deluge of rain; Sir Walford Davies, as conductor of the music, had his robes soaked, as did Dr. Lang, the Archbishop of Canterbury. In his sermon he said:

Twenty-one years ago a soldier dreamed a dream. . . . His dream was that the spirit of the good Scout might make the boys of his own nation healthy, happy, and helpful, and fit them for loyal service to their country and their God. To-day 'Behold this dreamer cometh', and he comes not alone, but with a comradeship of nearly two million boys belonging to forty-two countries. His dream has become one of the great realities of the world.

These words were driven home by B.-P. towards the end of the Service: 'We are assembled here, as a great family of brothers, all sons of one Father—God—to thank Him for our happy Brotherhood on its birthday and to pray also for strength to go on to greater heights and increase our brotherhood in love for one another and our neighbours.'

At luncheon in the Chief's tent, after the Services, the same thought was expressed in more intimate fashion by Cardinal Bourne, Archbishop of Westminster. 'My dear Chief,' he said, 'I cannot conceive of any other Movement that could bring me, His Grace the Archbishop of Canterbury, Dr. Bateson (who represented the Free Churches), Rabbi Rabinowitz (who represented the Chief Rabbi), and these others present here together with one common aim and one common purpose.'

Amongst the distinguished visitors was George Lansbury, at that time a member of the Cabinet. In his speech after the displays he said:

I am quite certain that in the days to come, in the days that he has yet to live and in the days that will come after, the name that will stand and be remembered in the world of the nations will be Baden-Powell. Nothing in the world can add, I think, to the wonderful work that has been done. He won't mind me saying, and his friends will not mind me saying, that the one thing that people like me hope and pray for, if we ever pray at all—the one thing we really hope for is that all these great movements of the world amongst young people, and especially this great movement, may in the future remove all man-made evil of the world, not the evil that we cannot help, but man-made evil, and will also establish the sort of relationship which pervades this place amongst people of all nations meeting together to enjoy themselves and to learn from one another how to live.

On 10 August came the presentation from the Scouts of the World to the Chief Scout of the World.

On behalf of all, the presentation was made by Mr. Christien Holm, President of the Danish Scouts. He said to B.-P.:

I wish to thank you heartily for all the pleasure, happiness, and service you have given to the young through this vast Movement.

We thank you because you have succeeded in joining together the youth of the world and as a result the nations will be able to get to know each other. You have opened up the possibility of understanding and friendship between the people of all nations. Chief Scout, we ask you to receive our gift as an expression of admiration and affection of the Scouts of the World.

The Chief Scout, in returning thanks, said:

My brother Scouts, this is a wonderful day for you, as it is for me. I feel that much too much has been bestowed upon me, when you think that the work of raising a big family such as you are, is the work of a very large number of good men all working together in different countries. It has been a wonderful week, and it has been a wonderful day for all of us, and I hope it means that, like the original little camp at Brownsea Island twenty years ago, this camp is the beginning of a far greater extension of our family throughout the world, to be the bond of boys in all nations. God has been good to us in the past in bringing us up to this stage, and I pray He will go on and make us real agents of His throughout the world.

Scouts, I don't know how to thank you for what you have done for me. I feel undeserving of the many presents and honours showered upon me during the past few days, and now you have capped it all with this wonderfully fine present, representing the gift of boys from every nation in every part of the world, and I accept it with a feeling of something in the way of gratitude more than I can really express. It has come to me as a very great surprise, because it was kept a secret from me until just lately. Those who were organizing the present approached my wife and tried to find out from her what I wanted most in the world. When she asked me what I wanted, I said 'Nothing. I am the richest man in the world', for I believe that the richest man is not the man who has the most money, but the man who has fewest wants. My wife pressed me further, and said I must want something. I thought again, and then remembered and said, 'Oh, yes, I want a pair of braces.' After that she reminded me that our motor car was getting into its old age—it's broken down twice in this camp and had to be towed home!—and I thought I really would like a car, but I never expected a splendid car like this, and I am most deeply grateful for giving me such a splendid toy. It will be more than a toy, for it will enable me to do more visiting of Scouts than I have in the past, and I am mighty grateful for it.

But, brother Scouts, let me say once more, I don't deserve your thanks. Give them rather to your Scoutmasters—those men who have devoted their lives, given up all sorts of pleasure and given all their time and energy to try to make you have a better time as Scouts, so that you will be better men in the future than you otherwise would have been. Thank those men rather than me, who merely made the suggestion. Above all, if you have had a good time as Scouts, if you have enjoyed your Scouting and enjoyed the comradeship you have made with other fellows, then you have someone higher to thank, and that is your God.

Whatever memories one has of those days, surely most unforgettable is that final scene when the Golden Arrows were passed to the nations as symbols of the peaceful tasks of Scouting.

This time the Scouts did not group together by nations, but mixed up and formed lines like the spokes of a gigantic wheel. B.-P. stood alone there at the hub of the wheel.

'Here is the hatchet of war, of enmity, of bad feeling, which I now bury in Arrowe', said the Chief Scout, at the same time burying a hatchet in a cask of gilded wooden arrows. 'From all corners of the world you come to the call of brotherhood and to Arrowe. Now I send you forth to your homeland, bearing the sign of peace and good will, and fellowship to all your fellow men. From now on the symbol of peace and good will is a golden arrow. Carry that arrow on and on, so that all may know of the brotherhood of men.'

Through a lane in the ranks the Chief Scout returned to the Royal Pavilion, where he addressed the boys again, saying:

I want to thank you all for coming here from the ends of the world to our happy Jamboree. It seems like only yesterday that we met in the mud and to-day we are going away, but in sunshine. There is sunshine in our hearts as well as in the air. I am glad to have seen you all. I have much to thank you for.

I want you to go back from here to your countries in different parts of the world with a new idea in your mind of having brothers in every country. You have seen them and you know them now, personally. I hope you have enjoyed your time here, you who come from other lands, and I hope that you have found England not so bad a place as you might have thought it. I want you all to take back to your countries a good account of Great Britain and all the boys you have met here, and the people who have tried to be good to you. Of course, any ass can see the bad points in people or a country, but a good Scout will look out for the good points in other people. I want you to remember the good points in us and forget the bad ones.

Tell your friends in your own countries all the good you can about

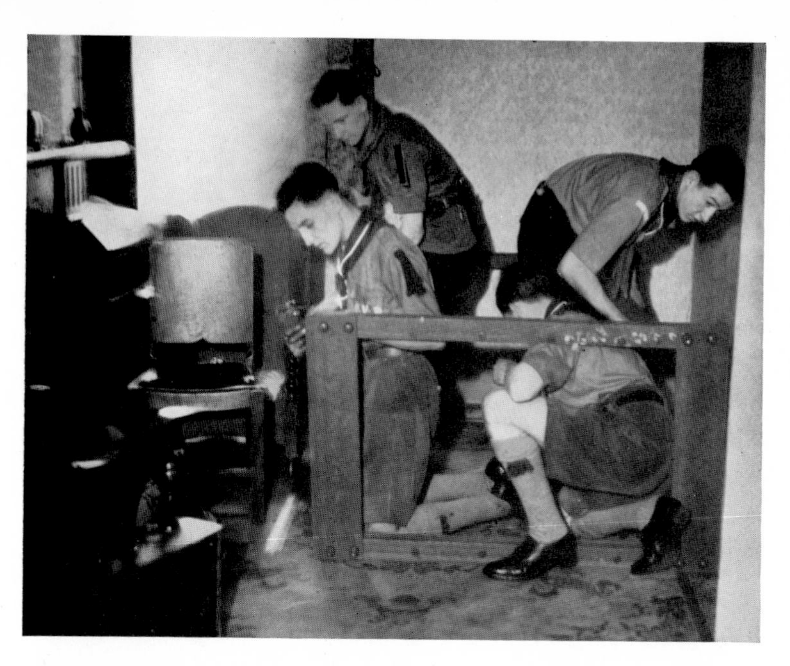

WAR SERVICE, 1939–45. PUTTING UP AN INDOOR SHELTER

EAST MEETS WEST AT THE 1947 JAMBOREE

WOLF CUBS

BOY SCOUTS TESTING THE BRIDGE THEY MADE

us, so that we can all think better of one another. Go forth from here as ambassadors of good will and friendship. Each one of you Scouts, no matter how young or small, can spread a good word about this country and those you have met here. I can only say now, 'Good-bye to you. Farewell.' I hope you will come again to our next Jamboree, as many of you as can, and make a success of it as you have made a success of this one. Try to carry on your Scout work in the meantime. Try to make yourselves better Scouts than ever, try to help other boys, especially the poorer boys, to come and be happy, healthy, and helpful citizens like yourselves. And now, farewell—good-bye—and God bless you all.

The Fifth International Conference was held during the Jamboree.

No very positive matters of policy or principle were discussed or resolved, but it was decided to hold the next conference in Austria and, more important still, to hold the First World Rover Moot at Kandersteg immediately after the conference in 1931.

The Fifth Conference had a unique distinction, one of the Bureau staff being challenged to a duel! The challenger was hastily removed from Arrowe Park by the leader of his delegation.

The concluding sentences of B.-P.'s final speech were both a congratulation and a challenge:

It seems to me little less than a miracle that we have arrived at this position of having almost every country running Scouts—to the number of two million—and it is entirely due to the men who have seen there are underlying the Movement possibilities for which they have brought their hearts and put their backs into it, and worked to bring it along to the happy stage we have now reached. And if we have arrived at this standing now after twenty-one years, look forward and visualize what we may do in the next twenty-one years if we start off now working to a great end, and with a great ideal when the nations are thirsting for peace.

⚜ ⚜ ⚜ ⚜ ⚜ ⚜ ⚜ ⚜ ⚜ ⚜ ⚜ ⚜ ⚜ ⚜ ⚜ ⚜ ⚜

CHAPTER TWENTY-ONE

DEVELOPMENT

IMMEDIATELY AFTER THE 1929 JAMBOREE, B.-P. WROTE:

> The standing which Scouting has attained through the Jamboree gives us a unique opportunity for making a bold advance, but this should be on well-considered lines and should be set in train without delay before the inspiration of the Jamboree has died down.

With this in mind he appointed a small Development Committee to discuss

> the inauguration of a definite scheme for extending the Movement, so that instead of merely touching the fringe of the boyhood of the country as at present, we should make a steady push forward to influence a considerable proportion of the rising generation.

Suggestions were collected from the counties and with these before them the members of the Committee set to work to such effect that their report was ready by March 1930. The main outcome was the setting up of a Development Department at Headquarters under a separate Commissioner. Sir Alfred Pickford was persuaded to undertake this work, and to help him as Adviser he had Colonel Charles Watson. This Department did much valuable work between the wars and undoubtedly helped to extend the range of Scouting and to co-ordinate many activities that had so far been carried on almost independently.

The Department was responsible for the general direction of publicity, publications, relations with religious, educational, and other bodies, and for the arrangement of speakers at public meetings. The latter were supplied with notes for their guidance. A religious panel was formed to advise on problems connected with the Churches.

The Committee had given much attention to the question of camping. From time to time reports had been received of bad camping; this was doing harm to the reputation of Scouting. In the early days few could criticize camping, for it was a rare activity; but by 1930 there were not only thousands of Old Scouts and Guides to note inefficiencies, but camping had become a popular sport. The difficulty was to devise a method of supervision that would not be irksome. For many years it had been a rule that Scouters taking boys to camp in districts other than their own should notify the local Scout authority. This was more a matter of courtesy than of regulation. The Committee felt that two improvements were possible without causing too much interference with the liberty of the Scoutmaster. The first was that the District Commissioner of the visited area should have authority to inspect, and report upon, the camps of visiting Scouts. The second was based on a scheme that had proved effective in Canada. A booklet had there been published entitled *Minimum Standards for Scout Camps*, and this had stimulated Scoutmasters to improve their camping. In this country a similar booklet *Camping Standards* (published in 1931) was prepared at Gilwell Park. Troops undertaking to work to the suggested standards were given a certificate to display in camp recording their intention to follow the lines laid down; a space was provided for the comments of the visiting District Commissioner. This voluntary scheme soon became popular and Troops kept their certificates as interesting mementoes of their camps. Parallel with this was the improvement in camping that resulted from the spread of Wood-badge training. Inferior camping will never be entirely banished, but it can be safely said that the standard reached in the majority of scout camps is a high one considering that the boys are bursting with energy and some are still in the Tenderfoot stage.

Camping Standards was only one of the many publications for which Gilwell Park was to be responsible during this inter-war period. Francis Gidney had opened this branch of the training work with a book entitled *Spare Time Activities*. The Spare Time Activity early became part of the Gilwell legend; each Scouter on a practical course was set a number of things to do in what was termed his 'spare time'; he might be told to make a splice, or a sketch, or to bake an edible twist over an open fire. As a crowded time-table left little margin it was felt that the talk about 'spare time' was rather forced! In his book Gidney gave short accounts of a number of such small tasks that might appeal to a boy and set him on the road to more constructive achievements. The book quickly proved popular. The title-page bore the pseudonym 'Gilcraft'; this had already appeared in *The Scout* and *The Headquarters Gazette*. Gidney adopted this pen-name as a convenient label for those who wrote under the sponsorship of Gilwell; he wanted to avoid, as B.-P. also did, the production of official handbooks giving the Scouter a ready-made programme; books by Gilcraft were intended as sources of ideas and as syllabuses. At the same time the name 'Gilcraft' implied an assurance that the books could be accepted as in keeping with training policy. At first no planned series was contemplated, but after the 1929 Jamboree it was decided to proceed in a more orderly manner. In all some twenty volumes were published in the Gilcraft Series by 1939. The subjects dealt with included pioneering, tracking, exploring, knotting, games, and first aid; others dealt with the principles and methods of the several sections. A number of writers were concerned, but most of the books were written by the Camp Chief or by members of his staff. In addition to this output of general books, there were half a dozen volumes of training notes for the private use of Deputy Camp Chiefs or Akela Leaders as well as some for those conducting District Training Courses. All these sets of notes were revised periodically.

It is impossible to estimate the influence exerted by these Gilwell-sponsored books; they reached thousands of Scouters who could not get to training camps; new-comers found the benefit of having reliable guidance, and more experienced Scouters received fresh ideas as well as encouragement. Thus by the gradually spreading influence of the training courses and by these auxiliary means, B.-P.'s interpretation of Scouting became more firmly established.

One pleasant event in 1930 should be recorded. A knighthood was conferred on P. W. Everett in recognition of his services in the Scout Movement. No one welcomed this more than B.-P. who felt that this honour would bring encouragement to the rank and file more than the many honours he himself received. Sir Percy Everett well deserved this honour, but his knighthood was the only one conferred for Scouting during the first forty years of the Movement's history.

Ernest Young felt obliged to give up the editorship of *The Scouter* in 1928 owing to his many other obligations. He was succeeded by G. Dymoke Green, son of the Secretary, as full-time editor. It was a serious loss to Scouting when he died in 1930, for he had already shown considerable enterprise as editor as well as in other fields. A gateway of Scandinavian design was erected to his memory at Gilwell. For some months D. Francis Morgan acted as editor until Dr. F. W. W. Griffin was able to join the staff.

A new stage was reached in 1930 in the evolution of the Rover section. Some changes had been made in the scheme in 1929; experience had shown that Rovers were not interested in the gaining of badges, so the First Class Rover badge was dropped out of the scheme. But this negative action left the position as to the training of these young fellows rather vague. One school of thought wanted the emphasis to be put on Service as a condition even of admission. The supporters of this view were mainly those who urged that all Scouters should be Rovers, and that the aim should be to attract men of all ages. Reference has previously been made to this attitude. Others put the emphasis on the need for some kind of training that would result in service to the community but would not overlook other claims on a young man's time. Those who thought along these lines were concentrating on the 17 to 21 age-group and were thinking of Rovering as a continuation of Scout training, not as its consummation. This split in the Rover section did much harm. The situation was vitiated by the fact that older men liked to regard themselves as Rovers without appreciating the fact that their presence in the same Crew as younger men created an insoluble problem for training. It became necessary to resolve this conflict of views. After much inquiry and discussion the Committee of the Council issued new Rules in 1930. These were explained at a Conference at Birmingham in April of that year. The emphasis was put on the training of the young fellow for Service including 'the first service or duty he owes—to establish himself in life—and make every endeavour to consolidate his position so that he is not a burden on others'.

A somewhat heated discussion took place at the Conference. One speaker maintained that with this new policy 'we shall not see many years before Rovering goes', while another called it the 'salvation of Rovering'. B.-P. summed up his own views in the following note:

My own feeling is that the Rover stage is the third progressive step in the education of the Boy Scout, and its importance is that it completes his education and also holds him under good influences and in good companionship at the critical period of his life.

But you can't hold a lad without giving him some definite objectives and activities. So we offer Service. For this his previous Scout life, both as Cub and Scout, has been a progressive preparation.

Under 'Service' I should include three progressive steps:

1. *Service to Self*, viz.
   (*a*) To get himself established in a career so that he is not a burden to his relations.
   (*b*) To develop his health by outdoor activities, hiking, &c.
   (*c*) To work energetically at his employment as his contribution to the national welfare.
2. *Service to the Scout Movement*. In this direction (until they become too numerous) Rovers can give a lot of help in various degrees according to their respective capabilities; but should be the main source of our supply of Scouters.
3. *Service to the Community*. This gives point to the Rover's study of 'Civics' and is the final step in making him a good citizen.

The rendering of 'Service' of any kind is, of course, the Scout's method of expressing his promise of Duty to God.

I am against making the Rover branch in any way a form of religious movement, otherwise it will be shunned by the wilder spirits, and those are the lads we want to hold straight.

If men from outside, i.e. non-Scouts, want to come in as Rover Scouts attracted by the good companionship and worth while aims and Service—so much the better.

To a conference of Rover Leaders he sent the following six points for their guidance:

1. That Rovers are *Scouts* and the Scout spirit and the out-of-door atmosphere are essential.
2. That Service is not extraneous to the Rovers' daily life and work. Carrying on their professions well is part of their service for the community.
3. That Rovering is partly preparation for life and also a pursuit for life.

4. That stickability is a branch of character that is most rare and most valuable and therefore most needed in the youth of to-day. It can be developed through Rovering.
5. That in formulating any rules or schemes for Rovering, for goodness sake let them be elastic. Look wide, since if broad-mindedly set out, they will apply not merely to London or Puddlington-in-the-Marsh, but to our far-reaching Dominions overseas and to foreign countries who all look to us for direction and example.
6. That Rovering is not intended to make a man a self-satisfied prig or a melancholy saint, but to help him to direct his joyous youthful energy into paths which will bring him greater happiness through living a life that is worth while in its service to others.

Unhappily neither the new Rules, nor B.-P.'s clear statement of opinion, resolved the conflict. The argument went on. The peak year of Rover membership was 1933 when the total in the United Kingdom was 38,043. From then onwards it slowly declined. A solution might have been the development of a vigorous Old Scout organization to absorb the over-25s; but this scheme never came to life; its importance was urged by both the Development Committee and the Conference of 1930, but the results were discouraging.

It must not be thought that these differences of purpose within the section paralysed the Rover scheme. Much good work was being done in quiet ways by Rovers who were not worried about such discussions. In spite of the noise made by some of the leaders, young fellows were being trained on B.-P.'s lines; they helped the Scouts and the Cubs where they could; they ran camps; they did much of the organizing of displays and other combined events in Local Associations; they went on adventurous hikes at home and abroad. How sound was their spirit was demonstrated at the Moot held at Auchengillan near Glasgow in August 1930. Over 1,400 Rovers camped together there, and the arguments at Birmingham seemed irrelevant. No doubt the fact that the Chief Scout was present helped to modify the differences.

In the following year the first International Rover Moot was held at the Scout ground at Kandersteg. This was attended by 2,500 Rover Scouts from twenty-two countries in addition to fifteen parts of the British Commonwealth and Empire. The Chief Scout was deeply moved by this event; this is shown by a passage he wrote at the time:

> Rover Scouts they are: a brigade, as it were of storm-troops of the larger army of over two million Boy Scouts. Their arms are alpen-stocks, their discipline that of good will from within; their service consists not so much in fitting themselves for war as in developing the spirit of universal peace. . . . To myself, possibly, the most inspiring part of their varied programme was when one saw the endless succession of these splendid specimens of the young manhood of all nations setting out in comradeship together with heavy packs on their backs and ice-axe in hand to tackle the neighbouring mountains.

This Moot had been preceded by the Sixth International Conference at Baden-bei-Wien, Austria. The delegates of twenty-seven nations attended. Nothing of special note marked this gathering, but it once again demonstrated the solidarity of the Movement in the five continents.

During these years of economic depression, the problem of unemployment, especially that of young men and of boys just leaving school, was constantly in the minds of all concerned with the training of the rising generation. Could Scouting do anything to help such young fellows in their periods of enforced idleness, or prepare Scouts more effectively to meet the future? Such questions presented themselves to B.-P. who was always alive to the needs of the day. He collected all the information he could and discussed the problems with those in contact with the areas most affected. Then he circulated the following suggestions:

> 1. The first effort of every Scoutmaster must obviously be to keep his 14–16 year old boys in his Troop and not allow them to drift away to join the unemployed crowd. This in very many cases will mean the introduction of greater variety in the Troop programme; and for preparing lads for occupation or employment it involves increased incentive and opportunity for taking up hobbies and handicrafts. We have to realize that an increasing number will be out of work but they should have at least hobbies to occupy their enforced leisure. They should be taught to rely on themselves and not expect amusement to be provided for them. This may involve more frequent Troop nights and the provision of tools and possibly workshops or

allotments. More Troop nights will be possible if Rover Scouts come in to help the Scoutmaster by taking charge of the Troop on different evenings, and by showing an example of keen and interesting Scouting. Senior Scouts should be encouraged themselves to organize games, sports, hiking, camping, &c. As regards the provision of tools and workshops, materials, &c., here lies a definite job for members of Local Associations. The sites and materials might be provided by them and the work of building by the Rovers and Scouts themselves.

2. The next point for Scoutmasters and possibly Local Associations is to get hold of the unemployed boys in the neighbourhood, probably through co-operation with the local school authorities and Employment Exchanges, &c., and to bring them in as Honorary members of the Troop to participate in the Troop activities and comradeship.

If every Troop took on only five 'younger brothers' this would mean 55,000 unemployed boys coming at once under good influence instead of drifting towards uselessness or crime.

3. In view of the coming increase of unemployed boys which has to be faced we already need a big increase in the number of Troops to receive and take them in hand. The first step in this direction must necessarily be a campaign to secure more Scoutmasters and instructors in hobbies and games. There are thousands of young men in the country to whom it has never occurred that they can, and ought to, do something in the way of social service. An intensive campaign to secure them could best be devised by Local Associations both through press appeals and personal solicitation. The fish are there in the river right enough, but whether you are to catch them depends on whether you offer the right kind of fly in the right kind of way.

4. Training must be made available for new Scoutmasters. Commissioners are in a position to see to this; Local Associations can second their efforts, especially in regards to meeting places, books, transport and expenses.

5. For the provision of gymnastic apparatus, workshops, allotments, tools, and materials, &c., funds are of course essential. But funds only come when you have got something to show as a reason for them. Local Associations have a corporate responsibility in this matter. Show people what you are doing and what you have done and give them an idea of what you might yet do, and purse-strings will be loosened. Begging letters are of very little use compared with personal visits to explain. Here again is work for individual members of the Local Association. Ladies' Committees or public banquets in large cities, if adequately organized, can give valuable help in this direction.

This appeal encouraged Scouters to do all they could both within their own Groups and also in co-operation with other organizations, to ease the situation. One scheme calls for special mention. Miss M. Majendie opened a centre at Hedingham Castle in 1930 for training unemployed Rovers and others for various domestic occupations. Under her enthusiastic guidance the scheme quickly proved its worth and gained the approval and support of the Government. Other centres were opened at Quendon, Ossemsley, Cirencester, Badminton, and Llanfrechfa Grange. By this means hundreds of young men were found jobs, and, of great importance, were saved from that feeling of not being wanted that beset so many in those difficult times. A further aid was the running of camps by one of the Gilwell staff for Scouts in areas so poverty stricken that they could not have their usual summer camps.

A Travelling Commissioner was appointed in 1931. It has been noted that in the early days there had been Travelling Inspectors or Organizing Secretaries to tour the country and help in establishing local Committees and Troops. The new scheme was on rather different lines. The Travelling Commissioner settled in a county for several weeks or for a month or two; during his stay he could gain a thorough knowledge of the conditions of Scouting and be available for consultation. In this way it was possible to get a fairly complete picture of how the Groups were functioning and of how the County and Local Associations were working. The first Travelling Commissioner was A. M. Chamberlain, who was later an Assistant Camp Chief at Gilwell.

Another development was the Deep-Sea Scout scheme; this had started in 1928. Deep-Sea Scouts are defined as 'members of the Royal Navy, the Merchant Navy, the Fishing Fleets, crews of ocean-going yachts or of Sea Training Establishments'. There were two purposes: one was to bring together those on a ship who had been Scouts (not only Sea Scouts), and the other was to provide these former Scouts with a means of getting into touch with Scouts in the ports they visited. A small journal *Scouts in Ships* was circulated to give them up-to-date addresses of liaison Scouters.

Great efforts were made to increase the number and efficiency of Sea Scouts. The successive Chief Sea Scout Commissioners

Vice-Admirals E. K. Loring and A. V. Campbell were assisted by the Rev. Leonard Spiller and R. H. Hole. The difficulties in the way of establishing and maintaining Sea Scout Troops have always impeded the growth of this section. It is essential that the Scoutmaster should be an experienced seaman, and many do not care to accept the considerable responsibility involved in this work. The cost of boats and of keeping them in condition is a serious deterrent.

Training courses of varying lengths were held for Scouters in charge of Sea Scout Troops or attracted by this kind of Scouting. Some courses were held on the *Foudroyant* and *Implacable*; others were held in Cheshire and Northumberland and at other centres. R. H. Hole was in charge of this work and he also paid visits to many parts of the country to stir up interest in Sea Scouting. In spite of all these efforts the total number of Sea Scouts in the United Kingdom has tended over a period of years to fluctuate between 4,500 and 6,000.

1934 saw the first St. George's Day Scout Service at St. George's Chapel, Windsor. A thousand King's Scouts and First Class Scouts representing all counties attended and after the service marched past King George V and Queen Mary.

⚜ ⚜ ⚜ ⚜ ⚜ ⚜ ⚜ ⚜ ⚜ ⚜ ⚜ ⚜ ⚜ ⚜ ⚜ ⚜ ⚜

CHAPTER TWENTY-TWO

SCOUTING OVERSEAS

DURING THE DECADE AFTER THE COMING-OF-AGE JAMBOREE, THE Chief Scout and Chief Guide made four major tours of the Dominions and Colonies in addition to shorter journeys. In the course of their passages they were able to pay brief visits to many outlying places, and at every port they touched there was a rally or meeting in their honour. Such passing calls did not give time for thorough inquiries into the state of local Scouting and Guiding, but both were experienced and shrewd observers and were able to get a useful idea of the position. The value of even the briefest of visits was that it brought renewed inspiration and encouragement to all; the feeling of being part of a great brotherhood was strengthened.

The longer and more thorough visits to the Dominions and Colonies gave the Chiefs a knowledge of problems and achievements that was invaluable both to the local organization and to Headquarters at home. It was B.-P.'s custom to record his impressions; these appeared in the pages of *The Scouter* and sometimes in book form. Such criticisms as he desired to make were passed on to the people concerned, and his advice and suggestions always proved of importance and of benefit.

A glance at the census figures shows that apart from a recession in 1937 (except in Canada) the Movement steadily widened its appeal. In the following list the totals of all ranks for every

	1930	*1932*	*1934*	*1936*	*1938*
Canada	50,224	58,868	64,771	81,138	86,290
Australia	37,274	55,201	55,788	50,546	51,571
New Zealand	11,103	12,900	13,512	12,664	14,858
South Africa	15,773	16,578	16,990	15,701	32,511*
Colonies, &c.	200,966	229,011	291,479	403,689	361,270
U.K.	438,096	477,423	459,980	448,396	460,234

* Includes 15,359 Pathfinder Scouts.

other year are given; the United Kingdom figures are added in order to complete the British total. If to these are added an annual average of 2,500 Scouts in British Troops in foreign countries, it will be seen that the million mark was passed in 1936.

If there were space in these pages to record the development of Scouting in each part of the Commonwealth and Empire it would be found to follow the same pattern as in Great Britain. This has not been due, as has already been noted, to any control being exerted from London; it is a tribute to the fact that Scouting suits boy-nature so happily that its progress anywhere is bound to follow much the same lines. Where local conditions have called for variations or modifications these have been made without destroying the mould. The picture of Scouting in Vancouver or Auckland is similar to that in Nottingham or Aberdeen. Some particular characteristics should, however, be noted.

Scouting has developed steadily in Canada since the visit of B.-P. with the Wolves and Beavers in 1910. A quarter of a century later he paid his last visit to the Dominion, and was delighted with the initiative shown in reaching out to remote townships and scattered farms; he was impressed with the share Scouting was taking in blending the many racial strains in the country; a Group might contain boys of half a dozen or more different national origins. It was for this reason that he welcomed the news of the linking up of the French-speaking Catholic Scouts of Quebec with the main Association. He noted one example of Scouting in unusual conditions. He wrote of one Prairie Scouter:

> He has come 275 miles with a party of Scouts and Guides from his parish to attend our Rally. The parish covers 8,000 square miles. The Scouts number 84, and the Girl Guides 98, but they are scattered over wide distances, and so work entirely as Lone Patrols, which he and his wife, as Guider, visit periodically in his 'rectory' (a Ford car).
>
> Once a year the whole Troop gather to a central spot to camp, and once a year both Scouts and Guides gather together with the members of the Local Association to a banquet. The Guides bring the salads and the Scouts bring the poultry. The youngsters sit down to their feed, waited upon by the Committee, and then the functions

are reversed. After the banquet each Patrol gives some sort of entertainment which it has previously prepared. Thus the whole district is brought together, which had never been the case before.

Most of the Scouts are 1st Class and there are several King's Scouts among them and all wear Scout uniform paid for by proceeds of plays performed by two Patrols. Yet many of them had never been in a town, or even on a railway, and none had ever seen a play!

The Scoutmaster and his party were delayed on this occasion in getting to our Rally because the ferry over a big river was not yet working owing to the floating ice, so they had to do an extra 120 miles to come round another way; and in addition they found difficulties with the snow.

The Scouter always carries food and blankets in his car because very frequently he gets held up by snow-drifts and blizzards. He has been at it ten years and loves the life!

Exchange visits between Canadian and United States Scouts on either side of the unguarded frontier are a regular occurrence; Troops of the same Troop number have established associations of this kind; thus Troop No. 3 of Detroit, Michigan, exchanges camp and other visits with Troop No. 3 of Chatham, Ontario. For a number of years there have been such visits between 100 representatives of six different Troops of Ontario and Troop 16 of Buffalo, N.Y. The visit of King George VI and Queen Elizabeth in 1939 greatly stimulated this close association.

Part of a report on 1934 gives a glimpse of varied activities:

Canada has now completed her first quarter of a century of the Movement. . . . The District Training Courses of the Home Country have been adopted with success. Six out of ten of this year's Canadian Rhodes Scholars to Oxford were, or had been, Scouts. The Christmas Toy Repair Shops for 1933, the tenth annual effort of this kind, established new records. A conservative estimate placed the number of children 'remembered' at over 80,000, including more than 9,000 located on prairie homesteads. In the Province of Quebec, Scouts collected over 1,000 fresh eggs at Easter for hospitals, needy families, &c. In various centres 'Scout Relief Barrels', marked 'Buy two: throw one in here', were placed in hundreds of grocery stores. At Hamilton, a Scout Circus ('Admission one can of soup') was very successful. In Vancouver, a number of Scouts paid for two weeks in camp, went for one week themselves, then came home, and sent some of their less fortunate boy friends to camp for the second week.

This toy repair scheme has become a traditional Christmas

Good Turn for Canadian Scouts; they collect broken toys, and repair them for distribution to children who would otherwise not get toys; other communal Good Turns include reafforestation and helping with the conservation of wild life.

Canadian Scouting owes much to the devoted service of John Stiles, who, for many years, was the Chief Executive Commissioner.

Australian Scouting has always been vigorous; it is, of course, organized by States but with close associations between them. One of their problems has been to help boys in the distant homesteads who cannot come together to form Troops. Lone Scouting, as it is called, has proved a second-best alternative to the full Scout life; other countries, notably South Africa and the United States, have also developed this way of helping boys in isolated places. These boys are linked by correspondence which is organized by a Scouter put in charge of a section of the country. On rare occasions he may be able to visit his Scouts in their homes, and, when practicable, he arranges camps to collect together the boys from a large area; to get to these centres may mean journeys of several hundred miles.

The Australian Scouts organized a Jamboree in December 1934 at Frankston, near Melbourne. This may be called a regional rather than an international Jamboree as its purpose was to bring together Scouts of the Southern Hemisphere; there were, however, representatives from Great Britain and the U.S.A. Some 10,000 Scouts were in camp to greet the Chief Scout and Chief Guide when they arrived for the opening rally. B.-P. was impressed with the friendliness shown to the visiting Scouts from India, China, and Japan, and from other eastern lands. He knew how strong was the 'white' feeling in Australia and that the Scout authorities had shown some courage in issuing their invitations. He commented:

Among their white brother Scouts, the coloured visitors were received with the same cheery hospitality which the Australian Scouts extended to all; while by the public they were given the fullest measure of applause when parading or performing in the arena. I am bound to say that on their part they largely reciprocated and earned this good will through their own cheery courtesy, their smartness and discipline. Their efficiency in woodcraft was put to an exacting test when the camp was assaulted one night by a tornado of wind and rain, but early morning inspection of the camp showed that without exception they had learned their business, for although the contractors' marquees were flat on the ground, not a Scout tent was down, and in spite of the soaking rain, breakfasts were cooking on glowing fires in all the camps.

Apart from its varied and interesting displays and impressive discipline, an outstanding feature of the Jamboree was the mixing of these boys of so many races in real mutual friendship for one another. This gave one visions and hope of what may be possible as they grow to manhood and increase in numbers.

These problems of race and colour present themselves throughout the Scout world in varying forms. Scout policy has been to encourage the friendliest relations amongst all, and in camps and at Jamborees not the slightest distinction is made between one and another. The difficulties are not within the Movement but in public feeling that may create awkward situations. In this matter B.-P.'s own long and varied experience was of the greatest value. He applied the principle of 'Softlee, softlee, catchee monkey'; he knew that any spectacular action by the Scout Movement would result in far more harm to Scouting than in good to the native Scouts. He did not, therefore, advise the local organizations to shock the public by trying to force mixed membership. The parallel organization, working towards the same objective and by similar methods, was, he felt, the next step. The Scouts meet at camps and Jamborees, and so, in its quiet way, the Movement helps to bring all to a better understanding of each other.

South Africa presents a particularly difficult problem. Four separate sections were formed there: the Boy Scouts Association of the Union for white boys, the Pathfinders for the natives, the Coloured Boy Scouts for the half-castes, and the Indian Boy Scouts. For a period these had no connexion with one another. South Africa held a high place in B.-P.'s affections (second only to England) and he dreamed of Scouting doing something towards welding the races into one community, but he was a realist and knew that progress must be cautious. It was, therefore, a special pleasure to him to be present during a tour in 1936 at a meeting of the South Africa Scout Council at Durban when it was decided to form a Federation of these sections under the Boy Scouts Association of the Union. The Twenty-eighth

Annual Report of the United Kingdom made this comment, 'it may be said that our policy of making the Movement open to all, regardless of class, creed or colour, is still not put into full practice. One has to admit that this is so, but a real advance towards the ideal has been made and with that one must at present remain content.'

A less pleasing feature of Scouting in South Africa was the formation in 1930 of the Voortrekker Movement for Afrikaans-speaking boys; many such boys were already in the Boy Scouts Association, and this separatist organization naturally caused difficulties, but it may well have hastened the tendency towards federation that has been noted above.

In 1937 South Africa applied to the International Bureau for separate recognition. Hitherto the Dominions had been covered by the registration of the United Kingdom. The International Conference approved the application and South Africa was separately registered. India followed this example in 1938, and Canada in 1946.

During a visit to New Zealand in 1931 the Chief Scout was impressed by the reports he received of the behaviour of the Scouts in the recent earthquake. He wrote: 'They kept their heads in that appalling catastrophe, and set to work individually on their own initiative everywhere to render first-aid, extricate the injured, rig shelters, cook food, take charge of children and property, and to make themselves useful in every kind of way.' Those who have met New Zealand Scouts at Jamborees will not be surprised to read this report, for they always give an impression of high-spirited keenness and efficiency. Scouting began in that Dominion at the end of 1908 when three Patrols were formed in Wellington. One of these pioneers notes that these Patrols 'proceeded independently with the aid of *Scouting for Boys*. Hats at first were unavailable, so with the aid of sugar and water we flattened out the brims of our fathers' wide felt hats.'

The conditions of Scouting are shown by this note from a Scoutmaster.

Many of the Scouts were farmers' sons and lived some distance away. Most of them rode to the meetings on sturdy ponies. Two boys lived twelve miles away but that did not prevent them attending meetings. We had several Maoris in the Troop, two of them stayed long enough in the Troop to gain their First Class and King's Scout

Badges, and were fine samples of their race. We had a mounted Patrol at one time.

Scouting in India developed steadily after the Chief Scout's visit in 1921. The institution of Wood-badge training has already been noted, and a further advance in standards was encouraged by the visit of the Camp Chief in 1933. Scouting is by no means confined to the main centres of population. In 1932 H. W. Hogg, Deputy Camp Chief, found Scouts in outlying parts of the Punjab when he made an extensive tour. A report states:

In some of the remote villages 13,000 to 14,000 feet high, where there is nothing but barren rock, and where the villages are shut off from the outside world nine months in the year with snow, Mr. Hogg found some of the keenest Scouts. In Lot, for example, which is seven days' walk from any civilized town, he discovered a Pack which he says was the equal of anything he has seen anywhere in the country. The six weeks tour covered over 500 miles extending right across the Himalayan mountains over the Babu, Rotang and Baralatcha passes. The last pass, 16,500 feet, led into a country over which the road passes at 17,000 to 18,000 feet, and for some days neither habitation nor human beings were to be seen, and at the end of that journey Mr. Hogg came across a Troop planted in a village which had no contact with the outside world.

Community Good Turns have always been a characteristic of Scouting in India. The Village Uplift movement of F. L. Brayne found support in the Scout Associations. An extract from the Twenty-eighth Annual Report of the United Kingdom gives an account of some of the communal work done.

During the earlier part of the year (1935) a very severe epidemic of cholera broke out in the city of Kolhapur, and as it showed no signs of abating the Kolhapur City Municipality asked the Scouts Association to give their services in tackling the problem. . . . The Scouters were authorised to inspect all hotels, distribute pamphlets and medicines, and to tell the people what steps they should take to make themselves immune from the cholera. The Scouts induced the citizens to be inoculated and told them how important it was that they should only drink water that had been boiled. Potassium permanganate packets and chlorogin were freely distributed among the people. The Scouts, under their Scoutmasters, worked for several days and nights together in carrying out the job they had been asked to do. Another Good Turn was in connection with the Mela last June when hundreds of thousands of pilgrims were drawn to Kurukshetra. The Punjab party of Scouters and Scouts numbered nearly 3,000, and their advance party of 100 had to clear away shrubs, thorny bushes and a large number of deadly snakes before producing a satisfactory camping ground. On the arrival of the main body the following services were organised: Information Bureau, Life Saving Brigade, Mobile Health Brigade, Messengers, Sanitation, Water Supply, Fire Brigade, Traffic control, Railway Station, Lorry Park, &c. A feature of this year's camp was that all Scouts were grouped in divisions and not in communities as in the past. Therefore, all question of communal rivalry was eliminated and the Scouts lived, worked, fed, and slept together irrespective of caste or creed. Some indication of the work that was done is shown by the facts that over 7,000 women and children who were lost were restored to their own people, while many thousands of pilgrims were escorted to safe lodging places or to the station. The work of life-saving was entrusted to 200 trained swimmers and although 300,000 pilgrims used the bathing ghats on the day of the solar eclipse, there was not one case of drowning. But perhaps what was appreciated most was the supply of drinking water to the pilgrims waiting for their trains.

The four Dominions have made the fullest use of the scheme of training established at Gilwell Park. Each has its Deputy Camp Chiefs who have been trained at Gilwell, and each has one or more permanent training camps modelled on the same lines as that at Gilwell. During the first twenty years of its work Gilwell welcomed to its courses 1,100 Scouters from thirty countries of the Commonwealth and Empire; many of these men and women had seized the opportunities presented by visits to Jamborees to get to Gilwell. In this way B.-P.'s practical interpretation of his ideas has been carried not only to the Dominions but also to the Colonies and Dependencies.

The story of Scouting in these Colonies could occupy a volume by itself. The scheme has been adapted to meet the most diverse conditions of climate and culture, and it has proved of special value as an auxiliary method of training outside the regular educational system. There has been no attempt to force on the Colonies a rigid system of a European pattern; local traditions and crafts are respected and, where possible, incorporated with the scheme of training given to the boys. Here it is possible to select only two or three examples to illustrate the diversity and adaptability of Scouting.

The following account is from a report on Nigeria:

Scouting is one of the few organisations in Nigeria which bring men of all tribes together. No man can expect help or kindness from any other than his own tribe, but in Scouting the Fourth Law brings all together. The most outstanding example is the Nigeria Camp, Ibadan, where Scouters from many parts of Nigeria may be in camp together, performing menial duties for each other, making friends, and inviting one another to their homes. A further example is shown by a party of Rover Scouts who recently hiked in a 'country' other than their own; at each village or town where there were Scouts they received hospitality.

Regularly Scouts are responsible for keeping village water supplies clean, and for clearing away refuse and mosquito breeding places.

We are making some changes in the Badge Tests to meet our conditions; for instance we have badges for Mud-builder, and Mat-maker. By adapting the system in this way we hope to encourage the use of the hands and to preserve crafts which are in danger of dying out. Non-Scouts very rarely leave towns and villages, so they are frightened of the country. It takes some courage to set off for a hike, and recently two Scouts doing the First Class journey test took it in turns to keep watch throughout the night. In Northern Nigeria the boys pass through a manhood test by flogging. We refer to the First Class journey as the manhood test.

There is a Scout Group at the Leper Settlement in South Nigeria; there are other Leper Groups, in Ceylon, for instance, and at Father Damien's Molokai there is a Troop of the Boy Scouts of America. The Scout method has indeed proved of help in many unusual conditions; note has already been taken of its use in bringing encouragement to children with physical or mental defects. Ceylon provides two examples of the application of the Scout method to particular problems. During the period of acute unemployment in the nineteen-thirties a Scout Colony was established at Kalatara to give training in agriculture to unemployed Scouts. A Troop was also formed at the Welikada Prison and soon proved a beneficent influence.

Even in remote islands such as Tristan da Cunha or Ascension Boy Scouts are to be found. The following account of how Scouting is carried on in one out-of-the-way place is typical of others. Nauru is an island on the equator between the Solomon and the Marshall Islands. It is administered by Australia.

Here Scouting took root in a small way in 1932, and now (1936) numbers well over 200 which is a remarkable figure out of a total population of some 1,500. Everything necessary for the sound working of an efficient Scout district is there and all is entirely done by the natives themselves under the guiding influence of an Australian Commissioner on his annual visits. The uniform consists of a lava-lava (a short skirt) of a brilliant red with white braid, a white singlet and a red scarf; no hat and no stockings or shoes. There are two complete Groups, one on either side of the island, and each has its own native meeting house, built of coconut thatches by the boys themselves. The training is always directed towards an increase in their native arts and crafts, and it is in this that Scouting provides that fresh interest in life that is so much desired, and to show how this Movement can be adapted to suit all the conditions and circumstances, the terms of the Handyman's Badge[1] may be instanced:

Make thatches, both pendunus and coconut
Make bibiscus string
Make matting for sides of houses
Cut coconut wood for rafters.

The Rover Scouts of Geelong (Victoria) correspond regularly with the Rover Scouts in Nauru.

Scouting is also at work in Papua, which comes under Queensland, and a Troop now exists there composed entirely of native medical students. This was formed on the return of the students from Sydney University.

While emphasis is constantly placed, and rightly so, on the value of Scouting as one means of fostering understanding amongst boys and young men of many nations, it is important to note its equally important mission as one of the links uniting the countries of the Commonwealth and Empire. The visits of the Chief Scout and Chief Guide did more than anything else to stimulate the sense of unity not only between the Boy Scouts of the great number of places they stayed at, but also with the Girl Guides. B.-P. himself, ever confident as he was of the influence that Scouting could exert in promoting world friendship, was most intent on the development of the Movement as a strengthening force in the Commonwealth and Empire. To him the *Pax Britannica* was the pattern of world peace. The increasing infirmities of age did not deter him from undertaking extensive tours that with their unending succession of rallies,

[1] This badge, in the U.K., covers such jobs as household repairs.

receptions, speeches, and consultations might have daunted a younger man. There were times when illness forced him to break his itinerary, but with regained strength he was as eager as ever to meet Boy Scouts whenever and wherever they could gather, in their thousands in a vast arena, or in their dozens in some remote outpost. Such was his enthusiasm that the smallest group in the smallest island felt that it was for their sakes that he had travelled across the world.

In addition to the Chief Scout many Commissioners from the United Kingdom paid visits to the Dominions and Colonies. Reference has already been made to Sir Alfred Pickford's tours. The complete list would be a long one, but a few may be recorded as representative.

In 1928 Arthur Gaddum and Major M. D. Mawe went to South Africa, and the latter also went to Bermuda in 1931. L. E. Mather was in East Africa in 1928. C. Dymoke Green visited Ceylon in 1931. Major A. Waley (Assistant International Commissioner) was in the West Indies in 1931. During the Chief's tours of 1933 to 1935 he was accompanied by Colonel Granville Walton. In 1926 Captain H. C. Mayo spent some months in Newfoundland chiefly in training Scouters. Sir Percy Everett attended the South Australian Corroboree in 1936 and three years later visited Canada. Lord Hampton (Chief Commissioner) attended the Australasian Jamboree in 1939.

Not least effective in promoting this sense of unity have been the tours of members of the Royal Family. The Prince of Wales (Edward VIII) attended Scout functions in many of the Dominions and Colonies and by his inquiries showed a constant interest in the Movement. His brother, the Duke of York (George VI), showed a similar interest during his visit to Australia in 1927, and the Duke of Kent saw much of Scouting in South Africa in 1933.

Visiting between Scouts of the Commonwealth and Empire is complicated by geographical facts, but many do manage to see something of each other. The year 1931 may be taken as typical.

Forty Scouts from Gibraltar came to London as guests of a Hendon Group which had previously visited Gibraltar.
Twelve Scouts from Sheffield went to Jamaica.
Eight Scouts from South Africa visited Australia and New Zealand.
Scouts from Fiji visited New Zealand.

These, and hundreds of other visits, are additional to the official parties attending Jamborees. Relatively few Scouts can join such parties, but on their return home they become carriers of goodwill, and, doubtless, as the months pass, so their travellers' tales become enriched.

The work of the Migration Department has resulted in large numbers of Scouts being helped to settle in the Dominions and Colonies. During 1934, for instance, 447 Scouts over 15 were sent overseas, more than half of them to Canada. Mr. T. H. Whitehead took a special interest in this aspect of Scouting; he presented a cheque for £5,000 to B.-P. during the 1929 Jamboree to assist migration. He had some difficulty in achieving his purpose, for B.-P. was so closely protected from unknown visitors that Mr. Whitehead nearly gave up his attempt. On his death in 1933, the Association became residuary legatees of his estate to the extent of over £40,000; this was left as a further aid to Scouts desiring to migrate. Whitehead Scholarships were founded giving two or more years' training at Agricultural Colleges in the Dominions. Up to 1935 there were seventy-seven of these scholars. The majority of these Scouts went into farming, but others were placed with the Hudson Bay Company, or in the B.S.A. Police of Southern Rhodesia. The work was slowed down by the reluctance of the Dominions at that period to accept emigrants unless they had guaranteed work awaiting them.

CHAPTER TWENTY-THREE

WORLD SCOUTING

HUNGARY WAS THE HOST COUNTRY FOR THE FOURTH WORLD JAMboree in 1933. The ill-fated Count Paul Teleki was Camp Chief. The site was the Royal Forest of Gödöllö, about eleven miles from Budapest. Some 9,000 Scouts from many parts of the Commonwealth and Empire and from thirty-one other countries were in camp. This number was smaller than had been hoped, but economic conditions were still bad. The Scouts began to arrive on 1 August; the last to get to the camp were five Rover Scouts from Somerset; they arrived at Antwerp on 30 July and cycled through Holland, Germany, and Austria, reaching the Jamboree on 8 August. Other Scouts coming through Germany were met by members of the Hitler Jugend whose attentions were somewhat embarrassing.

The intensely hot weather made activity unwelcome, but the usual pattern was followed in the programme of rallies and displays. The Chief Scout was handicapped by a bout of rheumatism; indeed this was so severe on the opening day that he had to be hoisted on to his horse for the inspection. His health made it impossible for him to remain for the full period of the Jamboree, and on 8 August a special farewell rally was held before he reluctantly had to leave.

His concluding message was as follows:

Let us pause for a moment for each of us silently to thank God for bringing us together as a happy family at Gödöllö.

After a moment's silence he went on,

Those of you who were at the last Jamboree in England will remember how the Golden Arrow was handed out to each country as a symbol of good will flying forth to all the ends of the earth through the Brotherhood of Scouting. Now at Gödöllö we have another symbol. Each one of you wears the badge of the White Stag of Hungary. I want you to treasure that badge when you go from here, and to remember that, like the Golden Arrow, it also has its message and its meaning for you.

The Hungarian hunters of old pursued the miraculous Stag, not because they expected to kill it, but because it led them on in the joy of the chase to new trails and fresh adventures, and so to capture happiness. You may look on that White Stag as the pure spirit of Scouting, springing forward and upward, ever leading you onward and upward, to leap over difficulties, to face new adventures in your active pursuit of the higher aims of Scouting—aims which bring you happiness. Those aims are to do your duty to God, to your country, and to your fellow men by carrying out the Scout Law. In that way you will, each one of you, help to bring about God's kingdom upon earth—the reign of peace and good will.

Therefore, before leaving you, I ask you Scouts this question—Will you do your best to make friends with others and peace in the world?

There was no lack of youthful enthusiasm in the reply.

In spite of the difficulties of the times the numbers of Scouts in the world increased as the following figures show:

1933	2,251,726
1935	2,472,014
1937	2,812,074

The Seventh International Conference was held during the Jamboree. Its deliberations were of value in promoting understanding, but the only resolution that calls for record here was the following:

This Conference again invites attention to the fact that political propaganda of any character, direct or indirect, national or international, must not be permitted in any camp or Scout gathering in which representatives of other nations are invited to attend.

This was an indication of the political tension that, as yet, was not alarming; Scouters of some nations had been known to leave provocative pamphlets in Jamborees and at training camps such as Gilwell in the hope of spreading knowledge of their national grievances.

In his talk to the Conference, B.-P. laid stress once again on the need for more extensive training. He said:

We have a tremendous opportunity before us, with the numbers of boys coming in and anxious to join—we have an immense opportunity of instilling the right principles and the right character into them if only we do it in the right way. And, therefore, it is that training of the officers is the valuable point and the most important one to work out on practical lines. I know that in most countries you have made a beginning in the way of training officers, but I would urge that you should go on with that and get it on a really sound basis, so that every officer has the opportunity of learning our true ideals and the best methods of imparting them.

Gilwell was increasingly being used by Scouters from foreign countries; in 1934, for instance, sixty-two Scouters from fourteen different countries passed through the practical courses. Many of these countries had established training centres on the pattern of Gilwell under the direction of Deputy Camp Chiefs who had been warranted with the approval of the Camp Chief. This linking-up was an important factor in developing Scouting along B.-P.'s lines.

Another link was forged by the British Scouts who year by year went across the Channel, or even farther afield, for camping, trekking, or hiking. In 1929, for instance, 475 parties of British Scouts totalling over 9,000 Scouts camped and hiked in Algeria, Austria, Belgium, Czechoslovakia, Denmark, France, Germany, Holland, Hungary, Norway, Poland, Sweden, and Switzerland. So it was to go on, year after year, without fuss or publicity. At times we hear of ambitious projects for taking children from this country for holidays to other countries, but ever since 1910 British Scouts have been visiting other lands in small groups; they seldom made much stir for they chose the country and not the town, and, as far as possible, wilder districts than can be found in the British Isles. They have saved through the months, and sometimes for a year or more, in order to enjoy these foreign camps; each party has been self-supporting and not called for financial aid on Scout Headquarters, still less on any Government Department. Few characteristics of Scouting have received less notice from the public, even from that section that is most conscious of the need for promoting friendships amongst the coming generation.

When he goes abroad the Scout carries with him an International Letter of Introduction. This does not, of course, entitle him to free hospitality, but it safeguards the Scouts of the country visited from those rogues who have at times posed as Scouts in the hope of material advantage.

A number of references have already been made in these pages to the development of Scouting in non-British countries. It is impossible here to follow their histories in any detail; a few notes must suffice.

One feature will strike the observer at once. Many countries have more than one Scout Association, and the distinction is generally based on religious belief. The way in which the Movement developed in France has already been described. The separate Association had a connecting link in a Bureau Interfédéral which was formed in 1922. A closer association came in 1940 under Scoutisme Français in which the Girl Guides were also concerned.

Similar Federations have been formed in Belgium, Denmark, Italy, the Netherlands, and one or two other countries. In Switzerland allowance is made for differences of language; the same organization is known by three different names, but they are really one body: Fédération des Éclaireurs Suisses, Schweizerischer Pfadfinderbund, and Giovani Esploratori svizzeri.

In this connexion a resolution of the International Conference of 1924 (Copenhagen) should be noted.

This Conference desires to emphasize that in pursuance of the main object of the International Bureau, applications from national Boy Scout organizations for registration are not only welcomed but cordially invited. To preserve the essential unity of the world Boy Scout movement and to ensure that the world movement shall have as its unalterable foundation the recognition of Scout brotherhood, regardless of race, creed or class, certain conditions are essential.

It is the sense of this Conference that the International Committee in adjudicating on applications for registration apart from compliance with ordinary conditions should in so far as possible insist:

(*a*) That where more than one organization exists there shall be a federation based on the common Scout objective.

(*b*) That there should be no discrimination as to admission to membership of fellow subjects or citizens for any reason of race, creed or politics.

Another resolution passed by the same Conference has a bearing on this world aspect of Scouting.

The Boy Scouts International Conference declares that the Boy Scout Movement is a movement of national, international and universal character, the object of which is to endow each separate nation and the whole world with a youth which is physically, morally and spiritually strong.

It is national, in that it aims through national organizations, at endowing every nation with useful and healthy citizens.

It is international in that it recognizes no national barrier in the comradeship of the Scouts.

It is universal in that it insists upon universal fraternity between all Scouts of every nation, class or creed.

The Scout Movement has no tendency to weaken but, on the contrary to strengthen individual religious belief. The Scout Law requires that a Scout shall truly and sincerely practise his religion, and the policy of the Movement forbids any kind of sectarian propaganda at mixed gatherings.

The various sections formed in Great Britain—Wolf Cubs, Rover Scouts, Sea Scouts, and special types of application such as Handicapped Scouts—have all been developed in turn in most other countries. In the United States of America, Sea Scouts were started for those over 15 years of age in 1912; this method of organizing special kinds of Scouting for older Scouts was later applied to Explorer Scouts in 1936, and to Air Scouts in 1942. Cubs for boys between 9 and 11 years of age were established in 1930 under the name of Cub-Scouts.

The organization of the Movement in the United States of America has taken a somewhat different shape from that in other countries. In one sense it has retained B.-P.'s original intention of Scouting being an activity added to the programme of existing organizations. An official statement of the scheme will make this clear.

Scouting is not something by and for itself. It becomes a part of the programme of the Institution which sponsors the Unit, and it should be integrated into the life of the community.

Scout leaders recognize the significant responsibility of the Sponsoring Institution for its own boys in Scouting. That is why the Boy Scouts of America do not operate Cub Packs, Scout Troops or Senior Units.

The Sponsoring Institution, as the parent body, owns and operates its own Scouting Programme. This sponsor may be a Church or other religious Institution, a Parent-Teachers Association, Service Club, School, Fire, or Police Department, Grange, or any other agency working with youth, or a group of citizens in a community. The Boy

Scouts of America provides a general programme, source material, trains the leaders selected by the Institution, and encourages the sponsoring Parent Institution to assume complete supervision over its own Pack, Troop, or Senior Group. The Scout Organization maintains Scouting standards, and carries out the basic policies established to safeguard all parent groups using the Scout Programme.

It is, therefore, of greatest importance that mutual understanding and co-operation exist between the Scout Movement and the agencies in the community.

When an Institution undertakes to sponsor a Cub Pack, Scout Troop, Air Scout Squadron, Explorer Post, or Sea Scout Ship, it says in effect, 'We are interested in the boys in our neighbourhood. We want them to grow into the right kind of men; that is, men of character, trained through participating citizenship. To this end we will use the Scouting Programme, and we assume a definite obligation to provide a meeting place for the Unit, supervision and leadership, and we will provide an opportunity for our boys to get an adequate year-round outdoor experience which meets Scouting standards'.

The founders of Scouting knew that they would have a much better opportunity to bring Scouting to all boys if they would promote it not as an organization, but as a Programme for the use of institutions which deal with boys.

This brings the control of the Units within the Parent Institution and gives a basis for closer co-ordination of the Scouting Programme with other phases of the programme to the Institution. There should be no conflict of activities and no dissipation of the boy's loyalty to the Parent Institution. The satisfaction the boy gets from his Scouting experience should produce increased loyalty to the Parent Institution.

Although there are no 'open' Groups as we know the term in the United States, the sponsoring system does not mean that the membership is necessarily limited to boys already members of the particular institution; if this were so, Scouting would be doing little more than retaining boys already under some kind of control; valuable as this would be, Scouting has a missionary function as well—to draw to it boys who would otherwise be without much guidance or under little discipline.

It will be noticed that the lay Committee in the U.S.A. representing the sponsoring authority has considerable control, and there is the risk that the laymen may interfere with the actual training of the boys. The Scout Executive is a full-time paid official for a Region or Local Council. The Boy Scouts of America make far more use of professional Scout Executives than any other national Association. The figures in 1940 were: 1,544,711 boys, 454,607 volunteer leaders (this number includes some thousands of lay committee men) and 1,393 full-time Executives. This last figure is not a high percentage of the whole membership, but even so it is beyond what any other country can afford. Every Scout pays a registration fee of half a dollar to the National Office, and a detailed record of the progress of every boy is kept at that office. This degree of organization and the funds available have their dangers; it tends to lead to elaboration and standardization.

The American standard of equipment is high. This was noted at the 1929 Jamboree when many a Scout raised his eyebrows at the way in which the American Scouts were provided with all kinds of commercial camp gear. This loss of simplicity is a serious weakness, and many attempts have been made to overcome it. Quite apart from the fact that the essence of practical Scouting is learning to do much with little, the poorer boy may be unable to become a Scout.

Scout uniform in America is also rather different from that of other countries. Hitherto it has been true to say that a Boy Scout could be recognized at a glance anywhere in the world. There are, of course, variations. The hat is not always of the cowboy type, but there are few countries where it is not worn. So, too, shorts and a scarf are part of the popular conception of a Boy Scout. There have been recurrent discussions in this country on the suitability of Scout uniforms especially for older Scouts and for Scouters. As no one has yet devised an attractive alternative, the discussions have resulted in no change. In the early days in the United States, knee-breeches were generally worn; but from 1922 shorts became more common, especially in camp. Since 1945 there has been a permissible uniform not unlike the battle-dress of wartime, with a forage cap.

The character of the development of Scouting in the United States is of the most vital importance to the future of Scouting as a world Movement. If we take four million Scouts as the total world membership in 1945, then two million came from the United States, one million from the Commonwealth and Empire, and the fourth million from about thirty-six other countries. The influence, therefore, of the Boy Scouts of America is bound to be a considerable and an increasing one. Far-seeing leaders in the United States are well aware of their own special difficulties, and they are also fully conscious of the responsibility their strength places upon them.

The expansion of Scouting has not been without its set-backs. Between the wars two countries, Russia and Italy, withdrew from the Movement. The Revolution of 1917 inevitably meant the disappearance of Scouts from Russia a few years later. The Pioneers and Komsomols that subsequently arose had some superficial resemblances to Scouts, but in essence they represent an entirely contrary view of life; the political materialist indoctrination of these boys and young men is sharply antagonistic to the ideals and purposes of Scouting.

Italy was one of the countries that adopted Scouting in the early period after 1910. Two vigorous Associations were formed, one Catholic and the other without any definite Church connexion. Italian Scouts were at the Jamborees of 1920 and 1924; their last official appearance was at the Kandersteg Conference in 1926. They were then facing dissolution in favour of the Balilla. Although for the next eighteen years there were no officially permitted Boy Scouts in Italy a few precarious connexions were maintained. B.-P. saw Mussolini in 1933 and discussed the problem with him, but the Duce made it clear that the Balilla would be the only permitted boys' organization.

The fortunes of Scouting in Germany have varied since 1910. Many efforts were made from both sides to develop a Scout Movement there that could stand on the same foundations as other countries. Two factors frustrated all these good intentions. The first was the rise of a number of rival bodies each claiming to be the true interpreter of B.-P.'s ideas; the second was more fundamental—a complete misunderstanding of the purpose of Scouting. Amongst the claimants to be Boy Scouts were the Pfadfinderbund, Deutsche Späherkorps, Neupfadfinder, and the Ringpfadfinder. Representatives of some of these bodies came to Jamborees as guests. A party of 200 German Scouts attended the 1929 Jamboree; they landed at Hull and then hiked across country to Birkenhead; but it is typical of the lack of unity that another group was not accepted by the first party (by no means happy amongst themselves) and toured the country without going to the Jamboree.

In 1924 an application by one German Association was made to the International Bureau for recognition. The answer was that there were three difficulties to be overcome. First there was too great a tendency towards military methods; secondly, political notions played too large a part in the training; and thirdly, interference with Scouting in Austria must cease.

A Conference was held in the following year between leaders of French Scouting and representatives of several of the German organizations. Some progress was made towards understanding, but immediately afterwards one of the bodies repudiated its own representative and declared that it desired no relations with Great Britain and France.

Another attempt to reach agreement was made at the end of 1929. This time it was Count Teleki of Hungary who acted on behalf of the International Committee. He visited the leaders of the various Scout or pseudo-Scout Associations but he came to the conclusion, with some reluctance, that internal rivalries and the political implications made progress impossible. The coming of Hitler to power meant that these many organizations led an increasingly precarious existence until they were absorbed by the Hitler Jugend.

During four years preceding the outbreak of the Second World War, there were three outstanding demonstrations of the unity of Scouting. The first was the Rover Moot of 1935; the second the World Jamboree of 1937; and the third the Rover Moot of 1939.

The Rover Moot of 1935 was held on the island of Ingarö in the Stockholm archipelago. A contingent of 1,200 left England at the end of July; this was made up of Rovers from the United Kingdom, Australia, Canada, South Africa, Southern Rhodesia, British Guiana, Jamaica, and India. There were very few organized activities at the camp as the purpose was to give these young men every opportunity for getting to know each other. The camp was under the leadership of Prince Gustaf Adolf who had as his chief assistant Count Folke Bernadotte—two leaders of Swedish Scouting who were to have tragic deaths. This was the last World Rover Moot that B.-P. was able to attend. He wrote of it in these words:

In these woods on Ingarö Island are collected some 3,000 Rover Scouts (that is Boy Scouts of over 17) coming from 26 different nations. They are camping together with the one main idea of making personal friendships with one another, so that the brotherhood of Scouts shall be something more than a mere name. By making personal contacts with their peers of other countries they may get to know something of their character, their national conditions and problems, and thus to develop a closer understanding and sympathy with them.

These young men have been brought to realize that within the next few years they will be among the men of affairs responsible for the fortunes of their respective countries. They see how at present the world is torn by unrest due to apprehension and uncertainty as regards the future, and to national fear and suspicion of rival countries; that all this leads to selfish individual effort on the part of each nation to protect its own interests as far as it can, whether in commerce, or industry, or by armament.

So this gathering at Ingarö, though it may appear to the ordinary onlooker to be a mere joy camp of a cheery lot of red-blooded youths, has in fact a serious side to it and one which is fully and inwardly realized by the lads themselves. Like their generation generally, they know that they are up against two great specific dangers—the danger of unemployment and the danger of War.

The Eighth International Conference was held in Stockholm during the Rover Moot. At the concluding session, B.-P. once more waged war against complacency.

I would urge this: Let us not go away from here with the feeling that, this Conference having ended, our duties are now over and we may rest content with our labours until the next meeting. Let us rather look on the Conference as the raising of the curtain for the performance of the next act of progress and development now to be performed during this coming two-year period. And let us go forward and perform it in such a fashion as will inspire all workers in the Movement to do the same for God, their Country, and the Boy—and to bring about concord and peace in the world.

Two years later came the Fifth World Jamboree. Holland was the host country, and the site was at Vogelensang—Bloemendaal—Bird Song—Flower Valley. The Jamboree was opened by the Queen of the Netherlands on 31 July. Some 27,000 Scouts were there, and to them Her Majesty said:

May the days that you are gathered here be marked by the true Scout Spirit, and may, through God's blessing, the friendships you form strengthen and deepen into a true and loyal brotherhood which remains long after you have scattered back to your countries all over the world.

It is not necessary to detail the programme of events, as this followed the usual lines of previous Jamborees. Perhaps the camp-fires should be specially mentioned; they were held in a lovely spot among the sand-dunes some distance from the camp, and the walk there and back (especially back) was something new in Jamborees! The first occasion was notable. A Scouter described it in this way:

Fully 20,000 people were present when 'Pom' signalled the flag bearers to take their places at the back of the raised platform. A grand sight those flags of every nation made against the rising slope at the back. On to the platform came the firemakers, ten Scouts of different countries each armed with bow and drill. Swiftly they got to work. Smoke rose in tiny spirals . . . a Scout dropped quickly to his knees, scooped up the smouldering tinder and, rising, whirled it round and round. The tinder burst into flame and dropped to the floor, and from it four torches were lighted and carried to four corners of the built-up camp fire. The torches were plunged into the wood, which quickly blazed up.

For the rest let a French Scouter speak:

Feu de camp en Hollande, thé en Hongrie, goûter en Pologne, danses en Suisse, accueil en Finlande, répétitions de danses en Écosse, visite en Roumanie, fraternité en Belgique, Luxembourg, ou Angleterre. Que d'émouvants souvenirs!

The days went by all too quickly, and at last came the final rally on 9 August. By the tall flagmast was a huge Jacob's staff, the symbol of the Fifth Jamboree.

The Chief Scout of the World spoke:

We have come to the end of our Jamboree. It seems as if we were only beginning it yesterday, and here we are already at the end. But during these few short days I am very glad that all of you Scouts gathered from all parts of the world have been making the most of your opportunities to make friends. After all, that was the main object of the Jamboree—to make with those of countries other than your own as many friends as possible.

We have been called a Boys' Crusade, the Crusade of Peace, and it is a very apt description of our Scout Brotherhood.

Youth of all countries represented at the Jamboree have been getting together and have pledged themselves to the crusade of friendship and good will. You will remember how in the times of the Crusades the great efforts to capture for Christianity the Holy City of Jerusalem failed. Then, when the boys saw that their fathers had failed in their efforts, they joined themselves together and said that they would undertake a Crusade to carry on the work of their fathers.

Unfortunately their attempt did not succeed, owing to its not being properly organized and owing to lack of adequate preparations. But at any rate it was an excellent effort, and it was in a great cause. This Brotherhood of Scouting is in many respects similar to that Crusade. You Scouts have assembled from all parts of the world as ambassadors of good will, and you have been making friends, breaking down any barriers of race, of creed or of class. That surely is a great Crusade. I advise you now to continue that good work, for soon you will be men, and if quarrels should arise between any nations it is upon you that the burden of responsibility will fall.

If you are friends, then of course you will not want to be in dispute, and by cultivating those friendships such as have been cemented at this great Jamboree, you are preparing the way for solutions of a peaceful character. This will have a vital and very far-reaching effect throughout the world in the cause of peace, and so pledge, all of you here in this great assembly of Youth, to do your absolute utmost to establish friendship among Scouts of all nations.

Thus you will find a better way for the removal of international disputes by the avenues of friendly discussion, of good will and of mutual understanding. The emblem of our Jamboree is the Jacob's Staff. This was the instrument by which the navigators in old days found their way across the seas. Let it also for us to-day be an instrument of guidance in our life. It is the Cross which for all who are Christians points the way; but it is also a cross with many arms; these are held out to embrace all creeds. Those eight arms, together with the head and foot of the emblem, remind us of our ten Scout Laws.

B.-P. then handed to the leaders of the contingents a Jacob's staff as a memento and a reminder.

I have handed to representatives of each country this totem to take home as an emblem of good will.

Go forth with this emblem to spread the spirit of good will.

Now the time has come for me to say good-bye. I want you to lead happy lives. You know that many of us will never meet again in this world. I am in my eighty-first year and am nearing the end of my life. Most of you are at the beginning, and I want your lives to be happy and successful. You can make them so by doing your best to carry out the Scout Law all your days, whatever your station and wherever you are. I want you all to preserve this badge of the Jamboree which is on your uniform. I suggest that you keep it and try to remember for what it stands. It will be a reminder of the happy times you have had here in camp; it will remind you to take the ten points of your Scout Law as your guide in life; and it will remind you of the many friends to whom you have held out the hand of friendship, and so helped through good will to bring about God's reign of peace among men.

Now good-bye. God bless you all!

He took off his hat, and in a voice charged with emotion added: 'God bless you!'

There is little doubt that the Chief Scout himself felt that this might be his last Jamboree; many of those who listened to him were conscious that, in the nature of things, they dare not hope to see his alert figure or hear his strong voice again at another such a gathering of Boy Scouts.

The Ninth International Conference, held at The Hague, 10–12 August 1937, was perhaps the most comprehensive Scout Conference ever held, the delegates of thirty-four different nations being present. The Conference took place after the Fifth World Jamboree at Vogelensang. Prince Gustaf Adolf of Sweden was in the chair for the greater part of the time, out of compliment to the position he had accepted as Honorary President of the Boy Scouts International Committee. At the opening he called on M. de Bruin, the Minister of Education of the Netherlands, to welcome the delegates on behalf of the Dutch Government. M. de Bruin said: 'You are going to deal with the international point of view. For ten days your boys from many States and nations, with their different languages and customs, have been here together. This is a splendid thing not only for the present, but also for the future. We cannot work together, or even genuinely differ in opinion, unless we approach each other more closely. A very large portion of the difficulties in this world is due to the fact that too often there is a lack of such meetings. You educate your boys on principles of understanding and appreciating each other by making them know one another.'

B.-P. was wearing the newly instituted Bronze Wolf, the highest and only award for International Scout work, and, after he had thanked M. de Bruin, he presented three others—to

Walter de Bonstetten for the founding and supervision of the International Scout Chalet at Kandersteg; to Hubert S. Martin for his indefatigable work at the International Bureau; and to J. S. Wilson for the work done at Gilwell Park in promoting an international understanding of Scouting.

Two resolutions passed at this Conference show the increasing tension that was to result in war two years later.

The Conference resolves that the International Committee be requested to do all that it can to ensure that Scouting and Rovering in all countries, while fostering true patriotism, are genuinely kept within the limits of international co-operation and friendship, irrespective of creed and race, as has always been outlined by the Chief Scout. Thus, any steps to the militarization of Scouting or the introduction of political aims, which might cause misunderstanding and thus handicap our work for peace and goodwill among nations and individuals should be entirely avoided in our programmes.

The Conference upon the recommendation of the International Committee resolves that in view of Scout Camp exhibits at this and previous Jamborees the International Bureau take steps to guard against exhibits at Jamborees of a political nature which might provoke brother Scouts from other parts of the world.

Part of B.-P.'s closing speech—the last he made at an International Scout Conference—is worth giving at some length.

With the process of time and the increasing number of experts amongst us there is always a tendency to add new ideas or to improve the old ones, to add rules and regulations that are thought to be good for the organization, but the original definitions and bases on which we have been working are apt to become obscured, and in some cases scrapped out of existence, and we tangle ourselves up with definitions until we run into the danger of over-organizing. This is a very real danger to-day, and I am so glad you are recommended to study Tage Carstensen's paper again, because it exactly deals with these points in the way I look at it also. Our remedy is to go back and study the original simple basis of our Movement. This might seem a retrograde step, but as one would probably say better in French: 'Revenir en arrière, c'est sauter en avant.'

We want to get back to the simple principles of training through the game of adventure. As Dr. West said yesterday, it is not the system that is at fault, but the method of applying it that has to be looked to, our ultimate object being to breed manly men for our respective countries, strong in body, mind and spirit, men who can be trusted, men who can face hard work and also hard times, men who can make up their own minds and not be led by mass suggestion, men who can sacrifice much that is personal in the greater good of the nation.

And when they have done that their patriotism must not be narrow, but with widened outlook they must be able to see with sympathetic eyes the ambitions of the patriots of other countries. . . . I want to remind you in this case, as indeed in what I have been saying of the original principles of our Movement, that all the steps in our history have been of automatic growth—not merely the problems, but the steps in growth and development. For instance, you can remember that it was not I who urged Scouting to the boys. It was only suggested to me to write a book, and the boys took it up for themselves. I wrote a book for certain institutions for boys, but boys outside those institutions took up Scouting on their own account. It was an automatic growth. . . .

Then, no propaganda was sent to foreign countries when we were busy with this Scouting at home, but within a very short time many countries took up Scouting, and now, before thirty years, countries over practically all the civilized world have taken up Scouting: another automatic growth. The whole thing is a natural growth, and therefore a natural movement and not an artificial organization made by rules and regulations. Of course, a few basic rules are necessary here and there, but they ought to be limited to the very basic ones, without refinements of little rules to cover every kind of possible question in the future. . . .

Three hundred and forty thousand new boys have joined the Scout movement in the last two years. We have now come up to 2,812,000 boys. . . . And so it is for us to go forward yet further, with full confidence, to do as the Cubs say—to do our best—and carry on and develop Scouting to the best of our ability.

⚜ ⚜ ⚜ ⚜ ⚜ ⚜ ⚜ ⚜ ⚜ ⚜ ⚜ ⚜ ⚜ ⚜ ⚜ ⚜ ⚜

CHAPTER TWENTY-FOUR

SCOUTING AT HOME 1935–9

IT HAS SOMETIMES BEEN ASKED WHY THE BOY SCOUT AND GIRL Guide Movements have not been more closely associated in this country. Part of the answer lies in the nature of the beginning of the Boy Scouts. As we have seen, B.-P. in 1907 was thinking of ways of helping existing boys' organizations to become more attractive. He was intent, as was his wont, on an immediate practical problem, and it may safely be said that the thought of providing a training scheme for girls did not enter his calculations. The need for some kind of parallel scheme was forced on his notice. The separate creation of the two Movements—separate in time as well as in conception—resulted in each developing independently. There has never been any lack of consultation both at the centre and in the local areas, but the possibility of joint training was not seriously considered. Here B.-P.'s knowledge of boy-nature once again served him well. He knew that boys of 11 to 15 years of age prefer to hunt in gangs and resent the intrusion of girls. Even after the age of 15 they prefer for some years to keep in separate compartments their relations with girls and their activities as boys.

B.-P. was content to leave the Girl Guides to evolve their own organization and he rarely interfered. The Movement went through a difficult phase soon after it had been formed, and it was not until Lady Baden-Powell was able to play a commanding part in the organization that the Girl Guides began to make real progress. They were helped by the greater freedom conceded to women during and after the First World War.

The two Movements have many associations together outside the actual training of the boys and girls. Combined rallies, social occasions, and other events provide opportunities for Guiders and Scouters to work together. The work done by Guiders and

Guides at the 1929 Jamboree in the camp hospital and in other ways may be regarded as typical. Even more effective than these special ways of helping each other is the steady influx of Guides into the Scout Movement as Lady Cubmasters, Assistants, and Instructors.

An exceptional kind of co-operation took the form in 1933 of a Goodwill Cruise. The *Calgaric* was chartered for the occasion and with 400 Guiders and 100 Scouters on board under the leadership of the Chiefs they visited the Baltic lands; it is hardly necessary to say what an encouragement this was to such countries as Lithuania, Latvia, and Estonia; both Movements were well established in those countries. Their subsequent 'liquidation' was a tragedy.

A second cruise took place in 1934; this time the ship was the *Adriatic* and the western Mediterranean the cruising-ground. The third cruise was made in 1938; in the *Orduna* the party visited Iceland and the Scandinavian countries.

This was an epoch of conferences; there were open ones for all Scouters; others were for Commissioners; another group dealt with the sections or were convened to discuss special activities. The Scout Movement became aware of that modern phenomenon, the conference-addict, who spends so much time on discussion or in listening to discussions that he can have little time for practical service; he at length comes to believe that the height of progress is marked by a resolution passed *nem. con.* Fortunately most Scouters were content to go on Scouting.

Certainly there were matters that called for consideration, but it cannot be said that, interesting as the discussions were, the conferences produced anything that had a marked effect. One problem above all others was worrying the Movement in the nineteen-thirties; why was membership declining? The following figures show the position in the British Isles.

1933 . . .	480,379
1934 . . .	459,930
1935 . . .	447,396
1936 . . .	445,411
1937 . . .	443,455
1938 . . .	460,234

All kinds of causes were put forward for this gradual decrease in membership; some saw in the economic difficulties of the time the explanation; others noted that in new housing estates there was no provision for meeting-places; some asked if the time had not come to overhaul the organization. No doubt all these helped to lessen the appeal of Scouting. It was not possible at the time to see a yet more fundamental influence—the slackening of moral standards, and the general lack of belief in the good life. That period has been well labelled 'the dismal thirties'. Scouting was fighting a rearguard action against the increasing scepticism of the times; the wonder was that the Movement was not more adversely affected. By 1938 the tendency was again upwards.

The unsolved problem of the older Scout was a further source of concern. Here the reasons were well known; the main one was that on leaving school for work at 14 or 15 the boy feels that he is a man and no longer wishes to associate with 'kids'. Yet some Troops always managed to retain a good proportion of these adolescents. They did so by keeping the training and activities varied and attractive at all stages. In the long run, the problem resolved itself into a question of the character and capabilities of the Scouters. While no new scheme was suggested, two lines of progress were followed. The first was the greatest extension possible of the training of Scouters, and the second was the drive to get more Scouts to the First Class stage.

The encouragement to carry the boy's training up to and beyond First Class had a measure of success as the following figures demonstrate.

	Scouters	*Scouts*	*First Class Scouts*
1934	25,205	211,195	7,348
1935	24,731	204,058	7,617
1936	24,305	200,660	8,874
1937	24,896	201,103	9,230

From the above figures it will be seen that in spite of a decline in the numbers of Scouters and Scouts, there was a substantial increase in the number of First Class Scouts. No one, however, could rest satisfied with this, for the number of First Class Scouts was too small compared with the number of Scouts.

Many felt that the real solution to the loss of older boys lay ultimately in having more trained Scouters. Here Gilwell gave all the help possible. In addition to the training courses held there, there were many courses run in counties by the Deputy

Camp Chiefs and Akela Leaders. Some counties had acquired training grounds of their own. The Camp Chief visited many of the courses and he and members of his staff ran occasional training camps both in the British Isles and in some foreign countries.

On all training courses the emphasis was placed on outdoor Scouting. There is always a temptation in towns, especially in the greater industrial centres, for Groups to spend too much time in their headquarters. The difficulties are, of course, formidable, particularly in the long winter evenings, but the full Scout programme demands a large measure of outdoor activity, otherwise it changes a Troop into a club; this does not imply any criticism of clubs for they do valuable work amongst boys and young fellows; it is merely to underline the fact that Scouting is not a club organization; it is based on 'the work and attributes of backwoodsmen, explorers, and frontiersmen'. To maintain that atmosphere and secure the essential outdoor experience is a tax on the enthusiasm, ingenuity, and imagination of the Scouters. The training courses set out to help all Scouters to realize the full programme, and more than a quarter of a century of the Wood-badge scheme proved that it raised the standard of real Scouting by providing Scouters with ideas, suggestions, and inspiration.

A further means of disseminating ideas was by means of books; of this something has already been said. Articles in *The Scouter* and in county and other Scout journals provided another means of stimulating outdoor Scouting. Dr. Griffin had made considerable headway in broadening the appeal of *The Scouter* before he resigned in December 1935; his successor was C. Beresford-Webb who also edited *The Rover World*, a journal that had been established without official backing; it was taken over by Headquarters in January 1935 but had to be abandoned three years later for lack of support. *The Scout* had to face the economic straitness of the times, but its editor, F. Haydn Dimmock (who took charge in 1918), was fertile in ideas and in devising new attractions for his readers. In 1935, for instance, he organized a Train Cruise from London to the north of Scotland; this proved so successful it became an annual event until the outbreak of war. By then the publishers of *The Scout* were reluctant to continue a boys' paper that was proving a financial liability rather than an asset. No doubt one of the difficulties was the changed needs of boys; the old type of adventure weekly was making less appeal, and several that were well known to boys a generation earlier had disappeared. The demand was for technical journals, and the craving for romance was satisfied more easily by the cinema. When war broke out the Association took over the publication of *The Scout* and its editor joined the Headquarters staff; in spite of paper restrictions and other obstacles, he built up the circulation and once more put the paper in a sound position.

With the spread of camping as a pastime and the growing demands from landowners and farmers for rents, the need arose for securing permanent sites that could be developed on Scout lines. Family camps and commercial holiday camps have little or no resemblance to Scout camping. The essence of the Scout camp is that there should be the greatest call for initiative and self-dependence; the wilder the site the better training it offers while at the same time providing better opportunities for getting to know more about nature. The Scoutmaster, if he really grasps the significance of camping for Scouts, prefers to find some out-of-the-way spot. Such places are no longer easily to be found, and many a Scouter has had the bitter experience of having discovered and used a suitable place only to find that others have profited by his pioneer work to crowd the site with holiday campers. Mention has been made of the serious difficulty in providing outdoor practical Scouting for Troops in large towns. The costs of getting out to open country are often prohibitive. The success of Gilwell Park as a boys' camping site for north-east London pointed the way to one solution of this difficulty. London Scouts acquired a site near Downe, Charles Darwin's old home in Kent; in 1933, as a result of a gift of £5,000 from the trustees of Sir William Dunn, it was possible for Headquarters to take over possession. This gave a badly needed outlet for south-east London Scouts. Three years later two most suitable areas were added to the growing list. W. D. Wakefield, one of the early Travelling Inspectors, presented to the Association Great Tower Plantation south of Bowness on Windermere; here was an ideal stretch of over 300 acres of absolutely wild country. The nature of the ground made it impossible to have large camps; Patrol camps were the only practicable type. In the same year, the Manor Charitable Trust offered for a nominal rent of a shilling a year 380 acres known as Broadstone Warren, part of Ashdown Forest in Sussex. This, too, was most suited to Scout purposes. Later on, the Trust added Wych Warren with a house that was used for convalescent Scouts during the Second World War, and ultimately replaced the old Rosemary Home. Other sites, smaller but still valuable, were added from time to time: Chalfont Heights (Buckinghamshire) and Phasels Wood (Herts.) are examples of camping grounds that came into Scout possession in various parts of the country.

Under the Public Health Act (1936) local authorities have the power of making by-laws to control camping. While the Bill was under discussion, the case for special treatment for such an organization as the Boy Scouts was successfully argued. A certificate of exemption from such by-laws was granted to the Association in 1937. This implied that Scout camping would be sound camping and placed a responsibility on all in the Movement to maintain a high standard. In this respect the permanent sites gained additional value as training grounds.

The work at Roland House expanded under the guidance of Stanley Ince who had been appointed Warden in 1929, a position he held until 1940. Ever since 1911 he had played an important part in Scouting in Hackney and in bringing 'backwoodsmanship into the backyard'. Serious disabilities resulting from the war did not hinder his service to East London Scouts. Increasing needs made it desirable to extend the premises. A gift from Sir Jeremiah Colman in 1936 made it possible to add the next-door house to the original settlement. The necessary funds for maintaining the work were provided by subscriptions from a large army of loyal friends; these were increased by the proceeds of an annual pantomime. In addition to its primary purposes of serving as a headquarters for east London Scouting and as a residence for Scouters, Roland House has an important place in international Scouting; many foreign Scouters have stayed there for a few days and have had an opportunity of seeing how Scouting can be developed in such a crowded area.

In another part of London, Holborn, an interesting method was used for raising funds; the 'Gang Show' devised and produced by 'A London Rover' gained a reputation that had a wide effect on Scout entertainments. This anonymous Rover was Ralph Reader, who, in April 1936, also produced at the Albert Hall, London, a magnificent spectacle entitled 'Boy Scout'. A cast of 1,500 Boy Scouts was drawn from London and the neighbouring counties, and, considering that full rehearsals could rarely be held, the result was astonishing and impressive. This was not a money-raising device, but a means of bringing Scouting to the attention of the public. The show was repeated in later years with undiminished success although with entirely fresh performers.

During this period there were many local rallies and Jamborees. In 1936, for instance, there was a West Country Jamboree near Plymouth, and a Northern Counties Jamboree at Raby Castle, Durham. At both the Chief Scout was able to be present.

Royal occasions called for the services of Scouts. The Silver Jubilee of the King and Queen in 1935 suggested some kind of special celebration; this took the form of a Chain of Beacons. There were 1,775 of these throughout Great Britain and Northern Ireland, and they were all lit at 10 p.m. on Jubilee Day, 6 May. The first, in Hyde Park, was ignited from Buckingham Palace by King George V.

After the third annual St. George's Day Service at Windsor, King Edward VIII addressed the thousand King's Scouts and First Class Scouts from the steps at the west end of St. George's Chapel. In the following November he toured South Wales and paid a visit to Llanfrechfa Grange to see the Domestic Training Centre there which was being run by the Association.

The year 1937 proved a busy one for the Scout Movement. The Jamboree in Holland has already been described; this came a few months after the Coronation of King George VI and Queen Elizabeth. The Chief Scout had returned from a tour of India where he had celebrated his eightieth birthday; the Movement was delighted when it was announced that the king had conferred the Order of Merit on its founder. The Scouts were responsible for two tasks at the Coronation; they were given the monopoly of selling the programmes; over 600,000 copies were sold which brought in a sum of £37,000 to King George's Jubilee Trust. The second duty was undertaken by London Rover Scouts; they assisted the police in erecting and looking after miles of barriers, and at the Abbey they organized the dispersal of the guests.

Coronation year brought fresh romance to the Sea Scouts. The Government of the Falkland Islands offered Captain Scott's famous ship *Discovery* to the Association. Acceptance was possible if the cost of upkeep could be met and the Port of London Authority would grant permission for the ship to berth in the Thames in a central position. Lady Houston provided the funds for upkeep and the P.L.A. gladly agreed to arrange for a suitable berth. The ceremony of handing over took place on 9 October; the Duke of Kent as Commodore of the Sea Scouts accepted the *Discovery* in the presence of the Chief Scout and of a company that included former officers and relatives of those who had served on board the ship. Moored off the Victoria Embankment, the ship soon began to attract hosts of visitors; more important, however, was its value as a headquarters and training centre for Sea Scouts.

Two important changes in the direction of the Movement have also to be noted for 1937. Lord Somers, who had been appointed by B.-P. in the previous year as Deputy Chief Scout, returned to England to take up his new duties. C. Dymoke Green retired from the position of General Secretary of the Association; he had rendered distinguished service to Scouting in that position for twenty-one years and it was indeed difficult to think of Headquarters apart from him; his wise counsel was sought by all, for they trusted a judgement that was based on long experience as a Scoutmaster and Commissioner. A curious experiment was made in appointing his successor. It was decided to have someone without previous experience of the Movement. P. E. Berryman was appointed. At the same time D. Francis Morgan became Legal and Parliamentary Secretary, and A. W. Hurll was appointed Secretary to the Deputy Chief Scout and Assistant General Secretary. He had entered the service of the Association in 1921 as a junior clerk. When war broke out P. E. Berryman returned to the R.A.F. and in 1941 decided not to resume his Scout work. A. W. Hurll, who had been acting as General Secretary for the past two years, then became General Secretary. In 1948 he was appointed to the new position of Chief Executive Commissioner.

B.-P. had been anxious for some time to see the financial

future of the Association placed in a stronger position. It was therefore decided to launch a Boy Scouts' Fund Appeal in 1937; Lord Somers was chairman of the Committee since B.-P. himself had been obliged for reasons of health to go to Kenya. It will be remembered that the first national appeal for funds had been cut short by the outbreak of war in 1914; this fresh appeal similarly had to be closed when war again broke out. By then the sum of close on £250,000 had been received.

World Scouting suffered a great loss in 1938 by the death of Hubert Martin who had been active in the Movement since 1909, and International Commissioner since 1918. His work as Director of the International Bureau since 1920 had been of the highest value to Scouting; his tactful handling of awkward situations had resulted in the closer union of the Associations of all countries in which Scouting played a part.

J. S. Wilson, the Camp Chief, was asked to become Acting-Director until the next meeting of the International Conference. This was held in Edinburgh at the end of July 1939. B.-P. could not be present but he sent a message from Kenya.

Considering the unrestful times around us, when all the world seems to be thinking of war, this particular Conference has a greater importance than any of its predecessors. War is a man-made infliction upon himself, bringing nothing but human misery in its train. It is therefore up to man to devise the remedy, and to restore to himself the blessing of peace with its prosperity and happiness for all. A first step should be to develop the spirit of good will and toleration, truth and justice, in place of envy, hatred and malice. It is difficult to teach old dogs new tricks, and our hope must lie with the oncoming generation to effect such change of thought. In a very few years our boys of to-day will be the men of their respective countries. To us, Scouts, the opportunity seems given to help in swinging back the pendulum to the practice of common sense and mutual understanding.

One resolution passed was to have a sad significance.

The Conference expresses its sympathy and extends greetings to fellow Scouts and Scouters who, through no fault of their own, have been forced to leave their native land. The Conference urges that every possible courtesy and help be extended to such Scouts and Scouters by the respective national Association, whether the residence is to be temporary or permanent, and that, wherever practicable, an invitation be extended for them to become associated in some temporary way with the local Scout groups, rather than the development of any separate national group in another country. It is to be understood that principles involved are not to be interpreted with any retroactive effect.

This Conference was held at the time of the Third Rover Scout Moot at Monzie Castle in Perthshire. It was attended by 3,500 Rovers from forty-eight different countries. Three, of whom two were Australians and one a Pole, had sailed a 50-foot yawl from Australia to Southampton, taking a year over the journey. The probability of war in the near future cast a shadow over the Moot, and many must have wondered how divided by national duty those young fellows might be within a few months. But this sense of strain was not allowed to lessen the high spirits of the Rovers or to weaken their goodwill one to another.

BOY SCOUTS ON TREK

SEA SCOUTS BOARD *DISCOVERY*

BLIND AND DEAF SCOUTS IN CAMP

ROVER SCOUTS ON HIKE

CHAPTER TWENTY-FIVE

THE END OF AN EPOCH

THE OUTBREAK OF WAR IN SEPTEMBER 1939 FOUND THE BOY Scouts Association prepared to render national service in the same spirit it had displayed in 1914. There was, however, an important difference between the situation then and in 1939. When the First World War broke out, there was no organized National Service scheme nor were there auxiliary units attached to the Forces. In 1939 these were all in existence, and Scouting, therefore, had to fit in with the arrangements made by the Government; rules about age and other regulations made it appear, at first, as though it was going to be very difficult for Scouts to do much. The exigencies of the times and the determination of the boys to help soon broke through the tangle of red tape. When, for instance, the evacuation of children from the big towns began in August Scouts very quickly found many ways in which they could help—it might be merely by carrying luggage or by cheering up the youngsters, but it was something not provided by regulations. There are bound to be unforeseeable gaps in large-scale plans which can only be filled by someone on the spot, and Scouts were certainly on the spot.

Scouters, Rovers, and Old Scouts underwent training in Air Raid Precautions and many of those not called up for active service joined one or other of the Civil Defence units. Later many served in the Home Guard and were grateful for their previous experience as Scouts or Scouters. Large numbers of Scouts were attached to Civil Defence units, to hospitals, and to other centres of relief and aid. The Thirty-second Report for 1941 contains a three-page list of the many kinds of national service rendered by Scouts. It would serve little purpose to reproduce that list here; it demonstrates beyond question that the training these boys had received as Scouts achieved the aim set by B.-P.—'to make the lads individually efficient, morally and physically, with the object of using that efficiency for the service of the community'.[1]

It would be possible to fill many pages with tributes paid to the services given by Scouts. The following extract from a letter written by a doctor to the Scoutmaster of a Troop on hospital duty must serve as typical of hundreds:

> May I take this opportunity of making known to you and all the boys the admiration of my colleagues and self for their splendid behaviour during the past night? I had ample opportunities of seeing your boys at work—sometimes unobserved—and was genuinely pleased at their cool and calm demeanour and their cheerfulness throughout the whole period. During those fateful early hours of this morning when we 'pros' were feeling the stress, I was still greeted on arrival with a bright smile and a cheery word which did help so very much. I should imagine that you feel immensely proud of them all and I, too, am happy at the thought of my small connection with them. Am just 'off' after 17 hours on duty, but simply had to write these few lines before turning in.

So, too, it would be possible to give many accounts of acts of courage and of heroism during air raids and other emergencies. In this respect the Scouts shared with the whole population a fortitude in adversity and an undauntable courage that made victory possible. Where the Scout or old Scout had an advantage over many was in having been trained to deal with sudden calls and to act on his own responsibility when the need arose. Moreover, his whole life as a Scout developed in him, as a kind of instinct, the giving of help wherever help might be needed. He was not more courageous than his neighbour; he was often better prepared.

The same point may be made regarding old Scouts in the Forces; the Movement is rightly proud of the large number of decorations for gallantry won by its members. Twenty-four were awarded the Victoria Cross, and six the George Cross. It would be impossible to establish that the fine achievements of such men were the result of Scout training; in some cases it could not be, since their Scout membership was brief. The testimony, however, of thousands who gained no awards is that

[1] The story of Scouting during the war both in allied countries and in the occupied territories is told in *The Left Handshake* by Hilary St. George Saunders. In these pages, therefore, it has not seemed necessary to go into much detail.

their Scout training in looking after themselves, in developing their powers of observation, in finding their way across country, in dealing with accidents, and in many other ways, provided an invaluable grounding for training in the Forces. These are intangible matters; they cannot be assessed; the best comment was that made by the Prime Minister, Mr. Winston Churchill, in a message to a Conference of Commissioners in January 1942:

I first met B.-P. many years before the birth of the Scout Movement. He was a man of character, vision and enthusiasm and he passed these qualities on to the Movement which has played, and is playing, an important part in moulding the character of our race. Sturdiness, neighbourliness, practical competence, love of country, and, above all, in these times, indomitable resolve, daring and enterprise in the face of the enemy, these are the hallmarks of a Scout.

You have many practical difficulties under war-time conditions in carrying on your work, but with persistence and ingenuity these can be surmounted in Scout fashion and I have no doubt that in your hands the Movement will carry on its task with the steadfast will and high courage with which it was founded. 'Be Prepared' to stand up faithfully for Right and Truth however the winds may blow.

The war had an unexpected influence on Scouting. It promoted what may be termed the mobility of Scouters; as units of the Forces were moved about, so Scouters and old Scouts came to know more of how the Movement worked not only in their own country but in other parts of the Commonwealth and Empire and in other lands. The man whose experience of Scouting had been mainly, if not entirely, in a large industrial town, might find himself in a scantily populated rural area where the problems of Scouting would be entirely fresh to him. It was common experience for a small town Troop, or a village Patrol, to receive a surprise visit from a London or Glasgow Scouter or perhaps one from Canada or the United States of America. Other Scouters were sent across the Atlantic for training and got to know something of the methods of the Boy Scouts of America or of Canada. The movements of troops might take a Scouter to the West Coast of Africa or to Burma. Innumerable contacts of this kind resulted in those discussions of methods and exchanges of experiences that are part of the conversation whenever two Scouters or Scouts get together.

This mobility of members of the Movement led to an increase in the numbers of Deep-Sea Scouts; many Crews (in the Rover terminology) or informal clubs were formed in ships and shore training stations, and wherever ships put into port, fresh Scout contacts were made. This pleasant experience was not limited to the sailors; soldiers on transports enjoyed the same delight in at once getting into touch with Scout people in whatever part of the world their service might take them.

In both the Royal Air Force and the Army facilities were approved for the formation of Rover Crews and clubs, and Commanding Officers in both Services were instructed to make it possible for serving members of the Boy Scouts Association to assist Scout Groups in areas where the men were stationed. A number of Crews were also formed in prisoner-of-war camps; these generally set themselves a course of training in preparation for becoming active Scouters on the return of peace.

In order to link up as many of these serving members as possible *The Forces Bulletin* was published by Headquarters and distributed free every month to all men whose names could be supplied by their old Groups. By 1945 the circulation had reached 23,000 copies.

Although the Sea Scouts were not given as responsible a task as in 1914, their training (under certain conditions) was recognized by the Admiralty as facilitating entry of Scouts into the Navy. Courses were conducted on the *Discovery* and on the *England* at Marlow. Many Sea Scouts were taken direct into the River (Thames) Emergency Service. Some Sea Scout craft rendered service at the evacuation of Dunkirk.

There was an inevitable drop in membership owing to the total dislocation caused during the first stage of the war. The greatest decrease was in the number of Scouters and Rovers due to their being called up on full-time service; within the first two years there was a decrease of 40,000 in the combined numbers of Scouters and Rovers. The evacuation of boys from the large towns meant that some Packs and Troops had to close down; wherever possible these town-boys were linked up with local country Groups, or new Packs and Troops were formed in their changed environment. A further cause of dislocation was the requisitioning of Group Headquarters; this temporary loss was less serious than the destruction of many a Scout Hut or Headquarters during air raids. By the end of the war the lost ground had been regained as the following figures for the United Kingdom show:

1938 . . .	434,471
1941 . . .	305,760
1943 . . .	424,083
1945 . . .	471,040

The remarkable fact was that the decrease in numbers was not more considerable and that this period lasted for such a comparatively short time. As in the First World War, the older Scouts and Patrol Leaders quickly filled many of the gaps caused by absent Scouters; men who had retired from active Scouting came back to keep things going, and many a Pack and Troop received valuable aid from serving members stationed in the neighbourhood. To help Patrol Leaders special training courses were held where possible, and a correspondence course was also conducted from Headquarters. During the first year of the scheme 686 Patrol Leaders completed the course. This was an exceptional war-time arrangement, as normally it is the Scoutmaster's job to train his leaders.

When war broke out the main Headquarters staff was transferred to Gilwell Park, but after a few months the situation was calm enough for a return to be made to Buckingham Palace Road. Fortunately the Headquarters building escaped damage although it was between Victoria Station and the Palace. Roland House was less fortunate and was twice damaged by bombs. The buildings at Gilwell were not hit, but a number of bombs fell in the grounds, and during one night over a hundred incendiaries were dropped across the estate. Camping was not possible there as it came within the restricted area, but this did not mean the suspension of all training for Scouters. The military requisitioned Gilwell in the autumn of 1940, and at the same time the Camp Chief received a commission in the army. His assistant, A. M. Chamberlain, carried on the training work; Youlbury became the main centre but courses were also run in some counties. Many a war-worker found that a Wood-badge practical course was a complete form of recreation in the best sense of the word. Many Scouters of foreign countries who came to Great Britain as exiles took advantage of the opportunity to be trained.

For some years before 1939 there had been discussions on the best way in which Scouting could make use of the increasing interest boys were showing in the aeroplane. An Airman badge had, in fact, been instituted before the First World War; this was not unconnected with the fact that B.-P.'s younger brother, Major Baden Baden-Powell, was an enthusiastic aeronaut, just as Sea Scouting owed much to the eldest brother, Warington. The Second World War stimulated the desire for something more definite than a single badge. In November 1940 it was decided to form an Air Scout branch. This at once proved popular under the excitement of war conditions, and provided a preliminary canter for boys who were too young to join the Government-sponsored Air Training Corps. Just as Sea Scouts have a distinctive uniform—dark-blue shirt or jersey and a blue-jacket's cap—so the Air Scouts were given their own colour, grey and a dark-blue beret. An attractive *Air Scout's Handbook* was a popular publication.

The census figures for Air Scouts for the United Kingdom show that the war-time enthusiasm did not last.

1941	5,736
1943	8,498
1945	6,694
1946	5,941

Quite apart from the passing stimulus of the war, the decline is not surprising. Air Scouts have problems of the same character as Sea Scouts. A boy will not be satisfied with being an Air Scout if he rarely gets into an aeroplane, just as a Sea Scout is an anomaly unless he has the use of a boat. Both branches will probably remain small in comparison with the total membership of the Movement, but they are important for holding boys whose interests are specialized in one or other of these two directions.

Another war-time expedient must be recorded. The Scouts' Defence Corps of 1914–18 had its parallel in the organization of War Service Scouts formed in 1942. The intention was to give, in keeping with the spirit of the times, energetic and strenuous activities for Scouts over 15. This might, it was felt, provide something for those too young to join one of the official preservice organizations set up by the Government. It was inevitable that these new units for young fellows would attract many away from Scouting; the call for getting as fit as possible for active service was strong, and the facilities offered were considerable—free uniform (Scouts had to give up clothing coupons for theirs) and service equipment and instructors were all there. The Association put no obstacle in the way of Scouts joining one or other of these formations, but it wished to provide something for Scouts who still preferred to train as Scouts. The *War Service Handbook* provided a working programme; it is interesting to note that it had a large sale amongst members of the Home Guard and of the Army Cadets. There was considerable initial enthusiasm for this new branch, but the numbers were never very great and the scheme was limited to certain areas where the right kind of leader was available. With the end of the war this branch died and dropped off. It had an important influence on the development of Senior Scouts; this will be discussed in later pages, but the experience gained with War Service Scouts was of value.

The Chief Scout was in Kenya when war broke out. He was anxious to return home so that he might do what he could to help the Movement in the ordeal of war. His doctors persuaded him to remain 'in the Africa we love', as he put it, and from there his 'Outlooks' in *The Scouter*, his articles in *The Scout*, and his tireless correspondence brought encouragement to all. He was seriously ill in the autumn of 1940, but a recovery raised hopes that he would regain a measure of strength, then came a relapse. He died on 8 January 1941. On 22 February he would have been eighty-four years old.

Although all knew that, inevitably, a few years must bring the end, the death of B.-P. came as a shock to the Scout world. The German propaganda declared that the Boy Scouts had been one of the most subtle methods of the British Secret Service! It was not possible for Scouts in the occupied countries to express publicly all that the news meant to them, but they devised their own ways of mourning their loss. In Holland, for instance, a photograph of B.-P. was secretly printed on a small card with a prayer on the back, and copies were circulated amongst the Scouts. It was not until after liberation that these followers of B.-P. were allowed to see the message he left to all Boy Scouts.

To Boy Scouts:

Dear Scouts,—If you have ever seen the play *Peter Pan* you will remember how the pirate chief was always making his dying speech because he was afraid that possibly when the time came for him to die he might not have time to get it off his chest. It is much the same with me, and so, although I am not at this moment dying, I shall be doing so one of these days and I want to send you a parting word of goodbye.

Remember, it is the last you will ever hear from me, so think it over.

I have had a most happy life and I want each one of you to have as happy a life too.

I believe that God put us in this jolly world to be happy and enjoy life. Happiness doesn't come from being rich, nor merely from being successful in your career, nor by self-indulgence. One step towards happiness is to make yourself healthy and strong while you are a boy, so that you can *be useful* and so can enjoy life when you are a man.

Nature study will show you how full of beautiful and wonderful things God has made the world for you to enjoy. Be contented with what you have got and make the best of it. Look on the bright side of things instead of the gloomy one.

But the real way to get happiness is by giving out happiness to other people. Try and leave this world a little better than you found it and when your turn comes to die, you can die happy in feeling that at any rate you have not wasted your time but have *done your best*. 'Be Prepared' in this way, to live happy and to die happy—stick to your Scout promise always—even after you have ceased to be a boy—and God help you to do it.

Your Friend,
Baden-Powell.

The authorities offered burial in Westminster Abbey. His last resting-place would have been between the tomb of the Unknown Warrior and that of David Livingstone, the great African explorer; nearby rests his godfather Robert Stephenson, the engineer, who gave his name to Robert Stephenson Smyth Baden-Powell. The difficulties of war-time made that burial impossible. A Memorial Service was held in the Abbey on 27 January and was attended by representatives of the King and the British Government, including C. R. Attlee (Deputy Prime Minister), by Ambassadors and Ministers of other countries, and by many distinguished men and women. For reasons of security it was not possible to announce publicly the place and time of the service, but Scouts and Guides were there to do honour to their Founder.

The funeral at Nyeri characterized those two lives of which he frequently spoke—the soldier and the scout; the body was escorted by officers of the highest rank in Kenya, with men drawn from regiments representative of Africa and of the services; four Rover Scouts and four non-commissioned officers were bearers. Scouts of many races—European, African, and Indian—were there as representatives of the millions of men and women, boys and girls, who owed him so much happiness. A reporter noted that 'not only the Governor-Generals, distinguished South African officers, but humble Kikuyu piccanins in Scout uniforms and Indian Wolf Cubs in fezzes stood silent at his last resting place'. So, even in the midst of the greatest of all wars, it was possible to bring together an assembly typical of the varied peoples who meet under the flags of the Scouts and the Guides.

The death of its Founder marked the end of an epoch in the Scout Movement. For a generation he had been its inspiration and guide. His life had been extended beyond expectation, and the fact that it closed at the darkest period of war for a time veiled the significance of his passing. It was not until the war was over that his followers saw more clearly all that the loss of his personal influence entailed. The consolation was that he had chosen as his successor a man who had quickly won the confidence and loyalty of all as Deputy Chief Scout. Unhappily the second Chief Scout died before the war was over—a brief three years of office. The problem of maintaining the tradition was thus intensified.

CHAPTER TWENTY-SIX

THE SECOND CHIEF SCOUT

AT THE COUNCIL MEETING ON 29 JANUARY 1941, LORD SOMERS WAS invited to assume the position of Chief Scout. He had entered the Movement in 1920 as a District Commissioner. Six years later he went to Australia as Governor of Victoria; as Chief Scout of that State he took a vigorous part in Scouting and continued his interest when Acting Governor-General of Australia and Chief Scout of the Dominion in 1930–1. A visit of B.-P. to Australia in 1931 brought the two men together, and the Chief Scout of the World was quick to see that Lord Somers was not a nominal Chief Scout of Australia but was a whole-hearted enthusiast who went hiking in the bush with Rovers and camping with Scouts. This enthusiasm found many outlets when Lord Somers returned to England, and it was in 1936 that B.-P. invited him to become Deputy Chief Scout. He headed the British Scouts attending the Jamboree in Holland in 1937, and in the following year took over the direction of the Appeal for the Scout Fund. He went through the training course at Gilwell Park, and later qualified for the Wood badge. His many visits to Scout rallies and camps and his presence at the Rover Moot in 1939 soon proved that B.-P. had chosen wisely, and this impression was deepened when Lord Somers became Chief Scout. In spite of ill health, he carried out exhausting Scout tours until failing strength made it impossible for him to do more.

The Movement lost a steadfast friend by the death of the Duke of Connaught in January 1942; he had been President of the Association since 1913. His place was taken by the Duke of Gloucester.

A Memorial Fund for B.-P. was launched on St. George's Day 1942; this was not a public appeal but a 'family affair' restricted to Scouts and others closely associated with the Movement. The intention was to have a B.-P. House in London as a meeting-place for Scouts and Scouters of all Scout countries; the need for this had long been felt and it was thought that there could be no more fitting memorial of the Founder than a centre of this kind. By the end of the war the sum of £130,000 had been contributed; this, for the time being, was invested in National Savings Bonds. It was hoped that action could be taken soon after the end of the war, but three more years of bombing resulted in so much destruction that the scheme had to be postponed indefinitely.

As part of the proposed memorial to B.-P. it is intended that the present contents of B.-P.'s Room at Headquarters should be removed to the House to more spacious quarters. Before he left for Kenya in 1937, B.-P. handed over to the Association a considerable collection of mementoes and trophies connected with his own life as a soldier and as Chief Scout. These were displayed in the former Council Chamber which was renamed 'B.-P.'s Room'. For the war period the most valuable of these exhibits, including the Jagger portrait, were removed to safety, but enough were left to attract Scouts and Scouters; during August 1943, for instance, 2,251 visitors signed the book. The room gained in significance by becoming a favourite meeting-place during the war. It was the headquarters of the Canadian Overseas Rover Crew, and Norwegian Scouts met there from time to time. Every month saw a gathering of representatives of the countries with war-time organizations in this country. This was an informal meeting under the leadership of the Director of the International Bureau or of the International Commissioner of Great Britain. On each occasion news was passed round that had been gleaned from various sources of how Scouting was being kept alive in the occupied countries; sometimes a Scouter who had recently managed to get to England was able to tell a story of hazard and adventure. An inevitable subject of discussion was the future of the Movement in these countries. It was soon evident that the problem would not be to revive the Movement for it was clearly very much alive, but how to use this vigorous spirit to the best effect.

One future need was foreseen; copies of *Scouting for Boys* and of other handbooks would be urgently required to replace those destroyed. An edition of *Éclaireurs* (the French translation of *Scouting for Boys*) was published in London in 1942. Then

Canada offered to print other editions. Scout books in Polish, French, Czech, Norwegian, and Dutch were produced, and a total of 55,000 copies presented by the Boy Scouts of Canada. This was part of their 'B.-P. Chins-up Fund'; the fund reached 67,000 dollars by the end of the war. About half of this sum was sent to the 'War Distressed Scouts Fund' raised in Great Britain to relieve immediate distress caused by the war. The Boy Scouts of America (U.S.A.) had a World Friendship Fund; by means of this, 60,000 copies of the World Brotherhood edition of *Scouting for Boys* (the first published in the United States) and *Aids to Scoutmastership* were sent to other countries as soon as conditions made it practicable; material aid, such as uniforms and equipment, was sent to forty-five countries.

Another suggestion came from Canada; Great Britain was asked to send over four King's Scouts with first-hand experience in air raids to tour the Dominion. It was not easy to select four from the large number eligible, but at length one was taken from each of four towns—London, Southampton, Birkenhead, and Glasgow. The farewell tea-party at Headquarters included the Deputy Prime Minister (C. R. Attlee) and the High Commissioner for Canada (Vincent Massey). The Scouts arrived in Canada in the middle of April 1942 and began a tour that took them from the Atlantic to the Pacific. They were then invited to tour the United States and it was not until the end of September that they sailed for home. At the request of the Ministry of Information they then toured this country until the end of the year. These bare facts give no indication of the success of this valuable experiment; the official report records that 'the Scouts have done a big job well and remain the same normal fellows as when they left—a remarkable thing in view of the way both Canadians and Americans did all they could to spoil them'.

On 22 July 1942 H.M. the King paid a visit to Imperial Headquarters. He saw various exhibits illustrating Scout war service and a film 'Men of To-morrow' which recorded what was being done by the Scouts. Members of the Council and Staff were presented to His Majesty, and he also talked with representatives of Belgium, China, Czechoslovakia, France, Holland, Luxembourg, Norway, Poland, and the United States.

One of the most important steps taken by Lord Somers as

Chief Scout was the appointment in May 1941 of a Commission 'to make recommendations to the Committee of the Council as to the post-war development of the Scout Movement'.

The Commission consisted of twenty-six members drawn from varying types of area throughout the country and of a diversity of Scouting experience. The first meeting was held in July 1941 when the members split up into nine committees to collect and study facts and opinions. Correspondence was invited and for the next six months these committees were busy analysing the six hundred letters received, carrying out personal inquiries, and interviewing Scouters. A preliminary Report was published in *The Scouter* in July 1942 as a basis for further discussion. Over 140 local conferences were held up and down the country during the next twelve months to consider this Report. This period fortunately came at a time when great numbers of Scouters in the Services were stationed in Great Britain for training; as a result no conference was an entirely local affair, for at each were visiting Scouters whose experience had been in other, and perhaps very different, districts. This gave a valuable breadth to the discussions. A Committee was set up to consider the reports of these conferences and the considerable correspondence the suggestions had stimulated; sometimes adverse comments were strongly expressed, but generally the discussions showed a serious desire to further the progress of the Movement. There was a further pause to allow time for Service Scouters in distant places and for the Dominions and Colonies to express their views.

The final decisions taken by the Committee of the Council were not published until September 1945, but it will be convenient to consider the most important of them here although chronologically it takes us beyond Lord Somers's period as Chief Scout.

At the outset the Commission laid it down that

> The carrying out of the Law and Promise should be regarded as the distinguishing mark of a Scout; and in particular more attention should be given to the importance of making Duty to God the inspiration of our work.

It reaffirmed that

> The Patrol System is fundamental in the Scout Troop and should be applied throughout the Movement.

In re-stating these principles the Commission was indicating clearly that, whatever modifications in structure changing conditions might require, there was not the slightest need for altering the basis on which B.-P. had built the Movement.

Various details of adjustments in organization need not detain us; these come in every Movement from time to time. When the Commission came to study the sections, there was nothing substantial to suggest as far as Wolf Cubs were concerned; for Scouts the main decisions were that the tests for Tenderfoot, Second Class, and First Class should be revised, and that a scheme for Senior Scouts was necessary. After much discussion the tests were revised in the following terms:

TENDERFOOT

1. *Preliminary*

Know the Scout Law and Promise, and their meaning in accordance with his age;

the salute as explained in Camp Fire Yarn 3 of *Scouting for Boys*; and

the composition of the Union Flag, and how to hoist, break, and fly it.

2. *Health*

Clean a wound, and make and apply a dressing.

3. *Observation*

Make the woodcraft signs given in Camp Fire Yarn 4 of *Scouting for Boys*.

4. *Pioneering*

Demonstrate with rope how to tie the following knots: reef, sheet-bend, clove-hitch, bowline, round turn and two half-hitches, sheepshank, and explain their uses. Whip the end of a rope.

SECOND CLASS

Before being awarded the Second Class badge, the Scout must pass the following tests:

1. *Preliminary*

Must be able to re-pass the Tenderfoot Tests.

2. *Health*

(*a*) Show how to deal with the following common minor accidents:

Minor cuts and scratches.

Sprains.

Bruises.

Bleeding from the nose.

Stings and bites.

Burns and scalds.

Know how to avoid sunburning and the importance of doing so.

Demonstrate the use of the triangular bandage as a sling.

Demonstrate how to summon help and to treat for shock (not electric).

(*b*) Know the general rules of health as given in Camp Fire Yarn 18 of *Scouting for Boys*.

(*c*) Demonstrate the Six Exercises described in Camp Fire Yarn 17 of *Scouting for Boys*.

3. *Observation*

(*a*) Kim's Game. Describe, in writing, 16 out of 24 well-assorted articles following one minute's observation, or follow a trail half a mile long containing not less than 30 woodcraft signs, in 25 minutes.

(*b*) Be able to recognize and name, from a list submitted by the Scout, six common trees, and know the values of their woods for fires.

4. *Pioneering*

(*a*) Tie the following knots and know their uses—timber-hitch and fisherman's. Demonstrate square and diagonal lashings by constructing a trestle of Scout staffs.

(*b*) Know the safety rules and care of a hand-axe and knife. Demonstrate how to chop firewood.

5. *Signalling*

Know the Morse or Semaphore sign for every letter in the alphabet and for the numerals—also the table of Miscellaneous Signals in Camp Fire Yarn 7 of *Scouting for Boys*.

Be able to send and receive a simple message accurately out of doors.

6. *Exploring*
    (*a*) Know the 16 points of the compass and how to set a map.
    (*b*) Lay and light a fire out of doors, with natural materials, using two matches only; cook over this fire porridge for two, and a twist or damper.

7. *Public Service*
    (*a*) Show that he understands the Highway Code

Paras. 1, 2, 4, 5, 6, and 7	(To all road-users).
Paras. 9–21	(To all pedestrians).
Paras. 62–75	(To cyclists).

    (*b*) If he has the use of a bicycle, demonstrate that he is keeping it properly maintained and that he is able to effect minor repairs.

FIRST CLASS

Before being awarded the First Class badge, a Second Class Scout must pass the following tests:

1. *Preliminary*
    (*a*) Must be able to re-pass the Second Class Tests.
    (*b*) Must have camped, as a Scout, for a total of 10 nights before completing his First Class Tests. One week-end camp, at least, must be included in the total.

2. *Health*
    (*a*) Demonstrate the proper method of dealing with the following emergencies—fire, drowning, ice-breaking, and electric shock.
    (*b*) Know the position of the main arteries and how to stop external bleeding from veins and arteries.
    Demonstrate how to deal with fractures of the collar-bone, arm, and fore-arm. Understand the importance of not moving other suspected fractures.
    Demonstrate the use of the triangular bandage as applied to the knee, head, and foot.
    Demonstrate how to deal with shock at all stages.
    (*c*) Swim 50 yards. If a doctor certifies that bathing is dangerous to a boy's health, the latter must, instead of this, pass one of the following badges: Camper, Handyman, Woodcraftsman, Naturalist, Backwoodsman, Pioneer, Stalker, Tracker, Starman, or Astronomer. The County Commissioner may allow a Scout to gain the First Class badge without passing the Swimming Test, provided he is satisfied that it is not practicable for the Scout to obtain facilities for learning to swim, and that the

HEADQUARTERS GENERAL PURPOSES COMMITTEE, *c.* 1924
Left to right: Lord Meath, C. Dymoke Green, Ernest Young, P. B. Nevill, Admiral Sir Bertram B. Thesiger, Sir Percy Everett, N. D. Power, Hubert Martin

ROLAND HOUSE, STEPNEY

GILWELL PARK: THE TRAINING GROUND

THE SCOUT CHALET, KANDERSTEG, IN 1924

Scout under 15 gains the Jobman badge and the Scout over 15 the Handyman badge as an alternative. The Scout should make every effort to pass the swimming test as soon as possible.

3. *Observation*

(*a*) Read the meaning of a series of simple tracks made in sandy or other suitable ground. These should include running, limping, carrying a weight, walking backwards, and blind gaits.

(*b*) Be able to recognize and name, from lists submitted by the Scout, 12 common trees and 6 common birds.

(*c*) Using improvised apparatus, such as a Scout staff, estimate three distances not more than half a mile, and three heights not more than 100 feet. In each case the estimate to be within 10 per cent. error above or below the actual.

4. *Pioneering*

(*a*) Demonstrate the following: sheerlashing; back- and eye-splice; fireman's chair knot; man-harness knot; rolling-hitch.

(*b*) Use a felling axe for felling or trimming light timber, or, if this is impracticable, be able to log up a piece of timber and demonstrate the theory of felling a tree.

5. *Signalling*

Send and receive a message out of doors, either in Semaphore at rate four (20 letters a minute), or in Morse at rate three (15 letters a minute). He must also understand the alphabetical check for numerals. Where it is desired to pass the test in Morse by buzzer, the test may be taken indoors provided the sender and receiver are out of sight of each other.

6. *Exploring*

(*a*) Read and be able to use a one-inch Ordnance Survey map (or its local equivalent). Use a compass and point out a compass direction by day or night without the aid of a compass.

(*b*) Go on foot, alone or with another Scout, a 24-hour journey of at least 14 miles. In the course of the journey he must cook his own meals, one of which must include meat, over a wood fire in the open; find his camp site and camp for the night. He must carry out any instructions given by the Examiner as to things to be observed en route.

A Sea Scout may do this journey partly by water and partly by land—at least 5 miles of the 14 to be done on foot. This test should be taken last.

7. *Public Service*

(*a*) Have a comprehensive knowledge of the Highway Code, including appendices and supplementary notes, and be able to answer any questions and give demonstrations in relation to any part in it.

(*b*) Demonstrate the principles of controlling traffic.

(*c*) If he has the use of a bicycle, demonstrate that he is keeping it properly maintained and that he is able to effect all reasonable repairs.

(*d*) Understand the procedure for reporting road accidents.

If these requirements are compared with those given in Chapter 7, it will be seen that the main pattern was retained but that adjustments were made to meet present-day needs. This is a good illustration of how Scouting can change the details of training without altering the fundamental principles and methods. Conditions that were suited to the standards of education of 1907 are no longer applicable to those that may now be reasonably expected of the normal boy. It should also be noted that a boy of 15 or 16 who gains the First Class badge has demonstrated an all-round capacity that is an asset to any community.

Before passing on to consider the Commission's proposals for Senior Scouts and for the training of Scouters, something must be said of the special conditions that made both problems matters of urgency.

At the end of 1939 the Board of Education (as the Ministry was then called) issued a circular to Local Education Authorities on the subject of the 'Service of Youth'—a somewhat vague label for the rising interest in the training of young fellows between the ages of 15 and 18. The Board asked that Youth Committees should be set up to promote the welfare of this group of young people. The introduction of an Education Bill (the Act of 1944) raising the school-leaving age to 15 (later 16), and proposing to establish county colleges for part-time education between this age and that of 18, further emphasized the need to review the position of Scouting in the new plan. Public discussions soon revealed that the training of leaders would be of first importance. It was therefore essential that the Scout Movement should make sure that the training it provided for

Scouters should be of high quality and fully suited to the new conditions. Clearly the matter could not be postponed until after the war for training colleges were already organizing courses for Youth Leaders.

It was with this need in mind that Lord Somers decided to take immediate steps to ensure that as much training as possible should be done during the war and that plans for extension should be prepared in readiness for the post-war period. At the end of 1942 J. S. Wilson intimated that he would resign his position as Camp Chief at the end of the war in order to concentrate on his work as Director of the International Bureau. Lord Somers then appointed R. F. Thurman as prospective Camp Chief. The pressure of the campaign for the Service of Youth increased; it died down very suddenly after the war, but at the time it seemed that Scouting would need to rally all its powers to maintain its position as a leading voluntary organization. So in July 1943 Lord Somers decided that R. F. Thurman's prospective appointment must be made substantive, and J. S. Wilson resigned the position of Camp Chief he had held since 1923. The Chief Scout's tribute to him should be recorded:

> Apart from the old Chief, our Founder, there is no name better known in the Scouting world, and the high standards he set are the standards accepted by his training team throughout. These standards were high because his own standard was high, and that, I think, is probably the secret of the immense influence for good he had with all who came under him.

Here a digression is necessary. R. F. Thurman came prominently to notice as the outstanding member of the first group of six Field Commissioners appointed in May 1942. The duties of these experienced Scouters may be regarded as an extension of the work of Travelling Commissioners; the latter, as has been already explained, spent a short period in a county or district where they could be of service in suggesting ways of improving organization and of raising the standard of Scouting. The Field Commissioners (it was originally proposed to call them Development Commissioners) were not to be peripatetic, but were to settle for a period of years in a county, or at a convenient centre for a group of counties, and be at the service of the County Commissioners to whom they were responsible though at the same time being members of the Headquarters staff. Within a few months of the beginning of the scheme it was evident that it served a valuable purpose; it may be noted, for instance, that a more thorough knowledge of the actual state of Scouting became available through their direct observations than had previously been obtainable. The post of Travelling Commissioner was not abolished; Rex Hazlewood, who later became editor of *The Scouter*, was appointed to this position in January 1942.

The President of the Board of Education appointed a Youth Advisory Council in 1942 to survey the needs of this new field of interest. R. F. Thurman was chosen as representative of the Boy Scouts Association, and he was thus in a central position at a critical period to share in the important deliberations of a Council that included leading men and women of the various organizations concerned with the training and welfare of young people.

If we add to his experience as a Field Commissioner and as a member of this Advisory Council, his practical knowledge as a Scoutmaster and as a Deputy Camp Chief, it will be seen that R. F. Thurman's appointment as Camp Chief was well founded.

We must now return to the Report of the Commission on Post-war Scouting. It contained the following passage on the training of Scouters:

> A quarter of a century has passed since Gilwell Park came into the possession of the Association and B.-P. started the regular training of Scouters. The scheme he then drew up, and the principles and methods he devised for carrying it into practice, have proved an invaluable aid to thousands of Scouters not only in this country but in the Empire and in other countries. It is gratifying that after so many years the system of Wood Badge training calls for no substantial change; some details have, of course, had to be altered to meet new conditions and fresh developments within the Movement, but the system as a whole stands firm. It is quite true to say that a man or woman can be a good Scouter without training—otherwise the Movement could not have got established—but it is equally true to say that the best Scouter will benefit from a training course, and those who are less efficient, or find it more difficult to grasp the principles and methods of Scouting, gain immeasurably. Moreover, it should be remembered that Gilwell Park and other training camps have become clearing houses for ideas, and all who go through these courses have at their disposal a store of experience which they would otherwise miss.

It is now necessary to make the courses more accessible to a larger number of Scouters, and to provide a greater variety of kinds of courses to suit different stages of the Scouter's life in the Movement.

The Report then discussed the various means for extending the range of training both in character and in appeal. It was, for instance, suggested that there should be explanatory courses suitable for the information of Youth Leaders; after the war a series of such courses was given at teachers' training colleges and similar institutions, the purpose being not so much to win new Scouters as to make sure of the principles and methods being understood. A considerable development was also proposed in preliminary courses for new Scouters or for those who were hesitating about becoming Scouters; these would provide guidance in first principles as a foundation for work with a Group and as a foundation for later Wood-badge training. Such courses proved popular after the war; their direction was placed in the hands of the county training team who organized courses at local centres to meet the needs of men and women who could give only spare time to Scouting. The basis of the syllabus was the old District Training Course which had been placed in the hands of the District Commissioners, but the new method of giving responsibility to the training team proved more successful in increasing the number of courses.

On the subject of the older Scout the Report said:

The Commission quickly found that, above all others, the question of how to retain the older boy was occupying the minds of thoughtful Scouters. It was realised that far too many Boy Scouts leave the Troop round about the age of 14 or 15; in 1941 there were no exact statistics of the position. The figures as at 31st March, 1943, and 1944, were as follows:—

	31st March, 1944.	*31st March, 1943.*
Scouts under 14	140,100	141,640
,, 14–15	36,281	58,594
,, 15 and over	32,409	

This is not a new story, but an old one, and the past volumes of *The Scouter* bear witness to the amount of uneasiness felt at what was usually termed 'leakage'. The Service of Youth scheme brought the matter to a head. It was disturbing, for instance, to be told by those officially concerned that Boy Scouts are all right for young boys, but that with those between the ages of 15 and 18, the Movement is less successful; it was implied and sometimes said, that we could therefore, not be of much use in the Service of Youth. Some Scouters have always been able to hold a fair proportion of their older boys but, unfortunately, they are in the minority.

In his 'Outlook' in *The Scouter* for August, 1943, Lord Somers wrote: 'I had quite a few talks with the old Chief before he left on his last journey to Kenya, and he was puzzled a lot as to what we could do to retain the older boy. His experience, which I have had since, showed what a splendid type First Class and King's Scouts are, fine, manly fellows and reliable in every way, and we both agreed what a lamentable thing it was that every Scout did not stick it until he reached that rung of the ladder. . . . There is one thing I am certain about, and that is that we must definitely recognise that a boy becomes a senior at a certain age, and if he has to spend his Scout life almost entirely with the younger boys of the Troop he will in nearly every case lose interest, gradually adopt the pace of the younger boys, or leave the Troop.'

Few aspects of Scouting have occasioned so much argument as this problem of retaining the older boy. As we have seen, it was lurking in the background during the period between the wars, and various suggestions were put forward as solutions of the enigma. Looking back now we can see how unfortunate it was that B.-P.'s Senior Scout scheme of 1916 (to begin at the age of 15) was never implemented. The Rover scheme (to begin at the age of 17) supplanted B.-P.'s idea, and it was a pity that he gave way to the opinions of his advisors; his genuine modesty proved, in this case, a misfortune.

The Commission reviewed the efforts that had been made to retain the older Scout; there was, for instance, the long campaign to stimulate an increase in the number qualifying as First Class Scouts; it was a hard-fought battle, and the gains were a poor return for the efforts made.

The Service of Youth project gave a shock to those who still felt that no change was needed, but that all would come right with more trained Scouters to produce more First Class Scouts. They were horrified to find that many educationalists and others engaged in training young people did not regard the Boy Scouts as an organization seriously concerned with adolescents. This attitude could not be dismissed as due entirely to the word 'Boy'; it was common knowledge that boys did tend to leave many Troops when they left school for work: this was just the period when the steadying influence of Scouting was most needed. The figures quoted above from the final Report (1945) were not available when the Commission was sitting, but they confirmed only too thoroughly the general impression.

A committee of the Commission drafted a scheme that was published in *The Scouter* in May 1943 and discussed at a County Commissioners' Conference that July. As a result of the criticisms received (some rather violent) the original suggestions were modified and the scheme made permissive and experimental. It was not until October 1946 that the Senior Scout section became a part of the Boy Scout system.

Certain important principles may be noted:

1. At 15 a Boy Scout becomes a Senior Scout and his status as such must be recognized by special training, preferably in a Patrol of Senior Scouts.
2. A suitable Scouter must be appointed whose sole concern is the Senior Scouts. This recognized the fact that it is only the exceptional man who is as successful with boys of the adolescent stage as with younger boys. Such exceptional men have always held their older Scouts, but their rarity is one explanation for the loss of older Scouts from most Troops. Hitherto, only one Scout in five has remained after the age of 15.
3. The first aim of the Senior Scout is the First Class badge, if he has not already got it; next the Bushman's Thong (for such subjects as camping, forestry, tracking, pioneering, naturalist), or the parallel award for Sea Scouts or Air Scouts. He should also qualify for the King's Scout badge (public service qualifications). This badge has been given additional significance since 1947 by the award of a certificate bearing the King's signature in facsimile, and by being personally presented by the Chief Scout.
4. All Proficiency badges have been revised and grouped in two series: one for Scouts under 15 and the other for those over 15. The purpose is to stimulate the older boy to reach a higher standard in his special interests and hobbies.

All this presupposes that the Senior Scout programme will

appeal to the older boy by reason of its demands on his skill, intelligence, resourcefulness, and sense of adventure. As an example the requirements for the Venturer badge may be quoted:

1. Make a journey of at least 20 miles on foot or by boat, with not more than two other Scouts. Route must be one with which the Scout is not familiar and should, if possible, include stiff country. Sleep out, using only kit carried in rucksack. Maximum weight 30 lbs., which must include food.

2. Complete an adventure journey as a member of a Patrol in which he shall play a leading part. The journey, which may be short in length, must include at least five 'incidents' such as rescues from fire or heights, compass work, night work, decoding. Water incidents to be included by Sea Scout Troops.

3. Be reasonably proficient in two of the following. Each of the two must be selected from *different* groups, as under:

(*a*) Boxing, fencing, wrestling.
(*b*) Rowing, riding, skating.
(*c*) Swimming, diving.
(*d*) Gymnastics, tumbling.
(*e*) Marksmanship, rock climbing, ropespinning.

4. Must be able to perform four of the following:

(*a*) Climb a tree to a height of 30 feet from the ground.
(*b*) Vault a fence two-thirds his own height.
(*c*) Throw a 60-foot line to fall between two pegs 4 feet apart at a distance of 50 feet, twice out of every three times.
(*d*) Swim 20 yards wearing clothes.
(*e*) Pole jump across a distance equal to his own height.
(*f*) Climb a rope to a height of 15 feet from the ground.

Some years must pass before the effectiveness of this scheme can be assessed. The signs are encouraging: the total numbers in this age-group increased by an average of about 2,000 a year for the three years 1945, 1946, and 1947.

During this period there were some Headquarters appointments that should be recorded. Great pleasure was given to the Movement when Sir Percy Everett became Deputy Chief Scout in November 1941. E. J. Bunbury became Treasurer of the

Association in July 1942 in succession to Sir James Leigh-Wood. J. F. Colquhoun was appointed Deputy Chief Commissioner and Chairman of the General Purposes Committee in 1943. Then in September 1943 T. G. Bincham became International Commissioner in place of R. A. Frost, who had succeeded Hubert Martin in 1938. The new International Commissioner soon communicated something of his own generous enthusiasm to this aspect of Scouting.

In April 1944 Lord Hampton resigned from the position of Chief Commissioner after twenty-four years of valuable service. Anyone who wishes to understand something of the inner spirit of Scouting could not do better than read Lord Hampton's *Scouting Sketches* in which he has embodied some of his own experiences as a Scoutmaster and Commissioner. Brigadier W. E. Clark was appointed Acting Chief Commissioner in May 1944.

Lord Somers did not live to see the end of the war. The illness that was to prove fatal slowly sapped his strength and he had reluctantly to give up the tours that brought so much encouragement to Scouts and Scouters in anxious days. His last 'Outlook' appeared in *The Scouter* in February 1944; he died on 14 July of that year. His loss was a heavy blow to Scouting; B.-P. died full of years and with his work accomplished; the successor he had chosen quickly won the loyalty and affection of the Movement and his decisions and actions as Chief Scout were based on a full appreciation of the principles and methods of the Founder.

No immediate successor was available.

⚜ ⚜ ⚜ ⚜ ⚜ ⚜ ⚜ ⚜ ⚜ ⚜ ⚜ ⚜ ⚜ ⚜ ⚜ ⚜ ⚜

CHAPTER TWENTY-SEVEN

FORTY YEARS AFTER BROWNSEA

IN THE SPRING OF 1944 THREE SCOUTERS LEFT THIS COUNTRY FOR the Middle East; they were the first of the members of the Scouts International Relief Service to go into the field. It was natural that the idea of doing something to relieve distress after the war should have arisen in the minds of many Scouters, and towards the end of 1942 the first steps were taken; a register was compiled of those who wished to volunteer for this service. There were many problems to face; how were men and women to get released for this work? Where was the money to come from? Would support be given by the Government? For months these and similar questions were discussed and negotiations, in co-operation with other societies, carried on with the authorities. It did not prove possible to get the numbers of men and women who could have been used; this was not for lack of volunteers, but simply because they could not be spared from essential work. The problem of funds was solved more easily than had been anticipated. The War Distressed Scouts Fund was ear-marked for Scout purposes; the Relief Service was not meant for the help of Scouts but for civilians. The new fund was raised in one day (20 May 1944) by Scouts doing odd jobs of work and sending in the money they earned. The organizers hoped for £10,000, and thought this was optimistic; actually £32,000 was raised, a proof that the object of the fund made a strong appeal to the boys.

This Relief Service lasted for just over two years; ninety-three Scouters took part, twenty-six of them being women. Service was rendered in Palestine, Syria, Cyprus, Greece, Yugoslavia, Italy, Egypt, France, Holland, and Germany; a team of five was sent out to Hong Kong at the end of 1945. The work varied in character according to the need and the Scouters had to adapt themselves to all kinds of situations at short notice. There was refugee welfare to supervise, hospital supplies to transport and distribute as well as food and clothing, and the care of camps for displaced persons. Much of this work was done long before U.N.R.R.A. teams were in the field and there was a constant call on initiative and resourcefulness as well as patience and cheerfulness.

Although this work had no direct concern with the Boy Scouts of the countries where the teams were stationed, there was much useful linking-up done and, when opportunities came, the Scouters did all they could to encourage and help the Scouts to re-organize themselves after their years of suppression. Few experiences were more enheartening, for instance, than those of the first team to land on the Normandy beaches in early September 1944; almost at once French Scouts came forward to help and to enjoy meeting again their comrades from Great Britain. As that team worked through northern France, helping with the evacuation of the old and the sick during truces at Calais and Dunkirk, and right on into Holland, so they found to their delight that Scouting was still flourishing in spite of prohibitions. They learned, too, of how Scouters had been sent to concentration camps or to forced labour and some to death.

The greatest part of the work was with the displaced persons in Germany. Teams were stationed at former concentration camps such as Dalum or Belsen; their function was to encourage these unhappy people to develop some kind of community life; the distribution and control of supplies was an important task, but the hardest work was to help these people without a country to win back their self-respect and their sense of responsibility. Unofficial Scout Troops were organized as well as clubs for the young people and social life for all.

When the time came to wind up the Relief Service after it had finished its first-aid job of carrying on until the official organization could get to work, some of the members joined the U.N.R.R.A. service and their experience proved of considerable value.

At the end of 1944 Gilwell Park was handed back to the Scouts. Much hard work had to be done to get it ready for the camping and training season of 1945, but there were many willing helpers and within a few months order had been restored, and by the end of the war Gilwell was again itself. Since then the training and the camping have flourished to the benefit of the Movement.

Meanwhile a successor to Lord Somers had been found in Lord Rowallan. He had started his Scouting as County Commissioner for Ayrshire in 1925, and he had been appointed President of the Scottish Scout Council in 1939. The Council of the Association invited him to become Chief Scout at its meeting on 22 February (B.-P.'s birthday) 1945. He went through the Wood-badge course at Gilwell that summer, and with his tours of Canada and West Africa in 1946 he renewed that personal association between Great Britain and the Commonwealth and Empire that B.-P. had done so much to strengthen.

Gradually Scouting got into its stride again; there were many difficulties; uniforms and equipment were difficult to get and were expensive. Group huts and headquarters had suffered from bombing or from requisitioning. Valuable gear such as tents had often been destroyed or seriously damaged. These limitations had their good effect; they compelled many a Group to return to the simple Scouting of earlier days when there were no enterprising firms to tempt Scouts to clutter themselves with elaborate equipment. Great as this difficulty was in this country, it was, of course, far more serious in those countries that had been occupied. Mention has already been made of the aid that came from Canada and the United States; all helped where they could, and true Scouting did not suffer.

The suggestions of the Commission on post-war Scouting that had been approved were one by one put into effect. The Commission had not reached any decisions about the future of the Rover section. Its report contains the following paragraph:

One of the most encouraging features of war-time Scouting has been the formation and success of Service Rover Crews. They have done much to bring together Scouters, Rovers and former Scouts now in the Services, and in Prisoner of War Camps. Some have carried on their excellent work for several years. Many of the members are eager to take up warrants when they return home, but others will look forward to being Rover Scouts. It is impossible to predict the circumstances under which Rovering will have to operate after the war. As long as there is a need for active service, or for occupation duties, many of our young fellows will remain in, or be conscripted for, the Forces. For them, everything possible must be done so that they may have vigorous Service Crews to help them. Some of those who return after discharge may be crippled or suffering; they will need all our sympathy and good-fellowship. Others will have to resume interrupted training for livelihoods; yet others will go through one of the courses for the training of ex-service men which the authorities are now planning. In such a complex situation there can be no simple solution. The Committee is, therefore, of the opinion that the Rover scheme of the future must be as elastic as possible in order to meet these varying needs. It has, therefore, appointed a Rover Advisory Panel to make recommendations.

The Advisory Panel brought out its plan in 1946 and this was accepted as a basis for development. The most important feature of this scheme is that it made a distinction between a Training Stage and a Senior Stage. The first ends for a Rover after about three years in the Crew 'but not later than his 25th birthday'. Here at last the crucial problem of age had been faced, and it was recognized that older men could not train with young fellows with any hope of carrying out a constructive programme. As with Senior Scouts, it is too early yet to judge how far this new plan will succeed; its working is complicated by the continuation of conscription; but Rover Crews in the Forces may well prove of increasing value.

Mention was earlier made of Scouting at the universities. Since the war this development has continued. Many universities can now have either Scout Clubs or Rover Crews. The position is explained in the following official statement.

The earlier student Scout organisations were Clubs, but the more recent pre-war ones were Rover Crews. Each group of students must decide upon the form of organisation most suitable in their circumstances. For instance, students who live at home are likely to have Scout obligations at home and little time to spare for Scouting at college. They may look for discussions rather than the practice of scoutcraft. Students at a residential college may feel the reverse. Again, the needs of postgraduates or students in training colleges and seminaries may differ; they may be tired of talk and want practical experience, or they may wish to test Scout practices in the light of their academic training.

The Scout Club and Rover Crew are not necessarily alternatives. At Oxford University the Scout Club includes a Rover Crew, while at Cambridge, the University Rovers arrange meetings of a club nature, and attract a high proportion of non-Scouts.

There are undoubtedly certain pitfalls to be avoided if it is decided to organise as a Rover Crew only:

1. The Rovers may become a sect of peculiar people, not attracting new men in as potential Scouters, and not being of sound propaganda value to the Movement.
2. The Rovers may remain overgrown boys rather than develop an adult outlook. Pre-war Rovers in Britain were apt to forget that their Boy Scout training had been a means to an end, not an end in itself, and that activities that should loom large in a boy's life can at most be hobbies in adult life. The post-war plan has given a new orientation to Rover Scouting, but it is too early to say how far this will affect Scouting in Universities.

The advantages of a Club are that it is the normal student organisation, and that it should more easily attract both old Scouts with little time and non-Scouts who wish to learn about Scouting. It need not be restricted to enrolled Scouts, and can include women members if desired. A happy solution seems to be a Rover Crew within the Scout Club, to provide practical activities and training in term-time for those who want it, and camping, etc., in vacations. It is, however, vital that the Rover Crew should be led by someone more experienced in life than the members themselves, and someone who will be available for several years, and who is *persona grata* with the college authorities. Without these conditions a Rover Crew may in the long run be a bad advertisement for Scouting.

An interesting development in the universities has been increasing co-operation between Scout Club and Guide Club; this may help to promote a more general working together than has, up to the present, marked these Movements that have a common Founder.

Mention has been made above of the Rover Advisory Panel. This method of mobilizing support has been extended to several sections of Scouting or to its aspects. Thus the Educational Panel and that for Religion have proved of great value; by the advice of the experts who serve on these, the Movement is kept in touch with living opinion and is more quickly stimulated to meet the needs of the times. The willingness of prominent men to serve the Movement in this way is in itself an encouragement quite apart from the value of their opinions and suggestions.

A fresh departure in Headquarters' policy was the beginning of a publishing department in 1946. The various handbooks by B.-P. and by Gilcraft have been published by established firms.

This has meant not only a loss of revenue but a limitation on style of production. The decision to publish its own books was a wise one for the Association, and promises well during its early experiments.

All through the war and with mounting enthusiasm afterwards Scouts were looking forward to the next World Jamboree. At the last an invitation had been accepted to hold the next in France in 1941. That date proved impossible, alas, but the French Scouts were determined that, whatever the year, the Sixth Jamboree would be held in their country. As the war clouds cleared, so hopes became brighter.

The International Committee met in London in November 1945 after an interval of six years. Prince Gustaf Adolf came from Sweden, Ove Holm from Denmark, General Lafont from France, Dr. James E. West from the United States, and Sir Alfred Pickford and Lord Hampton of Great Britain were also there with the Director, J. S. Wilson, and the Secretary, R. T. Lund. The Committee was received by H.M. King George VI. It was with mixed emotions that the Committee came together. They mourned the loss of the Founder and of those colleagues who had fallen in the war. There was encouragement in the news of how Scouting had more than survived in the occupied countries; most could report increasing membership. The Movement had been restarted in Austria and Greece, and even in Italy after being banned for eighteen years it had risen again.

It was agreed that the next Jamboree should be in France in 1947. Consideration was given to the position of Scouting in camps for displaced persons, and to its possible establishment in Germany. It was felt that much quiet preparatory work would be needed in that country before a genuinely indigenous Scout Movement could develop; an organization imposed by the victors would be doomed to failure and lead to a repetition of past difficulties. This policy was followed; it was not until 1947 that the first signs of real Scouting in Germany became noticeable. Some leaders were sent to Sweden or to Gilwell Park for preliminary training and to see Scouting in action. In the following year permission was given for the formation of Scout Troops as a controlled experiment, but several years must elapse before full recognition is possible.

The site of the Sixth Jamboree was at Moisson on the banks of the Seine about half-way between Paris and Rouen. An island in the river provided a Sea Scout base. Here on 9 August were gathered 24,000 Scouts from 70 different lands with some 200 guests from Displaced Persons Camps. The activities were much as at all Jamborees, but at Moisson there was a new feeling, difficult to define, but created by the knowledge that a dream had come true after the years of war and that Scouting was once more on the march. For the older men there was the joy of meeting old friends of whom nothing had been heard for years, but this was mingled with sorrow at news of how others had suffered and died.

It was the first Jamboree since B.-P.'s death, but the presence of his son, Peter, the second Lord Baden-Powell, and of the grandson, Robert, gave a feeling of continuity.

An observer's account of the last rally must suffice as a record.

When we arrived in the Arena we were puzzled at seeing a huge spherical balloon representing the world, and also at a number of wooden bridges which seemed to be placed according to no plan. Round the Arena stood the Scouts. Presently a line of Scouts representing the various countries made a human chain round the globe. Then they heaved it up and urged it forward to the waiting Scouts. It was then passed overhead right round the Arena. At first this World moved slowly, but gathered speed as the Scouts got the trick of passing it along. Afterwards crowds of Scouts dressed to represent the forces of evil attacked the World and were driven off by its defenders. Then followed the more formal part of the ceremony—the speeches of thanks and farewell. 'Auld lang syne' (which seems to have acquired international status) was sung with the vast gathering linked round the Arena.

Lastly came what proved to me to be the most impressive demonstration of the Jamboree—the march of the Scouts of the World. Now we saw the meaning of the bridges; they were so arranged that the Scouts marched along the pattern of a Carrick Bend, the symbol of the Jamboree. Just as the two ropes pass and re-pass over and under each other, so two columns of Scouts by marching over and under the bridges wove the pattern. The striking thing, however, was not the weaving of the knot but the number of different aspects of the marching Scouts—now being seen from the side, passing over one bridge or marching directly towards us over another; or passing over a bridge and then marching away from us. The total impression was of life and numbers; better than ever before we could realise what 24,000 Scouts mean in the mass.

There was an important symbolism that I hoped all understood. At the opening ceremony the Scouts had marched in by countries; at this closing ceremony each sub-camp was the unit, and bore at its head the many flags and banners of the Scouts of several countries who had been camping together and making friends during these days. This was a fitting conclusion of a gathering of Scouts of the World in a Jamboree of Peace.

The Eleventh International Conference followed the Moisson Jamboree. The census gave a total of 4,409,780 Scouts in forty-three recognized Associations; this was an increase of over a million members above the 1939 total in spite of the fact that the list of Associations no longer contained the names of Afghanistan, Bulgaria, Estonia, Iran, Iraq, Japan, Latvia, Lithuania, Poland, Siam, Spain, and Yugoslavia. Associations recognized for the first time or re-admitted were Austria, El Salvador, Haiti, Italy, Libya, Nicaragua, and the Philippines.

One of the most interesting topics discussed was that of Old Scouts; the following resolution was passed:

Recommends that member Associations should foster and inspire the mobilisation of the vast numbers of old Scouts and Scouters who have been members of recognised Scout Associations for the following reasons:

(*a*) To keep alive the spirit of the Scout Promise and Laws in their own lives,

(*b*) To bring that spirit into the communities in which they live and work,

(*c*) Whilst remembering their other responsibilities, actively to support Scouting in their communities, countries and the world.

(*d*) and further recommends: That the fortieth anniversary of the beginning of Scouting presents an excellent opportunity for launching and developing the formation of Old Scouts Branches.

In keeping with this resolution a conference was held at Gilwell Park in the autumn to consider the future of the Old Scout branch in Great Britain; this had been in being for some years but had not shown much vitality. It was decided to establish a B.-P. Guild of Old Scouts.

* * * * * * *

This is an appropriate point at which to break off this history of Scouting. The Jamboree at Moisson opened on 9 August 1947; B.-P.'s first camp on Brownsea Island closed on 9 August 1907.

'Break off' is the right expression, for the Scout Movement is in full vigour and the story is far from its end. B.-P. once said that the time would come when Scouting would not be needed, but though much has changed since 1907, the need persists in spite of differences in social conditions, in spite of improved educational opportunities, in spite of the advances in public health and general welfare. Scouting still appeals to the boy. It provides that outlet he needs for his spirit of adventure in a world that is becoming more and more organized; it satisfies his love of romance; he wants the freedom of the woods and he wants to live like the pioneers and explorers even in the midst of bricks and smoke. B.-P. saw into the heart of the boy when he wrote:

The underlying feature is the *spirit* of the Movement, and the key that unlocks this spirit is the romance of Woodcraft and Nature Lore.

Where is there a boy, or for the matter of that a grown-up man, even in these materialistic times to whom the call of the wild and the open road does not appeal?

Maybe it is a primitive instinct—anyway it is there. With that key a great door may be unlocked, if it is only to admit fresh air and sunshine into lives that were otherwise grey.

But generally it can do more than this.

The heroes of the wild, the frontiersmen and explorers, the rovers of the seas, the airmen of the clouds are Pied Pipers to the boys.

Where they lead the boys will follow, and these will dance to their tune when it sings the song of manliness and pluck, of adventure and high endeavour, of efficiency and skill, of cheerful sacrifice of self for others.

There's meat in this for the boy; there's soul in it.

Watch that lad going down the street, his eyes are looking far out. Is his vision across the prairie or over the grey backed seas? At any rate, it isn't here. Don't I know it!

Have you ever seen the buffaloes roaming in Kensington Gardens past that very spot where Gil Blas met the robbers behind the trees? And can't you see the smoke from the Sioux Lodges under the shadow of the Albert Memorial? I have seen them there these fifty years.

Through Scouting the boy has now the chance to deck himself in a frontier kit as one of the great Brotherhood of Backwoodsmen. He can track and follow signs, he can signal, he can light his fire and build his shack and cook his grub. He can turn his hand to many things in pioneer and camp-craft.

His Unit is a band of six, commanded by their own boy leader. Here's the natural gang of the boy, whether for good or for mischief. Here's responsibility and self-discipline for the individual. Here's *esprit de corps* for the honour of the Patrol as strong as any house-spirit in a public school.

To the outsider's eye the Scouts' staffs are so many broomsticks, but to the Scout they are different. His staff, decorated with his own particular totem and signs, is typical; like his staff, among a mass he is an individual having his own traits, his own character, his own potentialities.

He may be one of a herd, but he has his own entity. He gets to know the joy of life through the out-of-doors.

This record may fittingly end with the final words of *Scouting for Boys*.

In every country the aim of the Scouts' training is identical, namely, efficiency for Service towards others; and with such an object in common, we can, as an international Brotherhood in Service, go forward and do a far-reaching work.

In our training of the boy we develop the individual in both spirit and efficiency to be an effective player in his national team of citizenhood. Acting on the same principle in the case of a nation we should try to develop the right spirit of efficiency for helping that nation to work effectively in the team of nations.

If each, then, plays in its place, and 'plays the game', there will be greater prosperity and happiness throughout the world, there will be brought about at last that condition which has so long been looked for—of Peace and Good-will among men.

INDEX